Goldwin Smith

Essays on Questions of the Day

Political and Social

Goldwin Smith

Essays on Questions of the Day
Political and Social

ISBN/EAN: 9783337073022

Printed in Europe, USA, Canada, Australia, Japan

Cover: Foto ©Suzi / pixelio.de

More available books at **www.hansebooks.com**

ESSAYS ON

QUESTIONS OF THE DAY

POLITICAL AND SOCIAL

BY

GOLDWIN SMITH, D.C.L.

AUTHOR OF "THE UNITED STATES: AN OUTLINE OF POLITICAL
HISTORY," AND "CANADA AND THE CANADIAN
QUESTION"

New York
MACMILLAN AND CO.
AND LONDON
1893

PREFACE.

THESE Essays are the outcome of discussions in which the writer has been engaged on the several questions, and are partly drawn from papers contributed by him to different periodicals.

Of the subjects some are specially British, though not without interest for a citizen of the United States; others are common to both countries.

Some service may be done by bringing an important question into focus, even when the reader does not agree with the opinions of the writer. The opinions of the present writer are those of a Liberal of the old school as yet unconverted to State Socialism, who looks for further improvement not to an increase of the authority of government, but to the same agencies, moral, intellectual, and economical, which have brought us thus far, and one of which, science, is now operating with immensely increased power. A writer of this school can have no panacea or nostrum to offer; and when a nostrum or panacea is offered, he will necessarily be found rather on the critical side. He will look for improvement, not for regeneration; expect improvement still to be, as it has been, gradual; and hope much from steady, calm, and harmonious effort, little from violence or revolution. In his estimation the clearest gain reaped by the world from all the struggles through which it has been going, amidst much that is equivocal or still on trial, will be liberty of opinion.

It will be found that the subjects are treated for the most part historically, or on general principles, and that the political student has seldom encroached on the domain of the practical statesman.

The thanks of the writer are due to the proprietors and editors of the *North American Review*, the *Forum*, the *Nineteenth Century*, and the *National Review*, for their courtesy in permitting him to draw upon articles which appeared in their periodicals, as well as for the privilege which he has enjoyed of being one of their contributors.

CONTENTS.

QUESTIONS OF THE DAY.

SOCIAL AND INDUSTRIAL REVOLUTION.

The belief that the human lot can be levelled by economical change, and the desire to make the attempt, are at present strong; they are giving birth to a multitude of projects, and in Europe are threatening society with convulsion. In America the possession of property is as yet more widely diffused than in Europe, while the hope of possessing property is still almost universal. Eagerness to grasp a full share of the good things of the present life has been intensified by the departure, or decline, of the religious faith which held out to the unfortunate in this world the hope of indemnity in another. "If to-morrow we die, and death is the end, to-day let us eat and drink; and if we have not the wherewithal, let us see if we cannot take from those who have." So multitudes are saying in their hearts, and philosophy has not yet furnished a clear reply. Popular education has gone far enough to make the masses think, not far enough to make them think deeply; they read what falls in with their aspirations, and their thoughts run in the groove thus formed; flattering theories make way rapidly, and, like religious doctrines, are received without examination by the credulous and uncritical. The ignorant readers of a socialistic philosopher, while they are incompetent to understand or scrutinise the arguments addressed to their intellects, imbibe the appeal addressed to their feelings and desires, which are fortified by the impression that they have philosophy on their side. The number of actual Communists or Socialists in any country is as yet small compared with that of the population at large. Of what is called Socialism in Germany much appears to be mainly a revolt against the burden of military service and taxation. Yet Socialistic ideas and sentiments spread especially among the artisan class, which is active-minded, is gathered in commercial centres, lives on wages about the rate of which there are frequent disputes, is filled with craving for pleasure by ever-present temptations, and stirred to envy by the perpetual sight of wealth. Envy is a potent factor in the movement, and is being constantly inflamed by the ostentation of the vulgar rich, who thus deserve, almost as much as the revolutionary artisans, the name of a dangerous class. This is the main source of that sort of social revolution which may be called Satanism, as it seeks, not to reconstruct, but to destroy, and to destroy not only existing political institutions, but the established code of morality, social, domestic, and personal. Satanism manifests itself in different countries under various forms and names, such as Nihilism, Intransigentism, Petrolean Communism,[1] the dynamite wing of Anarchism; Nihilism being defined with more startling sharpness than the rest, though the destructive spirit of all is the same. Social innovation is everywhere more or less allied with, and impelled by, the political and religious revolution which fills the civilised world; while the revolution in science has helped to excite the spirit of change in every sphere, little as Utopianism is akin to science.

No man with a brain and a heart can fail to be penetrated with a sense of the unequal distribution of wealth, or to be willing to try any experiment which may hold out a reasonable hope of putting an end to poverty. By the success of such an experiment, the happiness of the rich, of such, at least, of them as are good men, would be increased far more than their riches would be diminished. But only the Nihilists would desire blindly to plunge society into chaos. It is plainly beyond our power to alter the fundamental conditions of our being. There are inequalities greater even than those of

[1] One of the French Communists, it seems, rejoices in the name Lucifer Satan Vercingetorix.

wealth, which are fixed not by human lawgivers, but by nature, such as those of health, strength, and intellectual power; and these, almost inevitably, draw other inequalities with them. Injustice is human, and where inequality is the fiat, not of man, but of a power above man, it is idle, for any practical purpose, to assail it as injustice. The difference between a good and a bad workman is, partly at least, the act of nature; yet to give the same wages to the good workman and the bad, as Communists propose, while it might be just from some superhuman point of view, from the only point of view which humanity can practically attain, would be unjust.

The universe may be tending to perfection, but perfection has not yet been nor is its general law. If Schopenhauer had said that this was the worst of all conceivable worlds, he would plainly have been wrong. It is possible to conceive a world without affection, beauty, or hope; but when he said that it was the worst of all possible worlds, that is, the worst of all worlds that could subsist without dissolution, though he might still be wrong, he was not so plainly wrong. Look where we will, we see disorder, destruction, cruelty struggling with order, achievement, and beneficence. Evolutionary progress itself has gone on since the beginning of geologic time by the elimination or decimation of races, with much suffering to the eliminated or decimated. Animals live by preying on other animals, inflicting pain and sometimes torture on their prey. This is part of the constitution of the world. Can anything be less like perfect justice than the distribution of lots amongst living creatures of every kind through the whole scale? The human frame is full of imperfections, and liable to a thousand diseases, some of which may be caused by imprudence or vice, but others by mere accident. The natural character of man is full of evil and destructive passions. The world in which man lives wears everywhere the same doubtful aspect. The weather ripens the harvest and blights it; the wind wafts the ship and sinks it. An earthquake engulfs Lisbon, while they are dancing at Paris. Beauty is intermixed with ugliness. The shapeliness of the horse, the brilliancy of the bird of paradise, are mated with the loathsomeness of the puff adder and the toad. Imperfection apparently extends as far as the telescope can range; to the solar system in which there are evidences of irregularity and wreck, as well as a moon devoid of atmosphere and covered with extinct volcanoes, and even to the universe beyond, if science has witnessed the destruction of a star. Yet some of us imagine that the law of the social frame is perfection, and that from the enjoyment of that perfection we are debarred only by iniquitous and foolish laws or by the selfishness of a privileged class, so that by repealing the laws and overthrowing, or as the Jacobins thought, guillotining, the class, we may enter into a social paradise. The French Revolution was a dead-lift effort to level the human lot and make felicity universal. It swept away abuses, a great part of which Turgot, had he been allowed to accomplish his task, might have quietly removed. But it brought on an avalanche of crime and suffering; it produced at once a disorganisation of commerce and industry, involving the deaths of a million of persons by misery; afterwards it gave birth to a military despotism and the Napoleonic wars; and it has left behind as its legacies the volcanic passions with which Europe still heaves, and which are always threatening it with earthquakes or eruptions. After all, the complaints of the French artisan about the inequalities of wealth and the distinctions of class are just as passionate as ever. Apparently, to lacerate and convulse the social organism is only too possible, to transform it is beyond our power. This does not make it the less our duty and interest to remove every social injustice that can be removed, and level every unrighteous inequality that is capable of being levelled. It limits effort only by regulating hope. It bids us look for improvement, not for regeneration, and prefer gradual reform to violent revolution.

The plans of innovation proposed vary much in character and extent. Those which here will be briefly passed in review are Communism, Socialism, Nationalisation of Land, Strikes, plans for emancipating Labour from the dominion of Capital, and theories of innovation with regard to Currency and Banks, the most prominent of which is Greenbackism, or the belief in paper money. This seems a motley group, but it will be seen on examination, that there runs through the whole the same hope of bettering the condition of the masses without increase of industry, or of the substantial elements of wealth, and without limiting the multiplication of their numbers. Through several there runs a tendency to violence and confiscation. It may be safely said, that all the movements draw their adherents from minds of the same speculative class, and that industrial revolution is not, like industrial reform, often recruited from the ranks of steady and prosperous industry. Lassalle, the creator of German Socialism, and the brilliant genius of the whole movement, is described to us as "a fashionable dandy noted for his dress, for his dinners, and, it must be added, for his addiction to pleasure." "Chivalrous," we are told he was, "susceptible, with a genuine feeling for the poor man's case and a genuine enthusiasm for social reform; a warm friend, a vindictive enemy, full of ambition both of the nobler and more vulgar type, beset with an importunate vanity and given to primitive lusts, one in whom generous qualities and churlish throve and strove side by side, and governed or misgoverned a will to which opposition was almost a necessary and native element."[1] He was tried for sedition when he was twenty-three, upon which occasion, though his opinions can hardly have been matured, he declared himself a social democrat and revolutionary on principle. Much of his energy was spent during eight years in championing the cause of a countess, for whom he at length procured a divorce and a princely fortune, receiving as his reward a handsome annuity.

Of Lassalle, of Karl Marx, of socialistic writers generally, it may be said that they think almost exclusively of distribution, paying little attention to production. Production is the more important factor of the two, but it affords no material for the agitator. Let the fruits of labour by all means be as fairly distributed as possible, still we cannot live by distribution.

[1] See *Contemporary Socialism*, by John Rae. Page 65.

By Communism is here meant the proposal to abrogate altogether the institution of property. The reply to that proposal is that property is not an institution but a fixed element of human nature. A state of things in which a man would not think that what he had made for himself was his own, is unknown to experience and beyond the range of our conceptions. A monk may abjure property even in the work of his own hands, but he feels that this is an abnegation and a sacrifice. The author of the saying that property is theft affirmed, by his use of the word theft, the rightful existence of property, and it is highly probable that as a literary man he would have asserted his claim to copyright, which is property in its subtlest form. In early times property in land was not individual but tribal; it is so still in Afghanistan, while in Russia and Hindustan it is vested in the village community which assigns lots to the individual cultivators; still it is property; squat upon the land of an Afghan tribe, or of a village community, Russian or Hindu, in the name of humanity, and you will be ejected as certainly as if you had squatted on the land of an English squire. In primitive hunting-grounds and pastures, property was less definite; yet even these would have been defended against a rival tribe. Property in clothes, utensils, arms, must always have been individual. Declare that everything belongs to the community, still government must allot each citizen his rations; as soon as he receives them the rations will be his own, and if another tries to take them he will resist, and by his resistance affirm the principle of individual property.

Religious societies, in the fervour of their youth, have for a short time sought to seal the brotherhood of their members by instituting within their own circle a community of goods. The primitive Christians did this, but they never thought of abolishing property or proclaiming the communistic principle to society at large. Paul distinctly ratifies the principle of industry, "Let him that stole steal no more; but rather labour, working with his hands the thing which is good, that he may have to give to him that needeth." "While the land remained," says Peter to Ananias, "did it not remain thine own; and after it was sold was it not in thy power?" Christian communism, so-called, was in fact merely a benefit fund or club; it was also short-lived; as was the communism of the Monastic orders, which soon gave way to individual proprietorship on no ordinary scale in the persons of the abbots.

Associations, called communistic, have been founded in the United States. But these have been nothing more than common homes for a small number of people, living together as one household on a joint-stock fund. Their relations to the community at large have been of the ordinary commercial kind. The Oneida Community owned works carried on by hired labour, and dealt with the outside world like any other manufacturer; nor did it make any attempt to propagate communistic opinions. A religious dictatorship seems essential to the unity and peace of these households; but where they have prospered economically the secret of their success has been the absence of children, which limited their expenses and enabled them to save money. Growing wealthy, they have ceased to proselytise, and, if celibacy was kept up, have become tontines. They afford no proof whatever of the practicability of communism as a universal system.[1]

What is the foundation of property? We do not seek for its theological foundation or for its moral foundation, but for its economical foundation. Its economical foundation is that it is the only known motive power of production. Slavery has its whip; but, saving this, no general incentive to labour other than property has yet been devised. Communists think that they can rely on love of the community, and they point to the case of the soldier who they say does his duty voluntarily from a sense of military honour. It is replied that, so far from being voluntary, a soldier's duty is prescribed by a code of exceptional severity, enforced by penalties of the sternest kind.

That the family and all its affections are closely bound up

---

[1] See Appendix.

with property is evident; and the Nihilist is consistent in seeking to destroy property and the family together.

Tracing property to its source, we find it has its origin, as a general rule, not in "theft," but in labour, either of the hand or of the brain, and in the frugality by which the fruits of labour have been saved. In the case of property which has been inherited, we may have to go back generations in order to reach this fact, but we come to the fact at last. Wherever the labour has been honest, good we may be sure has been done, and the wealth of society at large, as well as that of the worker, has been increased in the process. Some property has, of course, been acquired by bad means, such as gambling speculation, or unrighteous monopoly, and if we could only distinguish this from the rest, confiscation might be just; for there is nothing sacred in property apart from the mode in which it has been acquired. But the tares cannot be separated from the wheat; discrimination is impossible; all that we can do is to discourage as much as may be bad modes of acquisition and refuse to pay homage to wealth ill acquired. Hereditary wealth, owned by those who have themselves not worked for it, strikes us as injustice; often it is the moral ruin of the heir, who sinks into a worthless sybarite. To prevent its excessive accumulation is a proper object of the lawgiver, and in fact such has been the tendency of legislation wherever inheritance is not bound up with political institutions such as the House of Lords. But to abolish inheritance seems out of the question. Bequest is merely a death-bed gift; if we forbid a man to bequeath his wealth, he will give it away in his lifetime, rather than leave it to be confiscated. A great inducement to saving will thus be lost, and without saving where would be the means of increased production, and how would the economical world advance? The waste of hereditary wealth in idle hands is to be deplored. But we have admitted that this is economically as well as physically an imperfect world. After all, in an industrial and commercial community like the United States, or even England, the amount of inherited wealth must bear a small proportion to that which is the product of industry and for which service has been rendered to the community by its possessor.

That wealth is often abused, fearfully abused, is too true; so are strength, intellect, power, and opportunities of all kinds. It is also true that nothing can be more miserable or abject than to live in idleness by the sweat of other men's brows. But this is felt, in an increasing degree, by the better natures; private fortunes are more held subject to the moral claims of the community; a spontaneous communism is thus making way, and notably, as every observer will see, in the United States. Charitable and benevolent institutions rise on all sides. In the United States munificence was not arrested even by the Civil War. This under the dead level system of Socialism would necessarily cease, and would have to be replaced by taxation administered by State officials. The sight of wealth no doubt adds a moral sting to poverty. The ostentation of it, therefore, ought to be avoided, even on the ground of social prudence, by the rich. But the increase of wealth, instead of aggravating, improves the lot even of the poorest. In wealthy communities the destitute are relieved; in the savage state they die.

By Socialism is meant the theory of those who for free markets, industrial liberty, competition, private contract, and the present agencies of commerce, propose in various degrees to introduce regulation and remuneration of industry by "the State." What is the State? People seem to suppose that there is something outside and above the members of the community which answers to this name, and which has duties and a wisdom of its own. But duties can attach only to persons, wisdom can reside only in brains. The State, when you leave abstractions and come to facts, is nothing but the government, which can have no duties but those which the constitution assigns it, nor any wisdom but that which is infused into it by the mode of appointment or election. What, then, is the government which Socialism would set up, and to which it would intrust powers infinitely greater than those which any ruler has ever practically wielded, with duties infinitely harder than those which the highest political wisdom has ever dared to undertake? This is the first question which the Socialist has to answer. His school denounces all existing governments, and all those of the past, as incompetent and unjust. What does he propose to institute in their room, and by what process, elective or of any other kind, is the change to be made? Where will he find the human material out of which he can frame this earthly Providence, infallible and incorruptible, whose award shall be unanimously accepted as superior to all existing guarantees for industrial justice? The chiefs of industry are condemned beforehand as tyrannical capitalists. Will the artisan submit willingly to the autocratic rule of his brother? If he would, is it conceivable that a man whose life had been spent in manual or mechanical labour would be fit for supreme rule? The question, What is the government to be, once more, presents itself on the threshold and demands an answer. To accept an unlimited and most searching despotism without knowing to whose hands it is to be entrusted would evidently be madness. Curiously enough, from nearly the same quarter from which comes Socialism, with its demand for paternal government, comes also Anarchism, demanding that there shall be no government at all. It is idle to form theories, whether economical or social, without considering the actual circumstances under which they are to be applied, and the means and possibilities of carrying them into effect. This is the merest truism, yet it is one which, so far as we know, Socialism neglects.

Despotic a government must be, in order to secure submission to its assignment of industrial parts and to its award of wages, especially if the wages are to be measured not by the amount or quality of the work, but by some higher law of benevolence or desert. Despotic it must be to enable it to compel indolence to work at all. Its power, practically, must be made to extend beyond the sphere of industry to social, domestic, and individual life. Resistance to its decrees could not be permitted, nor could it be deposed in case of tyranny or abuse. Liberty, in short, would be at an end, and it is difficult to see how progress could survive liberty. The inventor of each utopia assumes the finality of his system. He takes it for granted that time, having now produced its perfect fruit, will bear no more. But history and science tell us that time is likely to bear new fruit without end.

Assignment of manual labour and payment for its performance by a paternal government are conceivable, though not practically feasible. But how could men be told off for intellectual labour, for scientific research, for invention? Could the socialistic ruler pick out a Shakespeare, a Newton, or an Arkwright, set him to his work and pay him while he was about it? What security would there be against a lapse into intellectual barbarism? Is not Socialism a manual labourer's dream? Of the artisans whom these theories flatter, all whose trades minister to literature, art, or refinement would be in danger of finding themselves without work.

Some Socialists propose to cut up the industrial and commercial world into phalansteries, or sections of some kind, for the purposes of their organisation. But industry and commerce are networks covering the whole globe. To what phalanstery would the sailors, the railway men, and the traders between different countries be assigned?

Take any complex product of human labour, say, a piece of cotton goods worth a penny. Let the Socialist trace out, as far as thought will go, the industries which, in various ways, and in different parts of the world, have contributed to the production, including the making of machinery, shipbuilding, and all the employments and branches of trade ancillary to these; let him consider how, by the operation of economic law, under the system of industrial liberty, the single penny is distributed among all these industries justly, "even to the estimation of a hair," and then let him ask himself whether his government, or his group of governments, is likely to do better than nature.

Socialists claim the Factory laws as a recognition of their principle and as opening the door of industrial revolution.

But it is difficult to see why the enforcement of hygienic regulations or safeguards for life and limb is more socialistic in the case of a factory than in the case of a city, or why the protection of women and children who cannot protect themselves against industrial cruelty and abuse is more socialistic than the protection of them against wife-beating or infanticide. How far legislation shall go in this direction must be determined not by any theory, socialistic or anti-socialistic, but by the character and circumstances of the particular community. In some communities strict legislation will be required in cases where in others individual intelligence and individual sense of duty will suffice. That the Factory Acts have not induced any radical change in the industrial system the complaints of the Socialists themselves are proof.

Ownership of public establishments and services, again, is a question apart, defined by the necessities of government, and involves nothing socialistic. Government obviously must own everything necessary to public order or national defence; it must own the postal service, to which its protection is plainly necessary, and to the postal service the telegraphic service may be reasonably united. On the other hand, the National workshops at Paris, the creation of the socialist Louis Blanc, were a failure; even the Government dock-yards in England, though rendered necessary by the exigencies of national defence, are said to be conducted less economically than private ship-yards. Australians tell us that with them government ownership of railways answers well. There is no reason why it should not, provided the government is pure. The cost of competing lines is saved, and if the stimulus of competitive enterprise is withdrawn, that of administrative emulation may take its place. Countries might be named which, if the government owned railways as well as subsidised them, would be plunged into corruption. In all government establishments there is danger of corruption, still more of laziness, torpor, and somnolent routine.

More truly socialistic is the assumption by the State of the duty of popular education. The prevailing opinion is that it is the manifest duty of the State to provide schools for everybody's children out of the public taxes. It might be thought that nothing was more manifest than the duty of every man to provide education as well as food and clothes for his own children, since it is by his act that they come into the world; or less manifest than the duty of the prudent man who defers marriage till he has the means of bringing up a family, to provide as a tax-payer for the schooling of the children of his less prudent neighbours. The wisdom which sets itself above justice ought to be very high. There are some, it seems, who would not only educate the children of the poor gratuitously, that is, out of the public taxes, but would give the school children meals and even clothes at the public expense. They can scarcely doubt that of such a system of almsgiving, widespread pauperism would be the fruit. When the duty is undertaken by the State, parental duty in regard to education and whatever goes with it of family character, must expire. Let those who think that the intellectual fruits of the State machine substituted for voluntary agencies are entirely satisfactory, read the series of papers in the New York *Forum*,[1] giving an account of a tour of inspection among the public schools of the United States. The formation of character and manners the system hardly professes. If it did, the manners would too often belie the claim. It lacks motive power in that line. The original New England school was the school of a small group of families carried on under the eyes of the parents, not unparental, therefore, and it was intensely religious. These conditions are changed. Politics too and ward-demagogism lay their hands on the election of school trustees. The high schools are largely accused of helping to set the farmer's sons and daughters above farm work, and sending them, for what they think higher employment, to the already over-crowded cities. If this or any other mischief is being done, there is no remedy. You cannot stop the State machine. What is voluntary, when it fails, stops of itself. However, State education is commended to us on the ground of political necessity. We are

[1] Vols. IV., V., and VI.

told that we must educate our masters. Popular ignorance with popular suffrage would be fatal to the community. This puts State education not on socialistic grounds but on that of political necessity, and necessity, whether political, military, or sanitary, must be supreme. The worst of it is that unless the truancy laws are more strictly enforced than is usually possible in a democracy, the dangerous classes are not in school.

Differentiation marks advance, and a centralisation which should reduce all functions to those of a single organ, would be not an advance but a degradation in the political as in the animal world.

A special form of Socialism is Agrarianism, which demands the Nationalisation of Land. This has received an impulse from recent legislation for Ireland. Not that the Irish tenant farmer is an agrarian socialist, or a socialist of any kind; what he wants is to oust the landlord, and have the farm to himself; if you demand, as a member of the community, a share of his land, he will give you six feet of it. He exacts a heavy rent for a little croft from the farm labourer in his employment. The sirens of Nationalisation have sung to him in vain. Nor did the framers of the Land Acts profess to abrogate or assail private property in land; they professed only to adjust by legislation a dispute between two classes of property-holders which threatened the peace of the State. But the natural consequences have been a general disturbance of ideas, and an increase of hope and activity among the apostles of agrarian revolution.

These theorists hold that private property in land is "a bold, base, enormous wrong, like that of chattel slavery." Mr. Herbert Spencer had said, "Had we to deal with the parties who originally robbed the human race of its heritage, we might make short work of the matter." To which the Nationalist replies: "Why not make short work of the matter anyhow? For this robbery is not like the robbery of a horse or a sum of money, that ceases with the act. It is a fresh and continuous robbery that goes on every day and every hour." It is proposed to forfeit, either openly, or under the thin disguise of a use of the taxing power, every man's freehold, even the farm which the settler has just reclaimed by the sweat of his own brow from the wilderness; and it is emphatically added, in language which sounds like the exultation of injustice, that no compensation is due; the man being merely ejected from that which never belonged to him, as a wrongful possessor is ejected by a court of law. That the State has, by the most solemn and repeated guarantees, ratified private proprietorship and undertaken to protect it, matters nothing; nor even that it has itself recently sold the land of the proprietor, signed the deed of sale, and received the payment. Aghast, perhaps, at his own proposal, the reformer afterwards suggests that in mercy, not of right, compensation for improvements, though not for the land may be granted. But if the nation compensates for all improvements, it may as well at once give a deed of quit claim for the land.

In the first place, how do the Nationalisers mean to carry into effect their schemes of resumption? They can hardly suppose that large classes will allow themselves to be stripped of all they possess, and turned out with their wives and children to beggary, without striking a blow for their freeholds. There would probably be civil war, in which it is by no means certain that the agrarian philosopher and his disciples would get the better of the owners and tillers of land; while, if they did, social peace would hardly ensue.

In the second place, as it is to the government that all land, or the rent of all land, is to be made over, we must ask the agrarian socialist, what form of government he means to give us? The theorists themselves denounce, as loudly as any one, the knavery and corruption of the politicians, who would hardly be made pure and upright simply by putting the management of all the land of the nation into their hands. Utopians are always forgetting that in introducing their systems they will have to deal with the world as it is.

Why is property in land thus singled out for forfeiture; and why are its holders selected for especial denunciation? Because, say the Nationalisers, the land is the gift of God to mankind, and ought not to be appropriated by any individual owner. This would preclude appropriation by a nation, as well as appropriation by a man; but let that pass. In every article which we use, in the paper and type of the very book which advocates confiscation, there are raw materials and natural forces, which are just as much the gift of God as the land. God made the wool of which your coat is woven to grow on the sheep's back, and endowed steam with the power to work the engine of the mill. God, for the matter of that, gave every man his brain and his limbs. Land is worth nothing, it is worth no more than the same extent of sea, till it is brought under cultivation by labour, which must be that of particular men. The value is the creation of individual labour and capital, in this case, as in the case of a manufacture. Circumstances, such as the growth of neighbouring cities, may favour the landowners. Circumstances may favour any owner or producer. They may also be unfavourable to any owner or producer, as they have been of late to the landowners and agricultural producers in England; and unless the State means to protect the holder of property against misfortune it has surely no right to mulct him for his good luck. The coal and iron beds of Wyoming and Montana, we are told, which to-day are valueless, will in fifty years from now be worth millions on millions, simply because in the meantime population will have greatly increased. They will be worth nothing unless they are worked, and where is the wrong if metals or beef or wool or anything else is worth more to the producer when produced in the midst of a swarming population than when produced in a desert?

Nor is there anything specially unjust, or in any way peculiar, about the mode in which the labourer on land is paid by the landowner or capitalist. Every labourer virtually draws his pay from the moment when he begins his work. He draws it in credit, which enables him to get what he wants at the baker's and grocer's, if not at once in cash.

All land will, of course, fall under the same rule. The lot

on which the mechanic has built his house, will be nationalised as well as the ranch.

It would appear that natural produce, being equally with the land the gift of the Creator, should be equally exempt from the possibility of lawful ownership, so that we should be justified in repudiating our milk bills because cows feed on grass.

Is Poverty the offspring of land-ownership or the land laws? Any one who is not sailing on the wings of a theory can answer that question by looking at the facts before his eyes. Poverty springs from many sources, personal and general; from indolence, infirmity, age, disease, intemperance; from the failure of harvests and the decline of local trade; from the growth of population beyond the means of subsistence. If the influence of the last cause is denied, let it be shown what impelled the migrations by which the earth has been peopled. Poverty has existed on a large scale in great commercial cities, which the land laws could but little affect, and even in cities like Venice, which had no land at all.

The increase of poverty itself is a fiction. The number of people, in all civilised countries, living in plenty and comfort, has vastly increased; and though, with a vast increase in numbers, there is necessarily a positive increase of misfortune and destitution, even the poorest are not so ill off now as they were in the times of primitive barbarism, when famine stalked through the unsettled tribes, though there was no "monopoly" of land. The London slums are hideous, but they are a mere spot in a vast expanse of decent homes, which is represented as not only the mate of poverty, but its source. The two or three millions of English in the days of the Plantagenets had more room and larger shares of the free gifts of nature than the thirty millions have now. But the working classes of those days lived in chimneyless hovels, and, as Dr. Jessop thinks, had, in Norfolk, but a single garment, not more wearing linen then than wear silk now. Loathsome diseases such as leprosy were common, and a third of the population was carried off at once by the Black Death. Local famines were frequent, owing to the want of machinery of distribution. If dissatisfaction was not manifested in strikes, it was manifested in the insurrection of Wat Tyler. Is there less poverty in unprogressive countries, such as the kingdoms of the East, or Spain and Italy, than in those which have been the seats of progress? That, of the increased wealth of England and other industrial countries, the largest share has gone to wages seems to be clearly proved. Nor can it be doubted that the remuneration of manual labour has risen, compared with that of intellectual work.

We cannot all be husbandmen or personally make any use of land. What we want, as a community, is that the soil shall produce as much food as possible, so that we may all live in plenty; and facts as well as reason seem to show that a high rate of production is attained only where tenure is secure. The greater the security of tenure, the more of his labour and capital the husbandman will put into the land, and the larger the harvest will be. It has been said, and though an over-statement, the saying has truth in it, that if you give a man the freehold of a desert, he will make it a garden, and if you give him the lease of a garden, he will make it a desert. The spur which proprietorship lends to industry is proverbially keen in the case of ownership of land. The French peasant is a remarkable proof of this. Originally, all ownership was tribal; and if tribal ownership has, in all civilised countries, given place to private ownership, this is the verdict of civilisation in favour of the present system. Where tribal ownership has lingered, as in Russia and in Afghanistan, general barbarism has lingered with it. The idea that a wicked company of land-grabbers aggressed upon the public property, and set up a monopoly in their own favour, is a fancy as baseless as the Social Contract of Rousseau, or any of the other figments respecting social origins which our knowledge of primeval history has dispelled. Did this extraordinary fit of spoliation come without concert upon every one of the countries now included in the civilised world? Where are the records or the traces of this series of events?

Is it intended that the tenure of those who are to hold the land under the State shall be secure? If it is, nothing will have been gained; private property, and what, to excite odium, is called monopoly, though there are hundreds of thousands of proprietors, will return under another form. The only result will be a change of the name from freeholder to something expressive of concession in perpetuity by the State; and this will be obtained at the expense of a shock to agriculture the immediate effect of which might be a dearth. That we have all a right to live upon the land is a proposition, in one sense, absurd, unless the cities are to be abandoned, and we are to revert to the primeval state; in another sense, true, though subject to the necessary limit of population. But what Nationalisation practically proposes is, that a good many of us, instead of living, shall, by reduced production, be deprived of bread and either be driven into exile or die.

The Nationalisation movement sometimes assumes the name of the Single Tax movement, which promises us unspeakable benefits if we will throw the whole burden of taxation on unimproved land. Who would be found to hold land? Shift the incidence of taxation as you will, it makes itself felt directly or indirectly by the whole community. If justice is to reign in the fiscal region, the service rendered by government, whether national or municipal, ought to be as far as possible the measure of taxation, and there is nothing to which government and police render so little service as unimproved land.

When we talk of Nationalising, it is well to remember, that though territory is still national, nations no longer live upon the produce of their own territory alone, and that the scope of plans of change must be enlarged so as to embrace the commercial world.

A milder school of agrarian socialists proposes to confiscate only what it calls the unearned increment of land, that is, any additional value which, from time to time, may accrue through the action of surrounding circumstances and the general progress of the community, without exertion or outlay on the part of the individual owner. Very sharp and skilful inspectors would be required to watch the increase and to draw the line. A question might also arise, whether, if unearned increment is to be taken away, accidental decrement ought not to be made good. But here, again, we must ask, why landed property alone is to be treated in this way? Property of any kind may grow more valuable without effort or outlay on the owner's part. Is the State to seize upon all the premium on stocks? A mechanic buys a pair of boots; the next day leather goes up; is the State to take toll of the mechanic's boots?

The fact is, that the vision of certain economists is distorted, and their views are narrowed by hatred of the landlord class. Too many landlords are idle and useless members of society, especially in old countries, under the operation of lingering feudal laws; but owners of other kinds of hereditary property are often idle and useless too. That the land should have been so improved as to be able to pay the owner as well as the cultivator, does the community no harm. This we see plainly, where the owner, instead of being a rich man, is a charitable institution. Nor, is any outcry raised, when the same person, being owner and cultivator, unites with the wages of one the revenue of the other. The belief that there is some evil mystery in rent, has been fostered by the metaphysical disquisitions of economists, who seem to have been entrapped by their disregard of any language but one. Rent is nothing but the hire of land, and there is no more mystery about it than there is about the hire of a machine or a horse. In Greek, the word for the hire of land and of a chattel is the same.

The desire of confiscating the property of landowners is, in European countries, closely connected with the objects of political revolution. But public spoliation, though it might commence, would not end here, nor would there be any ground for fixing this as its limit. Let a reason be given for confiscating real estate honestly acquired, and the same reason will hold good for confiscating personalty, the labourer's wages, and the copyright of the author and the plant of the journalist who wins popularity by advocating spoliation of his neighbour.   If property is theft, the property in the Savings Bank is theft like the rest.

Peasant proprietorship is as much opposed as anything can possibly be to nationalisation of land; so the Nationalisers, when they approach the peasant proprietor, speedily find. But there are some who look to it with unbounded hope.   The political arguments in its favour are well known; among them is the adamantine resistance which it offers to communism of all kinds.   Economical considerations are apparently against it, since a farmer on the great scale in Dakota will raise as much grain with a hundred labourers as is raised by ten times the number of French peasants.   Socially there are arguments both ways.   The advantage, and, indeed, the ultimate existence of the manorial system, must depend upon the presence of the landowner upon his estate and his performance of his duties to his tenants.   But the life of the peasant in France, and even in Switzerland, is hard, and sometimes almost barbarous, while he can scarcely tide over a bad harvest without falling into the money-lender's hands.   On the American continent, where the people are more educated, their tendency seems to be, when they can, to exchange life on the farm, which they find dull and lonely, for the more social life of the city.   Perhaps the time may come when agriculture will be carried on scientifically, and upon a large scale, to furnish food for an urban population.   The life on a great farm will be social, and will exercise higher intelligence than spade labour.   England, the enthusiasts of peasant proprietorship should remember, is organised on the manorial system, not only with manor houses but with large farms and large farm buildings to correspond. Do they intend to clear away the large farm buildings as well as the manor houses, and to construct a set adapted to small holdings in their room?

Liberation of labour from the exactions of the capitalist is the hope of those who set on foot co-operative works.   These, hitherto, have generally failed from inability to wait for the market, and tide over bad times, from want of a guiding hand, and from the unwillingness of the artisan to resign his independence and his liberty of moving from place to place; though the last cause is less operative with the submissive Frenchman than with his sturdy English or American compeer. Capital, spelt with a big initial letter, swells into a malignant giant, the personal enemy of labour; spelt in the natural way, it is simply that with which labour starts on any enterprise, and without which no labour can start at all, unless it be that of the savage grubbing roots with his nails. It includes a spade as well as factory plant that has cost millions; it includes everything laid out in education or training. We might as well talk of emancipating ourselves from the tyranny of food or air. Every co-operative association must have some capital to begin with, either of its own or borrowed, the lender, in the latter case, representing the power of large capital just as much as any employer. The aggregation of great masses of capital in one man's hands is a social danger, and one against which legislators ought, by all fair means, to guard, though it is sometimes not without a good aspect; witness the New York Central Railroad, which could hardly have been brought to its present state by managers under the necessity of providing an equally large dividend every year. But the operation of the joint-stock principle, it seems, is evidently producing a gradual change in this respect. It will often be found that the rate of profit made by a great capitalist is far from excessive, though his total gains may be large. Mr. Brassey's total gains were large, but the rate of his profits did not exceed five per cent, while it is very certain that without him ten thousand workmen, destitute of capital, scientific skill, and powers of command, could not have built the Victoria Bridge. Co-operative farming seems to hold out more hope than co-operative manufactures. Still it would need capital and a head.

To get rid of competition, and substitute for it fraternity among workers, is the other aim of co-operation. But the co-operative societies must compete with each other, while, as buyers, having regard to cheapness in their purchases, they will themselves be always ratifying the principle of competition, and, at the same time, that of paying the workmen not on the fraternal principle, but according to the amount and value of his work. Every heart must be touched by fraternity and wish that co-operation could take the place of competition, which, in its grinding severity, is too like many other things in this hard world. But, after all, choose any manufactured article, con- sider the multitude of people who in various trades and differ- ent countries have co-operated in the production, yet have not competed with each other, and it will be seen that, even as things are, there is more of co-operation than of competition among the workers.

Co-operative stores have nothing but a misleading name in common with co-operative works. They simply bring the consumer into direct relation with the producer, and give him the benefit of wholesale prices, which may be perfectly well done, so long as the officers of the association can be trusted to exercise for the society the same degree of skill and integrity in the selection of goods which the retail tradesman exercises for himself. Retail establishments, however, of the ordinary kind, but on a large scale, like that of the late A. T. Stewart, in New York, with low prices,.and, best of all, ready-money payment, afford the practical benefits of co-operation.

From Unionism and strikes, again, too much seems to have been hoped by the workingman. They have not seldom enabled him to make a fairer bargain with the master, and they are perfectly lawful; though it is daily becoming more apparent that the community, to save itself from the misuse of Unionist power, must steadfastly guard the liberties of the Non-union men. But the idea that strikes can, to an unlimited, or, even, to a great extent raise wages, seems unfounded. The screw may be put upon the master, but it cannot be put upon the community; and it is the community, not the master, that is the real employer. The community which buys the goods ultimately settles the price, and, thereby, finally determines the wages of the producers, notwithstanding any momentary extortion; nor can it be constrained, by striking, in the end to give more than it thinks fit and can afford. The workman who strikes himself buys everything as cheap as he can, and in so doing he is keeping down the wages of those whose labour produces the article to the lowest point in his power. By strikes, carried beyond a certain point, capital may be driven away, and the trade may be ruined, as trades have been ruined, but the rate of wages will not be raised. The master, though he is the immediate employer, is the agent through whom the community pays the workmen. To the men, his commercial relation is at bottom that of a partner, taking out of the earnings of the business the share which is due for capital, risk, and guidance. Masters are beginning to mark this fact in a kindly way, by giving shares in the concern or premiums to the men, while they retain the guidance in their own hands.

Strikers should never forget that they are themselves buyers as well as producers, and, therefore, employers as well as employed; so that if they can strike against the rest of the community, the other trades can strike against them, and wages being thus raised all round, nobody will gain anything. They ought also to remember that they are parts of an industrial organism, on the well-being of which as a whole that of all its members depends, and which is deranged as a whole by the disturbance of any portion of it. A strike in one section of a trade throws out of work hundreds of men, women, and children, in the other sections. A strike in certain departments, such as that of railways, will stop the wheels of commerce and industry; in others, it will cause incalculable loss and suffering. Suppose, when an artisan had been hurt by the machinery, the surgeons were to put their heads out of the window and say they were on strike.

Artisans are in the habit of speaking of themselves exclusively as workingmen. Everybody who is not idle is a workingman, whether he works with his brain or with his hands, and whatever part he may play in the service of a varied and complex civilisation.

We may relegate political economy to Saturn but we shall find that it will return. Malthus will return; not the immoral ogre painted by fancy, but the perfectly moral and benevolent observer, who pointed out a most important fact, though he partly overlooked the limitations. If the number of guests at the table of life is increased without limit, each man's share of the feast must be diminished or some must go unfed. If by the growth of the artisan population the labour market is overcrowded, strike as often as you will, there cannot be employment with good wages for all. The idea that multiplication of labourers, without increase of the natural means of production, will increase the produce seems to possess some minds, but it scarcely needs confutation.

It cannot be doubted that these unhappy wars between employer and employed have given birth to a set of men who subsist by industrial war. In the journals and speeches of these men nothing is said about the improvement which the artisan might make in his own condition by thrift, temperance, and husbandry of his means; he is told only of the advantage which he might gain by industrial revolution. Nor is anything said about the efforts which undeniably are being made by the employer and by society at large to raise the lot of the artisan. Before the men themselves the hope of rising into a higher grade of industry is not set. They are led to regard themselves as destined to the end of their days to be members of a union of wage-earners always doing battle with their masters. The artisan is always the "toiler," the other classes are "spoilers," and the drift of the preaching is that the spoilers ought to be made to disgorge, and are lucky if they escape condign punishment. The underlying notion seems to be that capitalists and the wealthy class, whatever may be done to them, will always be in existence and will present themselves like sheep for an annual shearing. But these sheep, once sheared, will grow no more wool. Men will not earn and save wealth for the despoiler.

Then there is the hope of vastly increasing the wealth of the world in general, and that of the poorer class in particular, by means of an inconvertible Paper Currency. Of this illusion, it may be truly said, that not the wildest dreams of the alchemist, or of those adventurers who sailed in quest of an Eldorado, were a more extraordinary instance of the human power of self-deception. Among the champions of paper currency there are, no doubt, many who know too well what they are about, and whose aim is to defraud the creditor, public and private, by paying off the debt with depreciated paper, an operation the sweetness of which, in the United States, under the Legal Tender Act, has been already tasted. But there are also honest enthusiasts, not a few, who sincerely believe that a commercial millennium could be opened by merely issuing a flood of promissory notes and refusing payment. This prodigious fallacy has its origin simply in the equivocal use of a word. We have got into the habit of applying the name money to paper bank-notes as well as to coin. The paper being current as well as the coin, we fancy that with both alike we buy goods. But the truth is that we buy only with the coin, to which, alone, the name money ought to be applied. The bank-note is an instrument of credit, like a cheque; not money itself, but an order and a security for a sum of money, which, the note being payable on demand, can be drawn by the holder from the bank, or the government, when he pleases. When a man receives a bank-note, he has virtually so much coin as the note represents put to his account at the bank by which the note is issued. The note is a promissory note, and the bank in increasing the number of its notes, like a trader who increases the number of his promissory notes, adds, not to its wealth, but to its liabilities. In the slip of paper there is no value or purchasing power; nor can any legislature put value or purchasing power into it. Greenbackers point to the case of postage stamps, into which, they say, value has been put by legislation. But a postage stamp is simply a receipt for a certain sum paid to the government in coin, and, in consideration of which, the government undertakes to carry the letter to which the receipt is affixed.

No paper money, it is believed, has ever yet been issued except in the promissory form, pledging the issuer to pay in coin, upon demand, so that each note, hitherto, has borne upon the face of it a flat denial and abjuration of the Greenback theory. Suppose the promissory form to be discarded, and the bill to be simply inscribed " one dollar," as the Fiat-money men propose, what would " dollar " mean? It would mean, say the Greenbackers, a certain proportion of the wealth of the country, upon which, as an aggregate, the currency would be based. What proportion? Let us know what we have in our purse, and what we can get in exchange for the paper dollar on presentation; otherwise commerce cannot go on. This, however, is not the most serious difficulty. The most serious difficulty is that while the coin, which a convertible bank-note represents, is the property of the bank of issue, the aggregate wealth of the country is not the property of the government, but of a multitude of private owners. The government is the possessor of nothing except the public domain and a taxing power, the exercise of which it is bound to confine to the actual necessities of the State. In issuing an order for a loaf of bread, a coat, or a leg of mutton, to be taken from the possessions of the community at large, it would be simply signing a ticket of spoliation.

Ask the Fiat-money men whether they are prepared to take their own money for taxes, and you will get an ambiguous reply. Some of them have an inkling of the fatal truth, and answer that the taxes must be paid in gold. The faith of others is more robust. But it has been reasonably inquired why the government, if it can with a printing machine coin money at its will, should pester citizens for taxes at all.

That the foreigner will take the national Fiat-money, nobody seems to pretend. Yet, if there is real value in it, why should he not? All the better, say the Greenbackers; if he will not take our money, he will have to take our goods. Then you will have to take his goods, and the commercial world will be reduced again to barter without a common measure of value, which would not be a great advance in convenience or in civilisation. Besides, trade is not merely a direct interchange of commodities between two countries; it is circulation of them among all countries, the United States sending cotton to England, England calico to China, and China tea to the United States, which, without a common standard of value, would be next to impossible.

In one sense, of course, government can, by its fiat, put value into paper. It can make the paper legal tender for debts; in other words, it can issue licenses of repudiation, and these licenses will retain a value till all existing debts have been repudiated, and all existing creditors cheated; but from that time their value will cease, since everybody, from the moment of their issue, will refuse to advance money, or sell on credit.

In all the cases known to economical history in which governments have issued inconvertible paper, depreciation has ensued, and such value as the paper has retained has been exactly in proportion to the hope of resumption. When cash payments were suspended in England, at the crisis of the French war, the depreciation was comparatively small, simply because the hope of resumption was strong. The guillotine was plied in vain to arrest the rapid fall of French Assignats, though these were not absolutely fiat-money, but bonds secured on the national domains, which were good security for the original issue. Confederate paper money, with the defeat of the Confederacy, lost the whole of its value, or retained a shadow of it only through stock-jobbing tricks. In San Domingo a gentleman, having tendered a silver American dollar in payment for his coffee, received from the surprised and delighted keeper of the coffee-house an armful of paper change. Washington, while he was saving his country, was being robbed through the operation of inconvertible paper currency of part of his private estate; and the effects, moral and political, as well as commercial, of the system, during the Revolutionary War, were such that Tom Paine, no timid or squeamish publicist, recommended that death should be made the penalty of any proposal to renew it. In all cases where specie payment has been resumed, the State, in addition to the loss incurred through disturbance and demoralisation of commerce, has paid heavily for the temporary suspension, because its credit has been suspended at the same time, and it has had to borrow on terms worse than those which it could have obtained in the money market, had its integrity been preserved.

The value is in the gold. It is in exchange for the gold that, whenever a sale takes place, the commodity is given. Trade was originally barter, and, in the sense of being always an interchange of things deemed really equivalent in value, it is barter still. I give a cow for three sheep, and then give the three sheep for a plough, which it is my ultimate object to purchase. What the three sheep here do in a single transaction, is done in transactions generally by gold. This fundamental and vital fact is obscured by the language even of some economists who are sound in principle, but who speak of the precious metals as though their value were conventional, and like that of symbols or counters. It is nothing of the kind. The first man who gave anything in exchange for gold or silver, must have done so because he deemed gold or silver really valuable; so does the last. The precious metals, probably, attracted at first by their beauty, their rarity, and their natural qualities; then, they were felt to have special advantages as mediums of exchange and universal standards of value, on account of their durability, their uniformity, their portability, their capability of receiving a stamp, of being divided with exactness, and of being fused again with ease. Thus they, and, in the upshot, gold, displaced all the other articles, such as copper, iron, leather, shells, which, in primitive times, or under pressure of circumstances, were adopted as mediums of exchange and standards of value. As was said in the time of Edward VI. in a protest against the debasement of the currency, " By the whole consent of the world gold and silver have gotten the estimation above all other metals, as metest to make money and be conserved as a treasure: which estimation cannot be altered by a part or little corner of the world, though the estimation were had but on a fanciful opinion, where indeed it is grounded upon good reason, according to the gifts that nature hath wrought in those metals whereby they be metest to use for exchange, and to be kept for a treasure: so as in that kind they have gotten the sovereignty, like as for other purposes other metals do excel." [1] But the precious metals have now the additional value derived from immemorial and immutable prescription, which would render it practically impossible to oust them, even if a substance promising greater advantages for the purpose could be found. The French Republicans tried to change the era, and make chronology begin with the first year of the Republic, instead of beginning with the birth of Christ. But they found that they were pulling at a tree, the roots of which were too.completely entwined with all existing customs and ideas to be torn up. It would not be less difficult to alter the medium of exchange and standard of value over the whole commercial world. A value which is moral, or dependent on opinion, is not the less real; the value of diamonds, as symbols of wealth and rank, may be dependent, not only on opinion, but on fancy, yet it is real so long as it lasts. An enormous find of gold would, of course, by putting an end to its rarity, destroy its value; this is a risk which commerce runs, but it does not seem to be great. Any inconvenience that might arise from the bulk and weight of the precious metals, is indefinitely diminished, while in use they are vastly, and in an increasing degree, economised by the employment of bank-notes and other paper securities, for gold, which are currency, though money they are not.

There ought surely to be no such thing as Legal Tender, even in the case of convertible paper currency, either on the part of the government or on the part of private banks. It is plain injustice to compel us to take anybody's paper as gold. If the government is solvent and its security is

---

[1] See Mr. Richard Bagley's *Ireland under the Tudors*, Vol. I., p. 371.

good, the paper is sure to be taken in preference to carrying about a weight of specie. Legal Tender confuses the ideas of the people, shakes commercial morality, and prepares the way for the attempts of the Fiat-money man, and for all the mischief which they breed.

Of Bimetallism we must speak with respect, since it has such an advocate as Mr. Grenfell. Yet the answer to the question seems to have been given with characteristic force and pungency by Lowe: " I congratulate you on the discovery of the philosopher's stone. If saying that one metal shall be equal in value to another can make it equal, you are fairly entitled to claim to have discovered the secret of boundless riches. But why bimetallism only ? Why not trimetallism or quadrimetallism? It is as easy to say that copper is equal to gold as silver." Gold and silver are two commodities, each of which has its value settled by qualities and circumstances over which legislatures have no control. Relative or proportional value can no more be legislated into a commodity than can absolute value. By the act of a government or a combination of governments, silver or any other metal may authoritatively be made legal tender in a certain proportion to gold, so far as the power of that government or combination of governments extends. This may be done with greater ease if the community or communities are not in active commercial intercourse with the rest of the world. To have two standards is to have none. It has been said that it matters not whether cloth is bought by the yard or by the ell. It matters, however, whether you have one yard measure or two, one of three feet and the other of three feet and a quarter. It was proposed, the other day, in America, to keep up the price of silver by making all the servants of the government wear silver buttons. It was asked in reply whether the servants were to pay for the buttons, or the public; as, in the first case it would be a tax on the servants, in the second, on the public, for the benefit of the Silver men, and the money might as well have been handed to them at once. But we should also have been told why the public was interested in keeping up the price of silver any more than the price of salt. It was mainly the influence of the Silver men, not the prevalence of the bimetallic theory that carried the Silver Bill. The market is flooded with silver, and if silver were monetised there would be a deluge. It is mournful that an industry should be depressed, but of all ways of relieving it the most costly is derangement of the currency. If the tobacco interest is depressed, are we to remonetise tobacco? Combined with the silver interest in the agitation was the recrudescence of Greenbackism and the desire of the debtor class, especially the heavily mortgaged, for an easy mode of paying their debts. Nor was the South unwilling to see a partial repudiation of the Federal war debt. The struggle against Greenbackism after the war was severe, though honesty and a regard for national credit prevailed. In the Silver law and its consequences we see one more proof of the formidable influence of sectional interests in party government when parties are nearly balanced. With the movement of the Silver men and Greenbackers in the United States concurred that of the Civil Servants in India, and a great point was made by Bimetallists of this concurrence. But in regard to such a question as a change in the world's currency, the pressure of two great special interests was surely a warning to be cautious. The interests themselves are part of the commercial world, and will lose in the end by derangement of the currency, though they may gain by a bonus for a time. Adherence to the gold standard does not preclude the " free coinage " of silver to any extent for auxiliary use, the range of which each country may determine for itself.

With belief in Fiat-money are often combined fancies about the tyranny of banks, and a desire to wreck and plunder them by an exercise of the legislative power, or to seize the business and its profits, and place them in the hands of the government. Especially it is proposed to take away the circulation of bank-notes, and the profits belonging to it. Banks are vital organs of a commercial community, which, in seeking their destruction, would show as much wisdom as a man would show in seeking the destruction of his own heart or lungs. They perform for us three indispensable functions, of which the first is the safe-keeping of our money, which, otherwise, we should have to keep in our houses at our own risk, as was the practice of Mr. Pepys in the reign of Charles II., and as is still the practice of the French peasant, who hides his hoard in a hole in the wall. The second function is that of economising gold, and at the same time sparing us the inconvenience of carrying about a mass of specie, by issuing bank-notes, which, being secured upon the whole estate of a chartered corporation, may, in general, be accepted without scrutiny, and thus form a paper currency; though it can never be too often repeated that they are not money. It is hard that those who are always declaiming against metallic money for its cumbrousness, and because, as they say, it lies dead and inert, should fail to acknowledge the service rendered by the banks of issue, in thus giving the metal wings, and making it do its work for commerce in a thousand places, while it is locally laid up in one. The third function, which is the offspring of comparatively modern times, is that of enabling us to trade on credit. This the banks do by discounting paper for the trader, whose resources they have satisfactorily examined, and whose commercial character they approve. In this way, they both substantiate and regulate credit, neither of which could be done without their agency, by the mere representations of the trader himself, or by private inquiry into his means. To stop the action of the banks in this department would be to stop trading on credit. Credit also is becoming a monster, and if there were no trustworthy means of measuring, regulating, and restricting it, a monster it would be.

The financial destructive grudges the banks the profits of their circulation, and wishes to transfer them to that which he calls the State, but which, it is necessary always to bear in mind, is in fact simply the men who compose the government. Why not grudge the banks the profits of the discount business, and propose to transfer that to government in the same way ? Why not do the same with all other trades by which profit, and often unfair profit, is made? Why not make the issuing of bills of exchange or promissory notes, why not make the supplying of the community with clothes or shoes, a monopoly in the hands of the government? What is there about the money trade in particular to make us desire that it should be put into the power of the politicians? Judging by experience, it would be about the last branch of commerce on which we should wish them to lay their grasp.

It is the business of government to put its stamp on the coin, in order to assure the community that the coin is of the right weight and fineness. This public authorities alone can satisfactorily do, and they may now be trusted to do it, though, in former times, kings were in the habit of defrauding the subject by debasing the coin. But here the duty and the usefulness of government in regard to the currency seem to end. The volume of bank-notes issued ought to be regulated, like that of all other commercial paper, by the requirements of the.day, that is, by the number and amount of the transactions; and it will be .so regulated while it is in the hands of the banks, which will not fail to issue all the bills for which there is real need, while, if they issue more than are needed, the bills will begin to come back upon their hands. But government can no more decide what amount of notes is required than it can decide how many promissory notes or bills of exchange or dock warrants ought, at any given moment, to be afloat. Setting government to settle the circulation of paper is having the barometer regulated by superior wisdom without reference to atmospheric pressure.

The Bank Charter Act of Peel and Overstone was the off-spring of the alarm caused by the failure of a number of private banks of issue. With deference to such high authorities, some would say that it might have been better to adopt proper safeguards in the way of inspection and other precautionary regulations. The Act has gone into operation only to a limited extent, having put an end to the existence of a few only of the private banks of issue, all of which it was intended gradually to extinguish. It has been thrice suspended at a commercial crisis, each suspension being attended with all the inconvenience and injustice of arbitrary intervention; and its general effect, whenever tightness is felt, appears to be to produce a sort of nervous contraction, which itself tends to the acceleration of a crisis.

Ordinary banks, being private institutions, are amenable to the law; in truth, there is nothing of which the politicians are fonder than harassing them with legislation. But a party government, supported by a majority, is its own law, and can do whatever its need or its cupidity inspires, without regard to the interests of commerce. Even the most commercial of such governments, when in want of money, does not shrink from issuing legal tender currency, without reference to the state of the money market. The American Silver Bill, again, shows what we might have to expect of the power to which it is demanded that the functions of the banks should be transferred. Would commerce have an hour of security, or be able to conduct any of her operations in peace and confidence, if the hand of demagogism were all the time upon her heartstrings?

Bank-notes, though not legal tender, cannot, in the ordinary course of trade, be refused, unless there is some public reason for mistrusting the solvency of the bank. This is the ground for subjecting this particular class of commercial companies to special legislation; and it is the sole ground; there would, otherwise, be no justification for an interference with the trade in money more than with any other trade. Nor has a government the slightest right to compel the banks to take its bonds, as the condition of permitting them to pursue an honest and indispensable traffic, or to levy tribute upon them in any other way. On the other hand, the stockholders of banks must not suppose that they, of all investors in commercial enterprises, are entitled to the intervention of government when their affairs are mismanaged by directors of their own choosing. If they invoke such aid, they will once more practically point the moral of the fable of the horse and the stag.

The notion that society is an organism or growth must not be carried too far; we have an individuality and a power of acting on the general frame, which the parts of an organism have not. But this view is, at least, nearer the truth than the idea which underlies all Socialism, that society can be metamorphosed by the action of the State, an imaginary power outside all personalities, superior to all special interests, and free from all class passions. Nothing, indeed, can be less free from class passions than the movements which have been here passed in review. Social hatred is a bad reformer, and the struggles to which it has given birth have almost always brought to the community, and even to the most suffering members of it, far more loss than gain.

To speak of Protection would be opening a wide subject, and one which perhaps scarcely falls within the scope of this paper. There are men, sensible in other things, who imagine that they can increase the wealth of a country by taxation. So long as governments and armaments are maintained on the present scale of expenditure, every country will need import duties, and must have its tariff. The only alternative, at all events, is direct taxation. Absolute free trade, therefore, is at present out of the question, and the different tariffs must be regulated according to the circumstances and the special industries of each community. Every nation will claim this right. England, who has her tariff like the rest, wisely lets in free the raw materials of her special industries and the food of her innumerable workmen, while she taxes finished articles of luxury, such as tea, wine, and tobacco. Free traders, British free traders, especially, have left this too much out of sight, and have compromised their theory by that error. But that taxation can add to wealth, that governments can increase production by forcing capital and labour out of their natural channels, that the interest of the people will be promoted by forbidding them to buy the best and cheapest article wherever it can be found, are notions which, if reason did not sufficiently confute them, have been confuted by experience. Under the free system the industries of England have been developed, and her wealth has increased out of all proportion to the growth of her population, and to an extent perfectly unrivalled. The verdict of economical history through all the ages is the same. Nobody proposes to draw Customs lines across the territory of any nation, and the commercial advantages of freedom of exchange know no political limit, though in passing from nation to nation fiscal necessity intervenes. What is the proper commercial area of Protection, Protectionists have omitted to explain. The workman does not gain by Protection; he is only transferred to an artificial industry from a natural industry, which would otherwise develop itself, and in which, as it would be more remunerative, employment would be more abundant. The master manufacturer is the only man who gains; to him the community, under the Protective system, pays tribute; accordingly, in countries where the system prevails, he is generally a Protectionist, and uses not argument alone, but the Lobby, and influences of all sorts, to keep up the tariff; he will even do his utmost to encourage expenditure, rather than that the scale of duties should go down. Nor can he be much blamed, when the government has induced him to put his capital into the favoured trade, and stake his future on the continuance of the favour. Political or social motives there may conceivably be for Protection, as well as for any other sacrifice of commercial interest, such as war itself; but the commercial sacrifice is a fact which cannot be denied. To foster by protective duties or bonuses infant industries, which may afterwards sustain themselves, and perhaps draw emigration to a new country, in itself might be a rational and legitimate policy, if the nation could really keep the experiment in its own hands. But artificial interests are created, a Ring is formed, and the nation loses control over its tariff. Such, at least, is the case with communities governed as are those of the American continent. The field of political economy, as a region not in the air but on the earth, and the tendencies, capabilities, and forces of society with which the economical legislator deals, must be treated as they really are. The connection of political economy with politics is a blank page in the treatises of the great writers.

Steady industry, aided by the ever-growing powers of practical science, is rapidly augmenting wealth. Thrift and increased facilities for saving and for the employment of small capitals will promote the equality of distribution. Let governments see that labour is allowed to enjoy its full earnings, untaxed by war, waste, or protective tariffs. The best of all taxes, it has been truly said, is the least. With equal truth it may be said that the best of all governments is that which has least occasion to govern.

----

[1] Among other signs of the social and industrial unrest of the age has been the production of a number of utopias such as "The Coming Race," "News from Nowhere," "Cæsar's Column," and "Looking Backward," the last named being the most widely circulated and popular of all. As the rainbow in the spray of Niagara marks a cataract in the river, the appearance of utopias, has marked cataracts in the stream of history. That of More, from which the general name is taken, and that of Rabelais, marked the fall of the stream from the Middle Ages into modern times. Plato's "Republic" marked the catastrophe of Greek republicanism, though it is not a mere "utopia" but a great treatise on morality, and even as a political speculation not wholly beyond the pale of what a Greek citizen might have regarded as practical reform, since it is in its main features an idealisation of Sparta. Visions of reform heralded the outbreak of Lollardism and the Insurrection of the Serfs. The fancies of Rousseau and Bernardin de St. Pierre heralded the Revolution. Rousseau's reveries, be it observed, not only failed of realisation, but gave hardly any sign of that which was really coming. The Jacobins canted in his phrase,

----

[1] The substance of this paper appeared in the *Forum* under the title of "Prophets of Unrest."

but they returned to the state of nature only in personal filthiness, in brutality of manners, and in guillotining Lavoisier because the Republic had no need of chemists.

There is a general feeling abroad that the stream is drawing near a cataract now, and there are apparent grounds for the surmise. There is everywhere in the social frame an outward unrest, which as usual is the sign of fundamental change within. Old creeds have given way. The masses, the artisans especially, have ceased to believe that the existing order of society, with its grades of rank and wealth, is a divine ordinance against which it is vain to rebel. They have ceased to believe in a future state, in which Dives and Lazarus are to change places. Of labour journals secularism is the creed. Social science, if it is to take the place of religion as a conservative force, has not yet developed itself or got firm hold of the popular mind. The rivalry of parties for popular favour has made suffrage almost universal. The poor are freshly possessed of political power, and have conceived vague notions of the changes which, by exercising it, they may make in their own favour. They are just in that twilight of education in which chimeras stalk. This concurrence of social and economical with political and religious revolution has always been fraught with danger. The governing classes, unnerved by scepticism, have lost faith in the order which they represent, and are inclined to timorous and hasty abdication. Some members of them, partly from genuine philanthropy, partly from ambition, partly perhaps from fear, are, like the aristocracy of the *salons* in France in the last century, dallying with revolution. The sight of accumulated wealth has stimulated envy to a dangerous pitch. This is not the place to cast the horoscope of society. We may, after all, be exaggerating the gravity of the crisis. The First of May hitherto has passed without bringing forth anything more portentous than an epidemic of strikes, which, though very disastrous, as they sharpen and embitter class antagonisms, are not in themselves attempts to subvert society. A writer who has surveyed all the democracies, says that the only country on which revolutionary Socialism has taken hold is England. German Socialism appears, as was said before, to be largely impatience of taxation and conscription. Much is called Socialism and taken as ominous of revolution which is merely the extension of the action of government, wisely or unwisely, over new portions of its present field, and perhaps does not deserve the dreaded name so much as our familiar Sunday law. The crash, if it come, may not be universal. Things may not everywhere take the same course. Wealth in some countries, when seriously alarmed, may convert itself into military power, of which the artisans have little, and may turn the scale in its own favour. Though social science is as yet undeveloped, intelligence has more organs and an increasing hold. The efforts which good members of the employer or wealthy class are making to improve social and industrial relations, though little recognised by labour journals, can hardly prove altogether vain. The present may after all glide more calmly than we think into the future. Still there is a crisis. We have had the Parisian Commune, the Spanish Intransigentes, Nihilism, Anarchism. It is not a time for playing with wild-fire. Though Rousseau's scheme of regeneration by a return to nature came to nothing, his denunciations of society told with a vengeance, and consigned thousands to death by the guillotine, hundreds of thousands to death by distress, and millions to death by the sword or by the havoc and pestilence which follow in the train of war.

The writer of an " utopia," however, in trying to make his fancy attractive by contrast, is naturally tempted to overpaint the evils of the existing state of things. " Looking Backward " opens with a very vivid and telling picture of society as it is:

" By way of attempting to give the reader some general impression of the way people lived together in those days, and especially of the relations of the rich and poor to one another, perhaps I cannot do better than to compare society as it then was to a prodigious coach, which the masses of humanity were harnessed to and dragged toilsomely along a very hilly and sandy road. The driver was hungry, and permitted no lagging, though the pace was necessarily very slow. Despite the difficulty of drawing the coach at all along so hard a road, the top was covered with passengers, who never got down, even at the steepest ascent. These seats were very breezy and comfortable. Well up out of the dust, their occupants could enjoy the scenery at their leisure, or critically discuss the merits of the straining team. Naturally such places were in great demand, and the competition for them was keen, every one seeking as the first end in life to secure a seat on the coach for himself and to leave it to his child after him. By the rule of the coach, a man could leave his seat to whom he wished; but on the other hand, there were many accidents by which it might at any time be wholly lost. For all that they were so easy, the seats were very insecure, and at every sudden jolt of the coach persons were slipping out of them and falling to the ground, where they were instantly compelled to take hold of the rope and help to drag the coach on which they had before ridden so pleasantly. It was naturally regarded as a terrible misfortune to lose one's seat, and the apprehension that this might happen to them or their friends was a constant cloud upon the happiness of those who rode."

And what are the feelings of the passengers toward the hapless toilers who drag the coach? Have they no compassion for the sufferings of the fellow-beings from whom fortune only has distinguished them?

"Oh, yes; commiseration was frequently expressed by those who rode for those who had to pull the coach, especially when the vehicle came to a bad place in the road, as it was constantly doing, or to a particularly steep hill. At such times the desperate straining of the team, their agonised leaping and plunging under the pitiless lashing of hunger, the many who fainted at the rope and were trampled in the mire, made a very distressing spectacle, which often called forth highly creditable displays of feeling on the top of the coach. At such times the passengers would call down encouragingly to the toilers at the rope, exhorting them to patience, and holding out hopes of possible compensation in another world for the hardness of their lot, while others contributed to buy salves and liniments for the crippled and injured. It was agreed that it was a great pity that the coach should be so hard to pull, and there was a sense of general relief when the specially bad piece of road was gotten over. This relief was not, indeed, wholly on account of the team, for there was always some danger at these bad places of a general overturn in which all would lose their seats."

These passages have their counterparts in "News from Nowhere," and "Cæsar's Column," the latter of which, inspired apparently by fear of the Vanderbilts and Astors, depicts New York as miserably enslaved by a bloated oligarchy of millionaires, with its demon fleet of ten thousand air ships. They will sink deep into the hearts of many who will pay little attention to the speculative plans of reconstruction which follow. For one reader of "Progress and Poverty" who was at the pains to follow the economical reasoning, there were probably thousands who drank in the invectives against wealth and the suggestions of confiscation. But is the description here given true or anything like the truth? Are the masses toiling like the horses of a coach, not for their own benefit, but only for that of the passengers whom they draw? Are they not toiling to make their own bread, and to produce by their joint labour the things necessary for their common subsistence? As to the vast majority of them, can it be said that they are leaping and plunging in agony under the pitiless lash of hunger, fainting at the rope and trampled in the mire? Are they not with their families living in tolerable comfort, with bread enough and not without enjoyment? Has it not been proved beyond doubt that their wages have risen greatly and are still rising? Have not the working classes, unlike the horses, votes? Is there really any such sharp division as is here assumed to exist between labour and wealth? Are not many who have more or less of wealth and who could have seats on the top of any social coach, labourers and producers of the most effective kind? Such a writer can hardly be the dupe of the fallacy that those only labour who work with the hands. What is the amount of the hereditary property held by idlers in such a country as the United States, compared with that of the general wealth? Do the holders even of that property really add by their existence to the strain on the workers as the passengers by their presence add to the strain on the horses? Supposing they and their riches were annihilated, would the workers feel any relief? Would they not rather lose a fund upon which they draw to some extent at need? The hereditary wealth which is here taken to be the monster iniquity and evil, what is it but the savings of past generations ?   Had those who made it spent it, instead of leaving it to their children, should we be better off ?   Then, as to the feelings of the rich toward the poor: can a Bostonian, as this writer is, look round his own city and fail to see that heartless indifference has its seat only in the souls of a few sybarites, and that sentiments at all events of philanthropy and charity are the rule ?

It is in these utopias that we see most distinctly embodied the belief that equal justice is the natural law of the world, and that nothing keeps us out of it but the barrier of artificial arrangements set up by the power, and in the interest, of a class.   Break down that barrier by revolutionary legislation, and the kingdom of equal justice, it is thought, will come.   Would that it were so !   Who would be so selfish and so ignorant of the deepest source of happiness as not to vote for the change, whatever his wealth or his place on the social coach might be ?   But equal justice is not the natural law, as the world is at present, toward whatever goal we may be moving.   Health, strength, beauty, intellect, offspring, length of days, are distributed with no more regard for justice than are the powers of making and saving wealth.   One man is born in an age of barbarism, another in an age of civilisation; one man in the time of the Thirty Years' War or the Reign of Terror, another in an era of peace and comparative happiness. No justice can now be done to the myriads who have suffered and died.   Equal justice is far indeed from being the law of the animal kingdom.   Why is one animal the beast of prey, another the victim ?   Why does an elephant live for a century and an ephemeral insect for a few hours ?   If you come to that, why should one sentient creature be a worm and another a man ?   In earth and skies, so far as our ken reaches, imperfection reigns.   He who in " Looking Backward " wakes from a magnetic slumber to find the lots of all men made just and equal, might almost as well have awakened to find all human frames made perfect, disease and accident banished, the animals all in a state like that of Eden, the Arctic regions bearing harvests, Sahara moistened with fertilising rain, the moon provided with an atmosphere, and the solar system symmetrically completed. All this is no bar to the rational effort by which society is gradually improved. But it shuts out the hope of sudden transformation. The social organism, like the bodily frame, is imperfect ; you may help and beneficially direct its growth, but you cannot transform it. To revolutionary violence the author of "Looking Backward" is himself wholly averse. He uses only the magic wand.

With private property, with which it is the dream of utopian writers to do away, go, as everybody knows, many evils ; among others that of inordinate accumulation, of which there may be instances in New York, though it is a mistake to think that accumulation is a matter of modern growth, or that the community was not just as much overtopped by the Medici and the Fuggers of the Middle Ages, the great feudal landowners, and the Roman magnates, as it is by the Vanderbilts and Astors; while the restraints of public opinion were nothing like so strong in those days as they are in ours. On the other hand, it is hard to see how without private property we could have the home and all that it enshrines. But let the evils be whatever they may, no motive power of production, at least of any production beyond that necessary to stay hunger, except the desire of property, is at present known. A score or more of experiments in Communism have been made upon the American continent by visionaries of different kinds, from the founders of Brook Farm to those of the Oneida Community and the Shakers. They have, as has already been said, failed utterly, except in the cases where the rule of celibacy has been enforced, and the members, having no wives or children to maintain, and being themselves of a specially industrious and frugal class, have made enough and more than enough for their own support. Collectively, the community has owned private property like other companies or corporations. The Oneida Community, the most prosperous of all, owned three factories, in which the workmen were employed on the ordinary terms. Barrack life, without the home, has also been a general condition of success.

So it is with regard to competition, that other social fiend of this and all utopians. Nobody will deny that competition has its ugly side. But no other way at present is known to us of sustaining the progress of industry and securing the best and cheapest products. It is surely a stretch of pessimistic fancy to describe the industrial world under the competitive system as a horde of wild beasts rending each other, or as a Black Hole of Calcutta "with its press of maddened men tearing and trampling one another in the struggle to win a place at the breathing holes." It is surely going beyond the mark to say that all producers are " praying by night and working by day for the frustration of each other's enterprises," and that they are as much bent on spoiling their neighbours' crops as on saving their own. Do two tailors or grocers, even when their business is in the same street, rend each other when they meet? Is there not rather a certain fellowship between members of the same trade? Does not each think a good deal more, both in his prayers and in his practical transactions, of doing well himself than of preventing the other from doing well.

The writer of "Looking Backward" himself says that "as men grow more civilised, and as the subdivision of occupations and services is carried out, a complex mutual dependence becomes the universal rule." What is this complex mutual dependence but co-operation?

As a normal picture of our present civilisation, the table of contents of a newspaper is presented to us. It is a mere catalogue of calamities and horrors; wars, burglaries, strikes, failures in business, cornerings, boodlings, murders, suicides, embezzlements, and cases of cruelty, lunacy, or destitution. No doubt a real table of contents would give a picture, though not so terrible and heartrending as this, yet rich in catastrophes. But it is forgotten that the catastrophes or the exceptional events alone are recorded by newspapers, especially in the tables of contents, which are intended to catch the eye. No newspaper gives us a picture of the ordinary course of life. No newspaper speaks of the countries which are enjoying secure peace, of the people who are making a fair livelihood by honest industry, of the families which are living in comfort and the enjoyment of affection. Buyers would hardly be found for a sheet which should tell you by way of news that bread was being regularly delivered by the baker and that the milkman was going his round.

Centuries unnumbered, according to recent palæontologists, human society has taken in climbing to what is here described as the level of a vast den of wild beasts or a Black Hole of Calcutta. Yet in one century or a little more it is to become a paradise on earth. Not Massachusetts or America only but the whole civilised world will have been regenerated and have entered into the economical Eden. So the writer of "Looking Backward" dreams; and to show that he does not regard this as a mere dream, he cites historical precedents of changes which he thinks equally miraculous, the sudden and unexpected success, as it appears to him to have been, of the American Revolution, of German and Italian unification, of the agitation against slavery. In two of these cases at least, those of German and Italian unity, the wonder was not that the event came at last, but that it was delayed so long. In no one of the cases, surely, is anything like a precedent for so wide and universal a leap into the future to be found. From Dr. Leete, who is the showman of the new heavens and new earth in "Looking Backward," the reader learns that society, in the year 2000, has undergone not only a radical change, but a complete transformation, Boston, of course, leading the way, as Paris leads in the regeneration proclaimed by Comte, and all the most civilised communities duly following in her train. Society has become entirely industrial, war being completely eliminated. No fear is entertained lest when the civilised world has been turned into a vast factory of defenceless wealth, the uncivilised world may be tempted to loot it. Yet this danger is not imaginary if there is any truth in what we are told about the military force lying latent in China, to say nothing of the people of South America, who, though politically unsuccessful, are always showing that they can fight.

The State has become the sole capitalist and the universal employer. How did all the capital pass from the hands of individuals or private companies into those of the State ? Was it by a voluntary and universal surrender ? Were all the capitalists and all the stockholders suddenly convinced of the blessings of self-spoliation ? Or did the government by a sweeping act of confiscation seize all the capital ? In that case, was there not a struggle ? Was not the entrance into Paradise effected through a social war ? A mere "recognition of evolution" by thinkers, the only means suggested, would hardly go far with capitalists or joint-stock companies, nor would they be likely to allow themselves to be stripped by a "political party" so long as they had the means of resistance in their hands. The seer was in his magnetic trance when the transfer took place, and he has not the curiosity to ask Dr. Leete exactly how it was effected. For us, therefore, the problem remains unsolved.

The inducement to the change, we are told, was a sense of the economic advantages produced by the aggregation of industries under co-operative syndicates and trusts, which suggested that by a complete unification of all industries under the State unmeasured benefits might be obtained. "The epoch of trusts ended in the great trust." This implies a practical approval of that tendency to industrial aggregation, which is a most momentous feature of the economical situation, and which in most quarters is viewed with extreme aversion and alarm. But these corporations, syndicates, and trusts, on however large a scale they may be, are still managed each of them by a set of persons devoted to that particular business, and they depend for their success on personal aptitude and experience. Between such aggregations and a unification of all the industries in the hands of a government there is a gulf, and we do not see how the gulf is to be passed. The tendency of industry appears, it is true, to be toward large establishments, the advantages of which over a multitude of petty and starveling concerns, both as regards those engaged in the trade and the consumer, are obvious. But the large producing establishments are still special, and the advantages of combining iron works with cotton works are not obvious at all.

To the objection that the task of managing all the industries of a country and its foreign commerce (for foreign commerce there is still to be) would be difficult for any government, the simple and satisfactory answer is that in utopia there could be no difficulty at all. The government of a purely industrial commonwealth is itself industrial. It consists of veterans of labour chosen on account of their merit as workers, the identity of which with administrative capacity and power of command, as it is not likely to be tested, may be assumed without fear of disproof. To banish any misgivings which we might have as to the practicability of such a government, the seer points to the part taken by alumni in the government of universities; surely as subtle an analogy as the acutest intelligence ever discerned. The government is to be "responsible" in all that it does. But how in the last resort is responsibility to be enforced and usurpation to be repressed by a community of industrial sheep?

The new organisation of labour has been followed by such a flood of wealth that everybody lives, not only in plenty, but in luxury and refinement before unknown. Everybody is able to give up work at forty-five, that being fixed as the procrustean limit for all constitutions, and to pass the rest of his days in ease and enjoyment. "No man any more has any care for to-morrow, either for himself or his children, for the nation guarantees the nurture, education, and comfortable maintenance of every citizen from the cradle to the grave." All the world dresses for dinner, dines well, and has wine and cigars after dinner. Under all this lurks, it is to be feared, the same fallacy which underlies the theory of Mr. Henry George, who fancies that an increase of population, being an increase of the number of labourers, will necessarily augment production, and consequently that the fears of Malthus and all who dread over-population are baseless. It is assumed that everything is produced by labour. But the fact is that labour only produces the form or directs the natural forces. The material is produced by Nature, and she will not supply more than a given quantity within a given area and under given conditions. Even in ·Massachusetts, therefore, which is supposed to be the primal scene of human regeneration, the people, however skilled their labour, and however utopian their industrial organisation might be, unless their number were limited or their territory enlarged, would starve. This is a serious question for a State which "guarantees to every one nurture, education, and comfortable maintenance from the cradle to the grave." As the guarantee extends to the citizen's wife and child as well as to himself, and they are made independent of his labour, the last restraint of prudence on marriage and giving birth to children would be removed. The people would then probably multiply at a rate which would leave Irish or French-Canadian philoprogenitiveness behind, and without remedial action a vast scene of squalid misery would ensue.

There is no more private property. In its place comes a sense of public duty urging each man to labour. Of the sufficient strength of this we are positively assured, notwithstanding the result of all the experiments hitherto tried. Reality peeps out when we are told that those who refuse to work will be put into confinement on bread and water. This is something like a reversion, is it not, to the coach and horses, with the "lash of hunger"? The occasional necessity of a "draft" is another intimation that Nature, though you thrust her out, will resume her seat.

The stimulus of duty to the man's family would exist no more, when the maintenance of his wife and children was taken off his hands by the State. For the lower natures, though not for the higher, there is to be emulation, which, it is taken for granted, will act on them with undiminished effect when all the substantial prizes have been removed. An appeal is also made to a semi-military sense of honour, and the community is organised as an army, with military titles, apparently for that purpose. But it has been shown, in answer to other theorists who have pointed to military honour as a substitute for the ordinary motives to industry, that military duty is enforced by a code of exceptional severity. Nor will the military forms and names have much meaning or be likely to animate and inspirit when war, with all its pride, pomp, and circumstance, has been banished from the earth.

All are to be paid alike, on the principle that so long as you do your best your deserts are the same as those of others, though your power may not be so great as theirs. Your deserts in the eye of Heaven, no doubt, are the same if you do your best, and Heaven has the means of ascertaining that your best is being done. But if it is asked what means a board of industrial veterans or their lieutenants, supposing them to be ever so excellent craftsmen themselves, have of ascertaining that every man is doing his best, the answer, we suspect, must be that in utopia such questions are not to be raised. In the present evil world most men do their best, or something like their best, because they have to make their own living and that of their wives and children. Some men, under the voluntary and competitive system, put forth those extraordinary efforts which make the world move on. But the State, though it might command the daily amount of labour by threat of solitary confinement on bread-and-water, could not command improvement or invention. Invention, or discovery, it seems to us, would be little encouraged under the utopian system, since no man is to be allowed to shirk labour on pretence of being a student, a regulation which might have borne hard on Archimedes, Newton, or even Watt. Newton would at all events have had, in obedience to an inexorable rule, to pass three years as a common labourer, and his labour during those three years would have cost the world uncommonly dear. Even the employment of Dr. Leete, the good physician of this piece, for some years as waiter in a restaurant was rather a waste of his, or, to speak more properly, of the State's time.

Money as "a root of evil" has been totally discarded. Its place is taken by credit cards, entitling the bearer, by virtue of his mere humanity, to a share of the national produce.

Wages are a thing of the past. The certificates are to be presented at the government store, for government is the universal supplier as well as the universal employer of labour. Money, it is said, may have been fraudulently or improperly obtained, but with labour certificates this cannot be the case. We hardly see how a government store-keeper at New Orleans is to tell that the certificate was not fraudulently obtained at Boston. How could the title to it be verified in foreign countries where, we are told, by international arrangement it is to be current? Probably in this as in other communistic schemes there is a lurking assumption that the members of the brotherhood would always remain in the same place, and that life will thus become stationary as well as devoid of individual aim. But the weak part of the arrangement betrays itself in the necessity of continuing to use the terms dollars and cents. They are used only, we are told, as "algebraic symbols." Surely the most obvious and the safest course would have been to discard the terms altogether, pregnant as they were with evil associations and likely as they would be to perpetuate the vicious desires and habits of the past. Let another set of algebraic symbols be devised, and let us see how it will work. In the case of the transition from the use of money to that of labour certificates, as in that of the transition from private commerce to commerce concentrated in the hands of government, we should have liked to be present when the leap was taken, or at least to have had some account of the process, especially as it must have taken place at once over the whole civilised world. For commerce, we have seen, there is still to be; the utopian of Boston could not get his wine and cigars without it.

Law as a profession has ceased to exist. Of course where there is no property there can be no chancery suits. As nineteen twentieths of crime arise from the desire of money — not from drink, as the prohibitionists pretend — it follows that in getting rid of money society has almost entirely got rid of crime. Of crime, in the present sense of the term, indeed, it has got rid altogether. A few victims of "atavism" are left as a sort of tribute to reality, but they generally save the judiciary trouble by pleading guilty, so high has the regard for veracity become even in the minds of kleptomaniacs.

In the present imperfect state of things, the distribution of employments, it must be owned, though partly a matter of choice, is largely a matter of chance and circumstance, the intellectual callings going to those who have the means of a high education. In utopia it will be entirely a matter of choice, after elaborate testing of aptitudes and tastes under the guidance of a paternal government. It is assumed that all employments will attract, since some men, after deliberate survey of all the walks of life, will conveniently choose to be miners, hod-men, "odourless excavators," brakesmen, stokers, or sailors on the north Atlantic passage. Danger is even attractive. Such is the exuberance of public spirit that the government has only to declare an employment extra hazardous and a rush of chivalrous candidates to it ensues. A rush might rather have been apprehended into the lighter callings, especially that of poet. Any repugnance to a particular kind of labour which there might be, will be conjured away by saying that all kinds of labour are equally honourable. Do we not say this now? Do we not feel this now much more than the pessimist admits? Does any one worthy of the name of a gentleman increase the burden which he imposes on his household "by adding to it contempt"?

Everybody is to be highly educated and thoroughly refined. This in utopia will not interfere with the disposition for manual labour, nor will it take away too much of the labourer's time. One question, however, occurs to us. The population cannot have been highly educated when the system was first introduced. How were the ignorant and unqualified masses brought to take part in its introduction, and how was its operation managed before they had been educated up to the proper mark? This is another problem of the transition, the solution of which remains buried in the seer's magnetic sleep.

The relations between the sexes and the constitution of the

family are, of course, to be revolutionised, and the revolution
has so far an element of probability that it follows what are
supposed to be Bostonian lines. The women are to be organised apart from the men as a distinct interest, under a "general"
of their own who has a seat in the cabinet. They would do
quite enough for society, they are gallantly told, if they occupied themselves only in the cultivation of their own charms
and graces; women without any special charms and graces but
those which belong to the performance of their womanly duties
as wives and mothers being creatures unknown in utopia.
However, for the sake of their health and to satisfy their feelings of independence, they are to do a very moderate amount
of work. They have in fact little else to do. They have
no household cares, as the State is universal cook, housemaid,
laundress, seamstress, and nurse; and "a husband is not a
baby that he should be cared for." Maternity, though recognised, is thrown into the background. It is an interlude in
the woman's industrial and social life, and as soon as it is
over the mother returns to her " comrades," leaving her child,
apparently, to that universal providence, the State. Hitherto,
it seems, men, like "cruel robbers," have "seized to themselves the whole product of the world and left women to beg
and wheedle for their share." By whose labour the world has
been made to yield its products for the benefit of both sexes,
we are not told. However, "that any person should be dependent for the means of support upon another would be
shocking to the moral sense as well as indefensible on any
rational social theory." Women in utopia, therefore, are no
longer left in "galling dependence" upon their husbands for
the means of life, or children upon their parents. Both wife
and child are maintained by the agency of the State, so that
the wife no longer owes anything to her husband, and the
child is at liberty, as reason and nature dictate, to snap its
fingers in its parents' face. Does the State give suck, and is
the baby no longer ignominiously beholden to its mother for
milk ? Is not the government composed of persons ? Why
is dependence upon the persons installed at Washington less

ignominious than dependence upon a husband, a father, or a mother? To some, dependence on the government might seem the most galling of all.

False delicacy is put out of the way, and the women are allowed to propose. They "sit aloft" on the top of the coach, giving the prizes for the industrial race, and select only the best and noblest men for their husbands. Ill-favoured men of inferior type, and laggards, will be condemned to celibacy. From them the "radiant faces" will be averted. These hapless persons are treated with a marked absence, to say the least, of the philanthropy which overflows upon criminals and lunatics, though it seems that the plea of atavism should not be less valid in their case. Has Dr. Leete, when he denies them marriage, found a way of extinguishing their passions? If he has not, what moral results does he expect? He will answer perhaps by an appeal to what may be called the occult "we," that mysterious power which, in an utopia, is present throughout to solve all difficulties and banish every doubt. Nothing can be more divine than the picture which Dr. Leete presents to us; but we look at it with a secret misgiving that his community would be in some danger of being thrust out of existence by some barbarous horde, which honoured virtue and admired excellence in both sexes without giving itself over to a slavish and fatuous worship of either, held men and women alike to their natural duties, and obeyed the laws of Nature.

The government is the universal publisher, and is bound to publish everything brought to it, but on condition that the author pay the first cost out of his "credit." How the author, while preparing himself to write "Paradise Lost," or the "Principia," is to earn a labour credit, we hardly see. The literature of utopia is of course divine. To read one of Berrian's novels or one of Oates's poems is worth a year of one's life. Would that we had a specimen of either! We should then be able to see how far it transcended Shakespeare or Scott. For love stories, we are told, there will be material in plenty and of a much higher quality than there was in the days of coarse and stormy passion. The actual love affair that takes place in "Looking Backward" certainly does not remind us of "Romeo and Juliet." Of the pulpit eloquence we have a specimen, and it is startlingly like that of our own century. One great improvement, however, there is; the preaching is by telephone and you can shut it off.

The physical arrangements are carried to millenarian perfection. Instead of a multitude of separate umbrellas, one common umbrella is put up by the State over Boston when it rains. The whole community is converted into one vast Whiteley's or Wanamaker's establishment. These visions of a material heaven on earth naturally arise as the hope of a spiritual heaven fades away. A material heaven on earth it is. The arrangements for shopping, like everything else, are divine. Public bands are playing seraphic music through the whole twenty-four hours, and you turn on the piece you like by telephone. Public buildings are palaces, and their equipment is a paragon of luxury. We only wonder how the unspeakable privileges of the city can be extended to the country, and who will be contented to stay in the country if they are not. The American dream is of city life. But let the material happiness be as brilliant as it will, supposing every shadow of economical evil to have vanished, there is one shadow that will not away. It is signified that at a man's decease the State allows a fixed sum for his funeral expenses. This is the only intimation that over the material Paradise hovers Death.

A vista of illimitable progress, progress so glorious that it dazzles the prophetic eye, is said all the time to be opened. But how can there be progress beyond perfection? Finality is the trap into which all utopians fall. Comte, after tracing the movement of humanity through all the ages down to his own time, undertakes by his supreme intelligence to furnish a creed and a set of institutions which are to serve forever. Progress, however, we do not doubt there would be with a vengeance. The monotony, the constraint, the procrusteanism, the dulness, the despotism of the system would soon give birth to general revolt, which would dash the whole structure to pieces.

It may seem that we are guilty of a platitude in seriously criticising a composition the author of which himself perhaps was hardly serious in what he wrote. But the destructive passages, we repeat, tell, while the constructive part, as soon as it is touched by the finger of criticism, vanishes into the inane.

THE QUESTION OF DISESTABLISHMENT.

Disestablishment of the Church in England and Scotland is a question evidently at hand. It is a subject to be approached not only by every religious man, but by every statesman, with tenderness and care. The village church in which "the kneeling hamlet drains the vintage of the grapes of God," with its altar at which the people of the parish have been married, the font at which they were christened, and its churchyard in which their forefathers sleep, has been the great feature not only of rural landscape but of rural life. The Rectory, if its occupant did its duty, has been the centre of rural civilisation, education, and benevolence. It has done more in this way than the Hall. The religious sentiment and poetry of the nation have had their centre in the Cathedral. In Scotland, if the aspect of the Established Church is less picturesque, the attachment of the people to it and the connection of their spiritual life with it, in spite of disruption, are still stronger. It will be a great misfortune if the problem were left to be settled by faction, and political gamblers were allowed to use disestablishment as the means of loading their dice.

That there is a current almost throughout the civilised world setting towards disestablishment can hardly be denied. It is true that, as we have been bidden to observe, in every monarchical country of Europe the Church is still established and endowed, while in some, as in Austria and in Russia, it is still in a high degree endowed, even monasteries with their estates remaining undisturbed. Almost everywhere there are Ministries of Public Worship. Even republican France has her Established Church, subsidised by the State. This is true, and it is true that in republican Switzerland there is still a Cantonal, though not a Federal, connection of the State with the Church. But on what sort of footing is the Church in the more advanced countries now established and endowed, compared with the footing on which she was established and endowed in the old Catholic days? No longer half mistress of the realm, or forming a great estate of it, she has sunk into a pensioner, and a not very beloved or honoured pensioner, of the government. In France, once the realm of her eldest son, where a century and a half ago she could put men to death for offences against her, she now shares her dole, not only with heretics but with Jews, while in the French province of Algeria she shares it with Mussulmans. In the land of Philip the Second, though almost the whole population still professes his creed, her position is hardly higher or more secure than in the land of Louis the Fourteenth. There, too, instead of dominating, she is a creature of the government, her enormous property has been secularised, and she has become a paid servant of the State. Education, the key of social character and influence, has been generally wrested out of her hands. Marriage, also, has been generally transferred from her domain to that of the magistrate. To take an instance from the Protestant side, how great is the change in the relation of the Church in general to the State since the days in which Calvin was dictator! If in Austria and Russia the process is not so far advanced, it is because they are behind the other nations in the general race. The Republics are the last birth of Time, they are the leading shoots of political growth, and in them the connection between Church and State is weakest. All the footprints point the same way. The only apparent exception is the restoration of the Established Church of France by Napoleon. The violence of the extreme revolutionary party had for the time outrun popular conviction, and thus a reactionary despot was enabled to take a step backward, and by his fiat reinstate an institution of the past. But how altered was that institution in its estate and in its relation to the government from the Established Church of the Bourbons!

Even Ministries of Public Worship, where they exist, are signs that the Church has become a subordinate department of the State, losing her independence and a part of her sanctity with it.

The Papacy itself, once the supremely established and imperially endowed Church of Catholic Europe, has it not been both disestablished and disendowed? Its chief is now the "prisoner of the Vatican," subsisting on the alms of the faithful and hopelessly protesting against the abolition of his temporal power. It is true his spiritual power over the people has been increased by becoming purely spiritual, and by the concentration upon him of the allegiance of the Catholic Churches which, having lost the support of the national governments, now look to their ecclesiastical chief alone. This is a fact suggestive of caution to the statesman, while it is reassuring to the churchman; but it does not affect our estimate of the situation.

Supporters of establishment bid us observe that in all the South American Republics except Mexico there is still an established Church. To Mexico must now be added Brazil, which, since it has cast off monarchy, has separated the Church from the State and placed all religions on a footing of equality. Mexico is a striking exception. So late as 1815 there was an *auto da fé* where now no religious procession can take place, no priest even can appear publicly in his priestly garments. In the other Republics, however, the connection between Church and State, though it subsists, is greatly altered, and the position of the Church is far different both in regard to establishment and in regard to endowment, from what it was in Spanish times. The priest has lost his political hold. Such hold as he still has he owes, not to the tendency of modern civilisation, but to the lingering influence of the religious despotism of old Spain.

In all the countries there is likely to be a halt and a breathing time after a great change. The union of Church and State is naturally followed by a period of half establishment, with reduced revenues, and toleration of all creeds, perhaps endowment of all of them alike, and Ministries of Public Worship. But the shadow will go back on the dial when the movement from religious privilege towards religious equality is reversed. What is the severance of the Church from the State whereby government declares its entire neutrality in matters of opinion, but the recognition of that freedom of inquiry which, while other results of political revolution are still doubtful or chequered, is the clear and inestimable gain of our modern civilisation? Free, opinion is not while one set of opinions is hedged about with artificial reverence and propagated at the expense of the rest. Disestablishment, if right in itself, will be not merely the destruction of an existing institution, it will give free play to the constructive agency of truth, which we trust will build the mansion of the future.

They are mistaken who tell us that in the communities of North America there never was a connection between Church and State, and therefore there can be no tendency to its destruction. The truth is that in most of the old colonies there formerly was a connection. In Virginia the Church of England was established, till religious equality, championed by Jefferson and Madison, followed in the wake of political revolution. In Massachusetts and Connecticut the connection was close, as in Massachusetts the Quakers found to their cost. Nor was it dissolved without a struggle. In Massachusetts, the law provided for the maintenance of ministers as well as of schools, and for the punishment of religious offences, such as profanity and disregard of the Sabbath. For a long time the political franchise was confined to those who were in close communion. In Connecticut, no church could be founded without permission from the general court, and every citizen was obliged to pay according to his means towards the support of the minister of the geographical parish of his residence. Ministers were exempt from taxation of everything. The Blue Laws, so far as they had any real existence, were legislation against sin, which implies an identification of the civil with the ecclesiastical power. Nothing of the connection now remains except the Sunday law, of which some agnostics complain as theocratic; restraints on blasphemous publications, which are as much dictated by regard for decency and for the public peace as by regard for religion; the exemption of Churches from municipal taxation; and a very slight religious element in the teaching of the public schools, not so much enforced by the State as generally demanded by public feeling. The exemption of Church property from taxation extends to the property of all Churches alike, nor is it probable that it continue long.

The Congress of the United States is expressly forbidden by the first amendment of the Constitution to establish any religion. There are some who would like to insert into the Constitution a recognition of the Deity, but this proposal makes no way. Congress has a Chaplain and is opened with prayer, but the chaplaincy is not confined to any particular Church. The President of the United States annually proclaims a "national thanksgiving day," and has sometimes proclaimed a fast, in compliance, however, with national sentiment, and without power of enforcement. This is manifestly an ancient system attenuated to vanishing point.

In French Canada, the Roman Catholic Church retains its revenues in virtue of an article in the treaty of cession, but it levies tithes only on its own members. The authority vested in the bishops for the regulation of parishes draws with it, though indirectly, a certain amount of legal power in municipal affairs. But the political influence which makes it more powerful in the province than any establishment could be, is entirely beyond the law.

In British Canada, the Church was originally established; reserves of land were set apart for its ministers, the university was confined to its members, and its bishop had a seat in the Council. But as soon as the colony obtained self-government, Disestablishment ensued; the clergy reserves were secularised, and the university was thrown open to students of all religions, while the high Anglicans seceded and founded a separate university of their own. A faint odour of departed privilege still clings to what was once the State Church, clergymen of which now and then allow it to be felt that they regard the members of other Churches as Dissenters, while the bishops, unlike those in the United States, retain the title of "lord." Of the endowments, there remain about forty rectories which were carved out of the clergy reserves before secularisation. Otherwise there are no traces of the connection between Church and State in nominally monarchical Canada, saving those which have their counterparts in the American Republic.

Not only does religious equality in all material respects prevail in the United States and in British Canada, but it is thoroughly accepted by everybody, and by the immense majority prized and lauded as an organic principle of New World civilisation. In British Canada, a few Anglicans may perhaps look back wistfully to the days of the clergy reserves. The Roman Catholic priest in the New World as well as in the Old World has in his pocket the Encyclical which declares that his Church ought everywhere to be established, and that government ought to use its power for her support. But, in the New World, the pocket is very deep, and there seems no disposition to draw forth the missive. In fact, we hear that some of the chiefs of the Roman Catholic Church avow a preference for the free system. In Ontario, and in Manitoba, the Roman Catholics have hitherto retained the privilege of separate schools, which, however, they owe, not to Canadian, but to Imperial legislation. In Manitoba they have come, and in Ontario they are likely to come, into collision with the commonwealth on this question. But the privilege, though a State favour, is in the line, not of connection, but of separation. The tribute in the shape of public subsidies, which the Roman Catholic Church extorts by her political influence in the States of the Union where there is a large Irish vote, is paid, not in the name of religion, but in that of charity. There is now a strong reaction against any such sectarian use of public funds.

The property of the American Churches, and the legal rights attached to membership of them or to their officers, are, of course, in the keeping of the civil law. This has been adduced as proof of the present existence in America of a connection between the State and the Church. But the same reasoning would establish the existence of a connection between the State and the Society of Freemasons or the Jockey Club.

The case in favour of Disestablishment in Ireland was particularly strong, and the cause of the State Church was weighted with a painful history. Yet the defence was able to show that the general principle was involved, and that the shafts of the assailants glanced logically from the Irish to the English Establishment, while they almost struck full on the Establishment in Wales. Let it be observed, too, that nobody thought of transferring the privilege and the endowment from the Church of the minority to that of the majority; while concurrent endowment, though it had much to recommend it from a political point of view, was proposed, only to be decisively rejected.

What proof of the drift of things can be stronger than the career of Mr. Gladstone? He who bestowed on Ireland religious equality, had once seceded from a government because it broke the principle of a State religion by proposing a small additional grant to Maynooth. He who is now apparently ready to put the question of Establishment to the vote, once wrote a treatise on the relation between Church and State in which, soaring above the ordinary arguments derived from the usefulness of religion to the commonwealth in promoting public morality, he maintained that the nation, like the individual, had a conscience which bound it to choose, support, and propagate the true faith. Nobody was to hold civil office or exercise political power who did not belong to the State Church. The members of the government were to be " worshipping men," and were to sanctify their administrative acts by prayer and praise.

Macaulay, in his review of Mr. Gladstone's essay, had no difficulty in showing that governments are meant to govern, not to settle theological questions, and that if no power was to be exercised except upon Church principles, much inconvenience, to which he might have added much hypocrisy, would ensue. He had no difficulty in dissolving the ingenious, but unhistorical, hypothesis of a restrictive treaty by which the essayist tried to escape the awkward consequences of an application of his principles to the Indian Empire. He had no difficulty in showing that such half-measures of persecution as the application of civil disabilities were at once unjust and futile. He might almost have contented himself with saying that only a person could have a conscience, and that the personality of the nation was a figment. But when he comes, as an orthodox Whig, to propound his own defence of a Church Establishment, saying that he will give Mr. Gladstone his revenge, he does give Mr. Gladstone his revenge indeed. His own theory is, in reality, as untenable as that over which he has been enjoying an easy though brilliant triumph. An institution, he says, besides the primary object for which it is intended, may serve a secondary object, just as a hospital intended for the accommodation of the sick may also serve, by its architectural beauty, as an ornament to the public street. Government is meant to take care of our temporal interests, and is properly fitted for that purpose alone; but if that is not employment enough for it, it may, as a sort of by-play, take to providing for our spiritual interests as well. A singular sort of by-play, surely, it would be. The appearance of a building belongs to architecture as properly as its arrangement. The encouragement of art by a political government, which Macaulay adduces as another illustration, is not less beside the mark, since it is art in general that government encourages, not a particular school of artists. The civil ruler in establishing a religion need not, Macaulay says, decide which religion is true, but only which is best for his practical purposes; he will give the Scotch Presbyterianism, though he may himself be an Anglican, because Presbyterianism, though not the most true, may be most suited for the Scotch. But what is his criterion? Is he to assume that the religion of the majority is the best? He helps to secure to the privileged religion a majority by establishing it, and thus vitiates his own test. Besides, how is he to measure and provide for changes of conviction, such as in the course of inquiry may take place ? Suppose he had been called upon to legislate in the period of the Reformation, when the majority was shifting from day to day. Nor does Macaulay wholly escape the charge, which he brings against Mr. Gladstone, of feeble and ineffective persecution. It is a kind of persecution, though a very feeble and ineffective kind, to compel the minority to contribute to the support of a religion which they believe to be false, perhaps destructive of souls, and to degrade their ministers by exclusion from the rank and privilege which those of the Established Church enjoy. Macaulay is acting as a philosophic politician, on the principle that all religions are to the statesman equally useful, and he forgets that to men of strong religious convictions any religion but their own is dangerous falsehood, to be forced to contribute to the support of which is of all tyrannies the most repulsive.

But are not these mighty opponents fighting in the clouds ? On earth we have had despots imposing their religions on conquered communities. Ferdinand the Second imposed his Catholicism on Bohemia when it was wrested from Protestantism, Louis the Fourteenth imposed his Catholicism on a German province when it fell into his hands. But has any king or governor ever selected a religion by the light of his own conscience and imposed it on the people ? Has the process ever been one of speculative reasoning or conviction ? For the origin of Establishment we must go back, apparently, to the days of tribal religion, in which every member of the tribe was, by virtue of his birth, a loyal worshipper of its tutelary divinity. Conversion as well as belief was not personal but tribal, the Saxon or Dane passing with the rest of his race, or the portion of it to which he belonged, and under his chief, by treaty or capitulation, to the allegiance of the conquering god. What is styled the conversion of Constantine was in all probability hardly a change of mind: it certainly was not a change of life; most likely it was the recognition, by a shrewd and thoroughly worldly politician, of the ascendancy which, partly through the manifest failure of the old gods to avert public disaster, Christianity had gained in the Roman world. ·

The Christian Church inherited the Establishment of the Pagan Empire. But to the primal tradition of allegiance to the national divinity was now added belief in the absolute and final truth of a religion guaranteed by supernatural revelation and by an Infallible Church whose authority excluded inquiry and made dissent treason at once against her and against the State with which she was united. Out of the Church Establishment of the Roman Empire grew, on the one hand, the Byzantine establishment now represented by the national Church of Russia, and on the other hand, the establishment of the group of European nations which framed a religious federation under the ecclesiastical sovereignty of the Pope. To what the identification of the Church with the kingdoms of this world and the consequent identification of heresy with treason led, as it could not fail to lead, is written on some of the most terrible pages of history. Religion has been accused of crimes of which the real source was in the union of the spiritual with the temporal authority, and in the temporal wealth of a State Church. Mere fanaticism has less to answer for than Papal tiaras and archbishoprics of Toledo.

Undoubting conviction and perfect unity of belief were throughout the conditions of the system. When doubt, inquiry, and disagreement came in with the Reformation, the basis of the system was withdrawn. At first, an attempt was made, at least by Protestant rulers, to fall back on national Establishments, to which it was the aim of statesmen, by legal constraint or politic compromise, to make all subjects of the realm conform. The belief that a nation was bound to have a religion, and to support it by legal privilege and endowment, had become thoroughly ingrained: its hold on the mind of the Puritan was strengthened by his uncritical acceptance of the Old Testament; and the Barebone Parliament of Independents wrecked itself partly in an attempt to disendow the Church. But geographical and political boundaries do not coincide with those of speculative conviction. Nationality, therefore, in the absence of coercion, could be no basis for churchmanship. The last expedient of those who, naturally enough, were reluctant to see the commonwealth finally divorced from religion, was to establish the religion of the numerical majority. But the weakness of such a principle has been already shown. You falsify your own test when you artificially draw people into a particular Church by giving it privileges and endowments. The principle was, in fact, renounced when endowment was refused to the Church of the majority in Ireland. The best religion, the Voluntaryist will contend, for the citizen as well as for the man, is that in which he sincerely believes; and belief, to be perfectly sincere, must be not only unconstrained but unbribed.

Stress has been laid, in the controversy with regard to the Anglican endowments, on the legal fact that the Church of England is collectively not a corporation, each of her incumbents being a corporation sole. She could hardly be a corporation in the Papal period, since, though locally *Ecclesia Anglicana*, she was part of a European, or, as her members contended, of a universal Church, transcending all local jurisdiction and with a law of its own transcending all municipal law. She could hardly be a corporation in the national period, because she was then identified with the nation, the king of which was her head. But, surely, such considerations, though they might be deemed decisive in a lawsuit, cannot go for much in determining the expediency of a great political and religious change. The same may be said with regard to the question as to the legal character and origin of tithe. As a matter of fact, tithe was in its origin neither an aggregate of voluntary benefactions, nor a tax imposed by the State. The payment was a religious duty, of the obligation to perform which the clergy had convinced the people, and which, like other religious duties, was enforced indiscriminately with civil duties by the kings and witenagemotes of those days. Nobody can doubt now that tithe is public property, to be dealt with according to the rules of public policy and justice, by both of which respect for vested interests is prescribed.

Arnold's ideal, apparently, was an Established Church, not only connected, but identical, with the commonwealth, embracing Christians of all doctrinal varieties, and making no distinction between clergy and laity but one of a merely official kind. This idea evidently was drawn from the commonwealths of ancient Greece, of the history of which Arnold was a passionate student. From Arnold it was transmitted to Stanley, who went so far in his love of State Churches and their champions as to show a slight tenderness for "Bluidie Mackenzie." The difficulties of application in a country like England, full of religious divisions, including the insurmountable division between Protestants and Roman Catholics, need no demonstration. How are the different sects to share the edifices and the endowments among them? How, if they are all to be domiciled under the same roof, is peace to be kept in such a family? The part of the Minister of Public Worship would not be easy. To the Empire, of course, with all its Mahometans and Hindoos, such an ecclesiastical polity could not be extended. But, above all, what object is to be gained by encountering all these problems and complications which would not be better gained through the self-adjusting simplicity of the free system? The function assigned by Arnold to the government seems to be that of ecclesiastical police, the needlessness of which the experience of Churches in America, where all goes on decently and without disorder, shows. Arnold appears to have forgotten that, in ancient Athens, such spiritual life as there was went on, at least in the time of Socrates, apart from the State religion, and that its pontiff sacrificed to Æsculapius a cock, not his spiritual convictions. The sacrificing of cocks innumerable to Æsculapius, with the provisions of stipends for his official ministers, would probably be the chief fruits of the Arnoldian system.

Arnold's ideal is a Christian commonwealth. This he would have, though he would not have conformity or orthodoxy, if his nation were made up of Christian Churches whose common principles would practically regulate public life and national action. In this sense the American commonwealth is Christian. It is far more Christian than England, or any one of the European nations with Established Churches, was in the last century. Ostensibly, of course, it is not Christian or religious; but surely it must be the practical, not the ostensible, character which has a value in the eye of Heaven.

In native American communities and in Canada, society and life, it may safely be said, are fully as religious under the free system, as they are in England under that of a State Church. Unquestionably there is far more respect for religion there than in France, where the Church is still established, but, in a "Librairie Anti-cléricale," the most hideous blasphemy is openly sold. The Church in America and Canada is, to fully as great an extent as in England, the centre of philanthropic effort and even of social life. There is fully as much building of churches and as much church-going, and the Sunday is as well kept. The very aspect of an American city or village, with its spires and steeples "pointing to heaven," though perhaps not "tapering" with consummate grace, proclaims the community religious. American missions to the heathen vie with those of England. If the public school admits only a very small element of religion, the Sunday school is a highly cherished and a flourishing institution. The churches are enabled to distribute large sums in charity; some of them in fact do fully as much as is desirable in that way. We hear of a single offertory in the church of a great preacher, with a wealthy congregation, of $50,000. While the choice of a religion is absolutely free, while no candidate for office is asked to what Church he belongs, while members of the same family belong to different Churches without domestic friction, to be entirely without a religion is to incur, with most people, a shade of social suspicion. In no reputable society would anything offensive to religious feeling be endured. All this is spontaneous and has the strength of spontaneity, while the religion of the peasantry in an English country parish is not so certainly spontaneous. In New York or Chicago, there is a large foreign population, much of it drawn from the moral barbarism of Europe. Yet even in

New York and Chicago, religion is strong, is well endowed, furnishes the basis of much social effort, and copes vigorously with the adverse forces.

It is difficult to compare the incomes of the clergy under the two systems, but probably the clergy in the Northern States are, on the average, as well off as in England, certainly since the reduction of the incomes of English benefices by agricultural depression. A first-rate preacher in a great American city has an income hardly inferior to that of an English bishop, when the bishop's heavy liabilities are taken into account. Clerical incomes might be greatly improved if the Protestant Churches between whose creeds there is no essential difference would, in the rural districts at least, instead of competing, combine, and give a good stipend to one pastor where they now give poor stipends to three. Nor does it seem impossible that something of this kind may be brought about. Though there cannot be said to be any present likelihood of formal union among the Protestant Churches, there is a strong tendency to mutual recognition and to interchange of pulpits, from which working union, at all events, may some day result. It is also difficult to draw a comparison between the social position of the clergy in the United States and their social position in England. There are not in America dignitaries like the English Bishop and Dean, enjoying precedence by virtue of their ecclesiastical office, nor is there a set of clergymen like the country rectors of England, combining the resident gentleman with the pastor. The balance perhaps is rather in favour of the clergy under the free system. No American clergyman can be an object of class-antipathy to the people, as it seems the English parson sometimes is in a country parish. That a clergyman, if he depends on his congregation for his pay, will become their theological thrall, is, perhaps, a natural fear. It certainly was strong in the writers of " Tracts for the Times," who, in reviving the doctrine of Apostolical Succession, avowedly sought a new basis of authority in place of the support of the State, which seemed to be failing them, in order that they might save themselves from becoming, like Dissenting ministers, dependent on their flocks, and being thereby constrained to pander to lay appetite in their teaching. Yet a complaint is not often heard upon this subject, and American congregations have been loyal to the pastors of their choice even when their loyalty has been severely tried. The layman, as a rule, is not a theologian; nor is it his tendency, so long as he gets on well with his pastor generally, to meddle with the teaching of the pulpit. Sometimes the stipend is paid, not by the congregation directly, but through the medium of a central administration. A clergyman of the American Episcopal Church states that under this plan he never heard a pastor complain of the loss of power or independence, that the tie of affection is as strong as in the most favoured parishes of England, that the congregations show no desire to tune the pulpit, and that if disputes arise they are easily settled. The clergy, he says, remain in their parishes as long and as securely as do the clergy in England; in his city they have just buried a rector who had been in the same charge over fifty years, one of his own predecessors held the cure for forty-six years, and all around him are men who have held their cures for twenty, thirty, or forty years. He knows of no differences between rector and congregation, nor does he believe that amongst their two hundred clergy there is one who wishes the Church to be " by law established." He admits that there are clerical failures, but he says that they rarely find themselves in positions of importance, and usually drop out early. In an Established Church they would, as a rule, not drop out, especially if they held family livings. Against any possible evils arising from the restlessness or caprice of congregations, are to be set the torpor which may be bred by security and the chances of irremovable incapacity or decrepitude. The parishioners of livings in the gift of colleges, when the colleges were close, and the presentees had lived many years in Common Room, would have had some strong evidence to give upon this subject.

The belief that religious extravagance will ensue upon the withdrawal of State control may, from American experience, be safely pronounced groundless. The effectual restraint on

extravagance is not State control, but popular enlightenment
Such works as Mr. Hepworth Dixon's "New America" and
"Spiritual Wives" have created a false impression. The wild
sects which he describes are, in the first place, as much social
as religious; and, in the second place, the space which they
occupy on the religious map of the United States is insignifi
cant. The great mass of the people belong to Churches im
ported from Europe, and identical in all essential respects with
their European counterparts. The only new Church of any
importance is the Universalist, which seems to be a liberal
Methodism with the doctrine of eternal punishment struck out
by the humanitarianism of democracy. Things are no longer
as they were in the earlier and less settled times. A camp
meeting now is little more than a religious picnic lasting
through several days. "Revivals" America has, and so has
England. The Salvation Army, if that is to be numbered
among extravagances, is an English product. Mormonism is
mainly recruited from England. No sect is to be found in the
New World comparable in wildness to some of which we read
as existing in Russia, where the connection between Church
and State, in its closeness, resembles the Caliphate. It is
needless to say that there is no superstition in the United
States so abject as that which has prevailed in the south of
Italy, in Spain, or in some parts of Russia.

It may be that in America preaching is more cultivated
than theology, and that this is partly the consequence of a
system which makes the power of attracting congregations
the passport to the high places of the clerical profession. It
is, however, fully as much a consequence of the rhetorical
tendencies of democracy in general. The tastes of the unedu
cated or half-educated are uncritical, and it is inevitable that
there should be, as unquestionably there is, rant in the popular
pulpit, as well as on the political stump. But there is also
preaching of the highest order, and such as, if good is to be
done by preaching at all, must do a great deal of good. It
may be doubted whether the English pulpit can vie with that
of the United States. It has hardly had a greater preacher

or in a higher style than the lamented Phillips Brooks. There is a tendency, perhaps, to overstrain for effect, but this is an intellectual characteristic of the age. People are no longer content simply to "hear the Word of God;" they crave for eloquence as they crave for ritual, and the result of the attempt to supply it is sometimes overstrain.

We cannot look far beneath the surface of religious life. Appearances, though strong and uniform, may deceive. Beneath all this church-building, church-going, mission-sending, and Sunday school-teaching, there may be growing hollowness and creeping doubts. That possibility is not confined to the Western hemisphere; but the tide of scepticism is less violent when it has no State Church against which to beat. The general tendency, even of those who lapse from orthodoxy in America, is not towards Atheism, but towards Theism, with Christian ethics and, perhaps, with Christian hopes. This, as a break, at all events, in a descent perilous to public morality, though orthodoxy may not value, statesmanship may.

If we turn to the Episcopal Church of the United States in particular, it could hardly be expected that the compromise between Catholicism and Protestantism devised by the Tudors and their councillors to meet the circumstances of the English people in the sixteenth century, or to satisfy at once the personal ritualism of Queen Elizabeth and her political antagonism to the Pope, would, when transplanted, strike its roots very deep into the soil of the New World. It is obvious that for certain classes of men, Methodism, Presbyterianism, and Roman Catholicism have attractions with which Anglicanism cannot compete. The Anglican Church is that of many of the rich and refined, whose tastes it suits by its hierarchical constitution, the dignity of its services, its historical associations, and its indulgent latitude. It also derives some social prestige from its connection with the State Church of England, with the episcopate and clergy of which its episcopate and clergy are identified. Not that it contains all the rich, or even a majority of them; many of the rich have risen from the ranks of industry and brought their Methodism, or some other popular religion, with them. Nor is it without an element drawn from the other social extreme. It counts among its members not a few of the very poor, especially among the new-comers from England, who have never been accustomed to maintain voluntary Churches, and to whom it is often liberal of its alms. We see here probably the position towards which it would gravitate if left to itself without State support in England. It must be remembered, however, that it has in England what it has not in the New World, cathedrals and parish churches, in which the religious life of the nation for ages has centred, together with a traditional hold on the minds of almost the whole of the wealthier classes. The elective episcopate of the United States, if it does not contain any one equal in learning to Lightfoot or Stubbs, is fully the peer of the English episcopate nominated by the Crown in excellence of personal character, in pastoral power, energy, and influence, in administrative capacity, and in the respect and attachment which it commands. The action of the laity when admitted to the Church legislature, which the English clergy dread, has been shown by experience to be conservative; they once were a check upon Evangelical, they are now a check on Ritualistic, innovation. No change of importance has been made in the Prayer Book beyond the omission of the Athanasian Creed. Of course there is trouble arising from the Ritualistic move-ment and the opposition to it; as trouble would arise from any attempt to combine two opposite codes of doctrine and spiritual systems in the same Church. But the laity may rejoice that no young incumbent has power, as in England, to change their worship from Protestant to Catholic, leaving them no remedy but a scandalous, costly, and precarious lawsuit. The election of a bishop sometimes ends, after a protracted struggle between the parties, in an unsatisfactory compromise. This is the inevitable result of the general division of opinion. Other evils there are which inhere in the elective system. Against these we have to set the evils which inhere in the system of nominations by the Crown, under which a Prime Minister, notoriously indifferent to religion, may capture the vote of a religious party by appointing its leaders to bishoprics.

It is true that, though severed from the State, the American Churches have not been entirely severed from politics. The Baptists appear creditably to maintain their traditional pre-eminence as the pioneers of spiritual freedom, but other Churches are more or less given to using their influence in politics to the detriment alike of Church and State; the Roman Catholic Church, with her control of the Irish vote, being the most political of all. The American Churches, or too many of them, sorely discredited themselves by bowing down before slavery in the evil day of its ascendancy, and repudiating or treating with coldness those who were striving to awaken the slumbering conscience of the nation; though as soon as the political and social pressure was removed the Churches, or such of them as were at heart opposed to slavery, stood erect again and lent the force of religious conviction to the nation in the mortal conflict. The foundations of all spiritual societies of men, as of the spiritual man himself, are in the dust; and it is too much to expect that, being composed of citizens and members of society, they shall entirely escape the political and social influences of the day. The Northern Churches might also plead, in excuse for their timorous attitude, the fear of rupture with their Southern branches, which in the case of the Baptists actually occurred.

Free Churches, if they cannot soar above humanity, have at least the power of self-adaptation and self-development. To a State Church this liberty is denied. It is in vain that clergymen of the Church of England speak as though in all the changes of doctrine and system it had been the Church that moved. By the will of Henry the Eighth the national Church was made Protestant so far as was required by the King's quarrel with the Pope and no further; by the will of Edward the Sixth and his Council she was made thoroughly Protestant and united to the Protestant Churches of the Continent; by the will of Mary she was made Catholic again and reunited to Rome; by the will of Elizabeth she was once more severed from the Papacy and settled on the principle of compromise. All this was done without any apparent evidence of a change of conviction on the part of the body of the clergy, which seems to have remained Catholic in sentiment throughout, to have welcomed the Catholic revolution under Mary, and to have been opposed to the Protestant revolution at the accession of Elizabeth, though no regard was paid in any case to its wishes.[1] James the First acted as a religious autocrat in his ecclesiastical proclamations and his appointment of deputies to the Synod of Dort. When he was at enmity with the Catholics he gave Low Church principles the ascendancy, by making Abbot archbishop; when he veered towards a connection with the Catholic Powers he gave High Church principles the ascendancy, by bringing forward Laud. Charles the First again in his reactionary changes acted as an autocrat, through Laud as his ecclesiastical vizier. Little attention appears to have been paid by the Primate to the opinions of the clergy, or even to those of the hierarchy at large. It was political power acting for a political purpose that, under the Restoration, finally cut off the Church of England from the Protestant Churches on the Continent, and, since the Romans deny her existence as a Church, while the Greeks practically will not recognise her, placed her in the strange position which she apparently holds of being the whole Church or no Church at all. In the next century, to use Hallam's scornful phrase, the State sprinkled a little dust upon the angry insects by depriving the Church altogether of the power of legislating for herself. She never had the opportunity of fairly saying what she would do with the Methodists, who were finally severed from her, not by excommunication or sécession, but by the necessity of registering their chapels under the Toleration Act. The Episcopal form of Church government was evidently perpetuated by the policy of the Monarchy. "No Bishop, no King." In Sweden the same influence retained Episcopacy though the religion was Lutheran. In countries such as Scotland, Switzerland, and Holland, where the religious revolution was made by an aristocracy or a democracy, other forms of Church government prevailed.

[1] See Dr. Child's *Church and State under the Tudors.*

Parliament, when it was thrown open to men of all religions and of none, became glaringly unfit to legislate for the Church. The Church thenceforth was condemned to legislative immobility. Change there has been and with a vengeance; the ritual has been turned from a Protestant service into what it is very difficult to distinguish from the Mass, while in other respects the Catholic system in place of the Protestant has been introduced. But this has been done, not by regular legislation, but by the irregular action of individual clergymen, at the expense of unseemly struggles and degrading litigation, sometimes before a tribunal of "Roman augurs." To give the change the colour of legality, it has been asserted that the Liturgy, not the Articles, is the standard of faith. Is it possible to believe that the standard is to be found, not in the original manifesto of which the object was explicitly to set forth doctrine, but in the ritual, the aim of the framers of which evidently was to retain as much as possible of the customary and familiar? The Church is the Keeper of all Truth: how came it to pass that down to the fourth decade of the nineteenth century she remained ignorant of this all-important truth respecting herself?

Few, surely, can look back with pride on the history of a political Church — her servile submission to the will of the sovereign; her boundless exaltation of the royal power for the sake of gaining royal favour and support; her sinister complicity with a political reaction which plunged the nation into a civil war; her alliance with the unholy powers of the Restoration for the purpose of crushing the Nonconformists; her preaching of passive obedience when the Crown was on the side of the clergy; her disregard of that doctrine as soon as clerical interests were touched by the tyranny; her courting of Nonconformist aid against James the Second; her renewed persecution of the Nonconformists under the leadership of the infidel Bolingbroke when the danger to herself was past; the wretched conspiracies of her Jacobite clergy against the peace of the country; the conduct of her clergy and bishops in Ireland, for the calamitous state of which they are partly responsible, and whence by their intolerance they drove forth Presbyterians, the sinews of Irish industry, to become the sinews of American revolution. For the obstinate violence of the government in its dealing with the Americans and the fatal rupture which ensued, clerical Toryism, as we know on the best of evidence, was largely to blame. Even with regard to questions of humanity, such as the abolition of the slave-trade and of slavery, the record of the State Church is inglorious, and we find its bishops voting against the repeal of the law making death the penalty of a petty theft. Was it possible that an institution morally and socially so little beneficent or venerable should exercise much religious influence on the people? True, besides her political history the Church of Hooker, Herbert, Ken, Butler, Wilson, Fletcher of Madeley and Simeon, has another history on which her friends may look with far greater satisfaction; but how far was this the fruit of legal establishment and State endowment?

To such an extent did the Church lose her spiritual and assume a political character that, as Somers said, absolute power, passive obedience, and non-resistance became, with her, doctrines essential to salvation. The good Bishop Lake said on his death-bed that " he looked on the great doctrine of passive obedience as the distinguishing character of the Church of England," and Bishop Thomas of Worcester expressed the same belief.[1] In the case of Monmouth, the bishops made the profession of this doctrine a condition of absolution. It is not with mere refusal to promote or countenance political innovation, that the State Church stands charged, but with playing an active and even a violent part in reaction. The torpor, the time-serving, the pluralism, the non-residence, the Trulliberian sensuality, as well as the scandalous place-hunting and the adulation of profligate Ministers and of kings' mistresses, which disgraced the clergy in the last century, are now, happily, things of the past. But when did they prevail? When the Church was most secure under the protection of the

---

[1] See *The English Church in the Eighteenth Century*, by Abbey and Overton, i. 138.

State. When did they cease and give place to a spirit of reform and duty ? When that protection began to be withdrawn.

The late Bishop of London, Jackson, is quoted by Dean Hole as saying that " when he recalled the condition of apathy, indolence, and disobedience into which the Church of England had fallen, it seemed marvellous to him that it continued to exist." The Dean himself remembers the days of pluralities and non-residence, when the people of his parish never saw or heard of their vicar, the church being served by the curate who lived five miles away, rode over for one dreary service on the Sunday, and was no more seen for the rest of the week, being much occupied with the pursuit of the fox ; when a pluralist who had come in a conscientious mood to visit the living from which he had long been an absentee, being offended by a bad smell, turned back and came no more; when the altar was represented by a small rickety deal table, with a scanty covering of faded and patched green baize, on which were placed the overcoat, hat, and riding-whip of the officiating minister ; when the font was filled with coffin ropes, tinder box, and candle-ends, and was never used for baptism ; when sparrows twittered and bats floated beneath the rotten timbers of the roof, while moths and beetles found happy homes below.[1] Since that time, the Dean says, there has been great reform, which he traces to the Oxford Movement. What was the age of decrepitude and abuse ? It was the age in which the Church of England felt herself most safely established. When did the revival begin ? When from the progress of Liberalism, civil and religious, the Establishment began to be endangered. What was the Oxford Movement ? It was practically a movement of dissent, though reactionary dissent, from the established system, and was at first so regarded and treated by almost the whole of the clergy of the Established Church. Its progress has been a perpetual conflict with the law and with the lay tribunals by which the law was upheld.

We have been warned that we must be very cautious in

<hr>

[1] See *The Memories of Dean Hole*, Chap. xi.

reasoning from the case of a new country like America or the British Colonies to that of an old country like England, where institutions are of ancient growth, and their fibres have become entwined with the whole political and social frame. It is a warning most true and most necessary to be observed, as is its converse, which forbids, for example, the attempt, apparently not yet abandoned, to propagate aristocracy in the Colonies. Yet it happens, curiously enough, that, just when this principle of relativity in politics is for the first time distinctly apprehended, it is beginning to lose somewhat of its force. Mankind is being unified by the increase of intercourse among the nations, and conscious intelligence is gaining the ascendancy over unconscious evolution. Of this, Japan, taking the most cautious estimate of her achievements, is a proof. America is brought close to Europe, and the success or failure of political and social experiments there already reacts upon the Old World.

The activity produced among the clergy by the effects of the Oxford Movement, and shown notably and most laudably in their ministrations among the poor, seems to have strengthened the hold of the Anglican Church upon the people in the cities. Among the people of the country, on the other hand, the Church appears to be losing ground, the reason probably being that the clergy are objects of suspicion to the peasantry from their connection with the squire. Perhaps also the parson sometimes is felt to meddle and dictate too much. To the attractions of Ritualism, while the minds of the people in the cities are sometimes open, those of the peasantry are completely closed. They lack the cultivated sensibility, they are utterly devoid of any historic link to the Middle Ages; their life is hard, and what they seek in religion is practical comfort, not the gratification of fancy and taste.

In Scotland, the Establishment is more strongly rooted than it is in England, as the last Midlothian election showed. It is more strongly rooted because having been founded, not by the Crown, but by the religious leaders of the Commons, it is more popular and democratic. For the same reason it is more orthodox, its creed being in the keeping, not of a clerical order, but of the people at large, who identify themselves with its doctrines and are little reached by sceptical speculation.

The policy of using a State clergy as a black police is, surely, not less shallow than it is insulting to the clergy who are to be so used. Let the people once understand that the pastor is a black policeman, and the influence on which this policy relies will be gone. A government gets fully as much support from free Churches in the maintenance of social order and for all moral objects as it does from any State Church. The American government got the most strenuous and effective aid from the Protestant Churches as organs of the popular conscience during the Civil War. On the other hand, that government escapes what, added to the storms of political faction, would certainly wreck it, entanglement with religious quarrels and with a chronic struggle between a privileged Church and her rivals. It has no Hampden Case, no Ecclesiastical Titles Bill, no Bills "for putting down Ritualism." Nor is it exposed to the chronic rebellion of a great body of Nonconformists irritated by social disparagement perhaps even more than by their religious grievance. An English Nonconformist minister is not, as such, disposed to revolution; he is not the natural ally of Jacobins; nor is there anything in his vocation which should lead him to desire the dismemberment of the United Kingdom. He is a Radical and a Home Ruler because it is from that party that he hopes to get religious equality.

None would be less disposed to hand over Ireland to the dominion of the Roman Catholic priesthood than the Welsh Methodists, if they were not tempted by the offer of Disestablishment for Wales. Church establishment in Wales is a stone hanging round the neck of a government swimming for life, and the integrity of the nation is imperilled in no slight degree by the obstinate determination to force on the Welsh Celt against his nature the fiat religion of Elizabeth Tudor. Anglicanism in Wales is the religion of the gentry, who are largely English. That of the Celtic peasantry it has not been and cannot be. The Celtic peasant may be a fervent Catholic, as he is in Ireland and Brittany, a fervent Presbyterian as he is in the Highlands, or a fervent Methodist as he is in Wales, a staid and decorous Anglican never. The overwhelming Gladstonian majority in Wales at the last election was a majority for disestablishment. The Anglican clergy of Wales are clergymen of the Established Church of England, and the interests of the Established Church of England are theirs. Are they wise in asking it to fight the decisive battle for its existence on a field so unfavourable to its cause as Wales?

Whatever is seditious and dangerous in the Irish priesthood arises not from its being unestablished, but from its being Irish, and Irish of the peasant class. It is also rendered anti-national by its allegiance to a foreign head; but this it would be in any case.

Some politicians have regarded religion as a disturbing force, for which legal establishment under State control provided salutary fetters. If religion is false, if the enthusiasm to which it gives birth is a kind of madness, and if the vices of its ministers are less dangerous than their virtues, the more it is kept under the control of statesmanship the better. But, then, why foster it at all? If it is true, and spiritual life is not a figment, that surely alone is genuine statesmanship which leaves conscience and worship entirely free. When one looks back over the history of religion, including the religious wars, persecutions, and massacres, one cannot help wondering, if all this has happened under the beneficent regulation of statesmanship, what worse things could have happened in the absence of such regulation.

There is looming up from the clerical quarter a danger of another kind, with which statesmanship may hereafter have to deal. If the subversion of religious belief by science and criticism goes on, it will by degrees withdraw that on which the ministers of religion rest for their influence, their position, and their bread. Their distress or their apprehensions may become a disturbing element in society. Such a body of men as the celibate clergy of the Church of Rome, striving to make up by social leadership for the loss of spiritual authority in an age of Socialistic agitation, might be a for-midable addition to the sources of trouble; nor have symptoms of such a tendency been wanting. But this is a liability against which, if it exists, no policy of Establishment can guard. On the contrary, Establishment aggravates the danger by keeping a standing army of clergy in its pay irrespectively of the popular desire for their ministrations, and thus preparing for a great crash, when otherwise the reduction might be gradual and no large body of men might be threatened at the same time with the loss of their livelihood and position.

Less coarse than the "black police" theory, yet not less objectionable or in reality less insulting to the ministers of religion, is the theory of certain *illuminati*, who would have a State Church of popular superstition for the vulgar, while the cultivated sit apart on their thrones of light. This implies that a number of men, presumably superior in moral qualities and highly educated, are to be set apart for the purpose of teaching useful falsehood. Suppose any of them become illuminated, are they still to remain in their profession? What but moral corruption of the profoundest kind can be the fruit of such a policy? Yet such a thing has been experienced as the erection of an Anglican Church by an unbeliever in Christianity in pursuance of some such view. It may be suspected that Establishment has even drawn some equivocal recruits of late from the scepticism which prevails widely and is often combined with Conservatism in politics, while the Churches which rest only on free conviction have been losing ground. It is time to bethink ourselves that a Church, established or unestablished, must be either an organ of truth or an engine of evil. Apparently, no small portion of the educated world in England has come to the conclusion that the evidences of supernatural religion have failed. If they have, to keep on foot an institution the function of which is to preach and propagate supernatural religion can surely be neither wise nor right. When evidences of religion fail, religion must go, and we must look out for some other account of the universe and some other rule of life. Let us have no politic figment or organised self-delusion, because, on any hypothesis, theistic or atheistic, they can only lead us to destruction. We have no chance of moving in unison with the counsels of the Power, whatever it be, which rules this world, or of prospering accordingly, except by keeping in the allegiance of the truth.

On the whole, it would seem that a statesman, looking at the matter from his own point of view, would be likely to prepare for a change, and consider how the change can be made with least shock to the spiritual life of the people and with least hardship to the clergy. It would seem that a wise Churchman would be likely to think twice before he rejected a compromise, on the general lines of Irish Disestablishment, which, taking from him the tithe, now reduced in value, as well as the representation of the Church in the House of Lords, would leave him the cathedrals, the parish churches, the rectories, the glebes, the recent benefactions, and give him a freedom of legislation, by the wise use of which he might, supposing Christianity to retain its hold, recover, by the adaptation of institutions and formularies to the times, a part of the ground which, during the suspension of her legislative life, his Church has lost. Democracy is marching on, and the opportunity of compromise may never return. It has been said in answer to such a proposal that the clergy are trustees, and that however desirable the compromise might be, they can surrender nothing of their trust. Trustees, however, can with the sanction of a court of law, and still more with that of the Legislature, consent to anything which is for the benefit of the estate. No power not acting under authority manifestly divine is qualified to say *non possumus*. Those who do say it can only mean that they are determined to go by the board. State religion perhaps had its day. Whatever had its day is absolved by history, who nevertheless says to it, *Vale in pace*.

There is, it is true, another course, besides Disestablishment, which may present itself to a statesman desirous of dealing cautiously with this question and avoiding a shock to natural religion, the policy of comprehension. This was embraced by

Cromwell, and was the most liberal course possible in his day, when the opinion that a nation was bound to profess and support a religion remained firmly rooted in men's minds, as the wreck of Barebone's Parliament on the rock of Disestablishment shows. Cromwell's commissioners, to use Baxter's words, "put in able and serious preachers who lived a godly life, of what tolerable opinions soever they were, so that many thousands of souls blessed God." It is certain that before the Act of Uniformity, Episcopal ordination was not necessary for induction to an English living, nor had the State Church of England severed the connection with the Protestant Churches on the Continent. If ever an act was tainted in its origin, it was the Act of Uniformity, and to repeal it in the present state of opinion would probably be easy. But the practical effect of the repeal would most likely be defeated by the sentiments of the High Church clergy, now the dominant party, and who believe in apostolical succession and in an episcopally ordained priesthood as alone competent to perform the sacramental rites which are necessary to salvation.

In such a case, as indeed in regard to all great and organic questions, every true patriot must wish that the party struggle which is tearing the nation to pieces could be suspended, and that the solution could be committed to the hands of some impartial, enlightened, and open-minded statesman, whose award would be framed in the interest, and would command the confidence, of the nation at large. We might as well wish for the descent of an angel from heaven!

THE POLITICAL CRISIS IN ENGLAND.

THE POLITICAL CRISIS IN ENGLAND.

In the political crisis through which Great Britain is passing there are some things peculiar to Great Britain. There are other things interesting to all nations organised or about to be organised on the British model, to all nations, indeed, of which the governments are elective. The apparent catastrophe of the party system appears to afford as much food for reflection to an American as to an Englishman.

Under the belief that she has a monarchical government and an hereditary upper chamber, which assure her stability and safety, England has plunged into a democracy more unbridled than that of the United States under conditions far more dangerous. The people of the United States have a written constitution which emanated from themselves, and is the object of their profound reverence. They have a Supreme Court to guard that constitution. They have a President whose veto is a salutary reality, and whose authority is being signally displayed at the present juncture. They have a Senate, elected on a principle comparatively conservative, and really co-ordinate as a legislative body with the popular house, whose Bills it amends or throws out without fear. The federal structure of their commonwealth, like that of a ship in compartments, is a safeguard against any sudden flood of revolution. In their constitution is an article forbidding legislation which would impair the faith of contracts. The conditions in their case are less dangerous because they have greater abundance of land, a far larger number of freeholders, less pressure on the means of subsistence, little Socialism, what they have being mainly imported, and, notwithstanding the Homestead business, comparatively little, on the whole, of industrial war, the native American workman as a rule not being given to conspiracy and striking. Nor is there in America any economical crisis like agricultural depression with its social consequences in England, for the present storm in the stock market is financial, and does not touch the substantial elements of prosperity. The American people are comparatively free from class division and jealousy. They are eminently law-abiding, and are on the side of government, regarding it as their own; while the masses in England, the artisans especially, have learnt to think of government as a power apart from them, if not as their natural enemy. Nor does the scepticism, which in England is unsettling society and shaking the nerve of authority, prevail so much or produce such effects in a nation which has no State Church to be assailed, the religion of which is voluntary, and which is given more to industry than speculation. There is happily much in the state of England now unlike the state of France on the eve of the Revolution. Above all, England has in her upper classes a reserve of moral and political force which France had not, and which extremity may call forth. She is also comparatively free from the financial difficulty which in France brought on the crash, though a large public debt, with power in the hands of the multitude, is always dangerous, and the fiscal system of England is not free from peril since it is totally inelastic, and the disuse of any one of the great articles of consumption on which the revenue is raised would produce a great deficit, while experience has shown that the people will not bear a new tax, and that the income tax with its political liabilities is the only resort.

In America, there can be no amendment of the constitution without the distinct announcement of the specific amendment to be made, or without the consent of three-fourths of the people, signified through the State Legislatures or Conventions. So conservative is the process that there was no amendment during sixty years. What takes place in England? Not an amendment of the constitution, but a fundamental change of it, involving a legislative dismemberment of the United

Kingdom, and probably entailing further revolution of the same kind, is concerted by a party leader with his Irish confederates behind the back of the nation, and forced upon the country by an unscrupulous use of the party machine. Not only was a distinct knowledge of the measure withheld from the people at the last general election, but with regard to its principal feature, retention of the Irish members, the people were totally misled, the framer having pledged himself that nothing would induce him to be a party to an arrangement such as that which he now proposes. The issue, instead of being submitted distinctly to the people, is mixed up with a dozen other issues, some of them purposely raised to obscure and prejudice it. The measure is then forced upon the House of Commons, most of its provisions without any fair discussion, by the closure, applied at the will of a party leader, whose real majority, subtracting the twenty-two Irish votes to which Ireland by his own admission has no title, is twelve. Nor is there anything to prevent any other revolutionary measure from being carried by the same means as the repeal of the union with Ireland.

For a few years under the commonwealth England had a written constitution. Otherwise she has had nothing but certain fundamental statutes, such as the Great Charter, with its confirmations, the Petition of Right, the Habeas Corpus Act, and the Bill of Rights, all of which are restraints on the tyranny of the Crown, not on the excesses of the people. Not only has England had no written constitution, paradoxical as the statement may seem, she has had no constitution at all, if by constitution is meant a settled system with fixed relations among the component powers. She has had nothing but a balance of forces which, oscillating more or less through her history, has now been finally upset, the Crown having been divested of all authority, the House of Lords of all but a suspensive veto, while supreme power is vested in the House of Commons or in the electoral caucus to which the House of Commons has itself in turn become a slave. What is complacently styled constitutional development has in fact been a secular revolution.

The hallowed word "constitutional" has been used as if it represented something real and capable of being ascertained, though rather occult, some supreme though somewhat mystical standard by which all political claims could be tried and all political excesses could be restrained. This was almost comically apparent on the occasion of the repeal of the paper duty in 1860, which made way for a cheap press. The Commons passed repeal, the Lords threw it out. Then arose the question whether the Lords, who could not constitutionally initiate or amend a taxing Bill, could constitutionally throw out a Bill repealing a tax, thus continuing the impost which the Commons had voted away. A grand display of political metaphysics ensued. Mr. Denison, then Speaker of the House of Commons, was asked what he thought. "Why," said he, "they talk about constitutional principle; but the whole matter is this, the Lords cannot initiate a money Bill because the Commons would throw it out; they cannot amend a money Bill because the Commons would disagree to the amendment; but they can throw out this Bill repealing a tax, because there is an end, and the Commons have no more to say."

The theory was government by a King and legislation by two Houses of Parliament, one hereditary and aristocratic, the other elective and popular, the two being coequal in authority, except that the popular House had the power of the purse, which it gradually improved into supremacy. In the reign of Edward I., the magnanimous perpetuator of a revolutionary creation, the fact may have tallied with the theory. The government was in the King, and the Commons, though in themselves weaker than the Lords, may have been strengthened by alliance with the Crown. Under Edward's feeble successor the balance was turned in favour of the aristocracy. It was redressed in favour of the Crown by the glories of Edward III., though the Commons at the same time, as holders of the purse, gained by the King's need of supplies for his wars; and Richard II., in spite of the miserable end of his father's reign, succeeded to authority, which his folly and that of his favourites threw away. Henry IV., with a doubtful title and a mutinous nobility, was thrown for support on the Commons, and on the Church, which was still a great power in the State. Agincourt restored to the Crown an authority which was again forfeited by the loss of France, the imbecility of Henry VI., and the misrule of those who had him in their hands. The suicide of aristocracy in the Wars of the Roses left the Crown almost despotic, and its despotism was enhanced by the ecclesiastical revolution under Henry VIII., after which the Church ceased to be a political power, and its influence was transferred to the Crown. What the Tudors had held the Stuarts lost, while they tried to extend it in altered times and against the decisive tendencies of the nation. The English Revolution in the time of Charles I., like the American Revolution and the French Revolution, cleared the ground for a new edifice. A written constitution became necessary. A written constitution was framed under the name of the Instrument of Government, with a Protector for life, a standing Council of State, in the appointment of which the Protector and Parliament went shares, and a single House of Parliament, with a property qualification high enough to be a test of responsibility and intelligence, yet not higher than industry and frugality might generally hope to attain. Had the Commonwealth of England, Ireland, and Scotland such a constitution now, it would be in little danger of dismemberment by the Irish Celts. Republican jealousy and the death of the Protector just when his system was taking root, prevented a fair trial of the experiment. Cromwell himself had been driven by the stress of his conflict with irreconcilable republicans in the Commons to have recourse to the revival of the Upper House in a nominative form. This failed, as other nominative Senates have failed, and by withdrawing the strength of government from the popular chamber, aggravated the difficulty which it was intended to remove. The Restoration, however, was a reaction, not against the Protectorate, but against the military anarchy by which the Protectorate was followed. During the reign of Charles II., there was something like equilibrium, though uneasy and unsteady, the Crown at the time of the Popish Plot being swept before the popular storm, while the close of the reign being almost despotic, though tyranny was exercised under strictly legal forms. James II. repeated the mistake of Charles I. in an aggravated shape, the Jesuit taking the place of Laud. With him the monarchy fell as a constitutional power, its fall being only broken by the personal ascendancy of William III., who to the last was his own foreign minister. Then power passed to the Peers, who besides their own House largely controlled the House of Commons through their nomination boroughs and their local influence in elections, while they had thoroughly perfected the system of holding together the economical basis of their ascendancy by the entail of their family estates. At its back, and as its constituency, the Peerage had the landed gentry, the class completely dominant at this time. The principal checks to aristocratic ascendancy were the rivalries and cabals among the families themselves. These, and the odium created by aristocratic selfishness and corruption, enabled George III. to recover a large measure, not of constitutional, but of backstairs authority. He was able to put a backstairs veto on Fox's India Bill. Once more there was a sort of equilibrium amongst the three powers in the State, the government being largely in the King or in the Minister of his personal choice, while each of the Houses had its share of power, the balance between them being dressed by the Parliamentary patronage in the hands of the Peers and the manifest inadequacy of the unreformed House of Commons as a representation of the people. But the equilibrium was totally and forever destroyed by the current of liberalism which set in when the war with Napoleon was over, overturning the Bourbon monarchy and the British aristocracy at the same time. When the Peers succumbed to the Reform Bill, supreme power passed definitively to the House of Commons, leaving nothing to the Peers on any great question but a suspensive veto. The last faint exercise of personal power by the King was the dismissal of the Whig Ministry by William IV. in 1834. Henceforth the Ministers who formed the executive government were appointed and dismissed, and the whole policy of the kingdom was determined by the majority in the House of Commons. Still the phantom wore the crown. Still the nation fully believed itself to be a monarchy, and prayed every Sunday that Heaven, which is supposed to enter kindly into the illusion, would dispose the King's heart to govern aright. A party leader bringing in a party Bill for the extension of the suffrage could say, and perhaps persuaded himself, that the effect of his measure would be to "unite the whole people in a solid body round their ancient throne." The same politician now points out the House of Lords to popular vengeance, as "a power not upon or behind the throne, but between the throne and the people, stopping altogether the action of the constitutional machine." Could self-delusion or constitutional hypocrisy further go? The House of Lords has still been taken for a co-ordinate branch of the legislature. European nations in quest of a constitution have continued to imitate the British model as they found it described in Blackstone or De Lolme, and a strange dance some of them have been led.

Still the House of Commons was a government. It had a tolerable measure of independence, of authority, and of dignity as a national council. Its electorate, after the settlement of 1832, was still tolerably responsible and intelligent. Nor was it by the fated advance of democracy or by any occult force, that the settlement of 1832 was broken up, though the current of European opinion was setting in a democratic direction. The settlement was broken up by the personal ambition of party leaders, who invoked the gale of popularity to fill their flagging sails. There was at the time little popular demand for the measure, and when, after its first announcement, its author had to withdraw it, nobody wept except himself. But he had set revolution going again. After that came a Dutch auction, in which Liberal and Conservative bid against each other, and the prize was finally knocked down to the Conservative party, then under a leader who, as Carlyle said, treated England as his milch cow, and who had found for himself a patron and a partner in a magnate instinct in politics with the spirit of the Turf. There is no reason to doubt, there is reason to believe, that the intelligent artisans would have acquiesced in an educational qualification; but the Tory leader had been advised by his election agents that ignorance would be on his side, and he had no scruple in acting on that advice. Qualifications of any real value have been swept away. Such as are left will presently go, and before long perhaps even that of sex will be abolished by the help of Conservatives who fancy that the women will vote upon their side. Of those who now possess the franchise, an immense number must be ignorant of all questions of State, liable to be misled by the grossest illusions, hurried away by the blindest passions, cozened by the lowest charlatans. It was generally, and not without reason, believed that the Tichborne claimant would have been sent to Parliament with immense majorities, could he have been a candidate at the time of the trial. But the constituencies are a sovereign power, unrestrained, and can, through their subservient representatives, at any time pass measures which would shake society to its foundation, and might bring ruin on themselves. They are sovereign not only over their own country but also over a vast empire. The British artisan who is shouting One man, one vote, forgets that he is the lord of two hundred and eighty millions of Hindus who have no vote at all,—and if they had votes might some day vote him and his cottons out of Hindustan. The American democracy, in spite of strong temptation, both material and sentimental, shrank from the annexation of Hawaii because it felt its unfitness for the government of dependencies even on so small a scale. Yet a democracy far less regulated, and on the whole far less intelligent than that of America, is taking on itself the government of vast dependencies all over the world.

Another scene has now opened. The House of Commons, after putting under its feet the Crown and the House of Lords, has in its turn been put under the feet of the caucus. Its independence, its authority, its dignity, and its self-respect are departing. By the closure it is reduced to a voting machine of which the caucus turns the crank. Its members, instead of regarding themselves as free counsellors of the nation, regard themselves as delegates of the caucus, pledged to do its bidding, and, if their conscience rebels, to resign. The other day a Gladstonian, seeing the deception which had been practised upon the country by the framers of the Home Rule Bill in the retention of the Irish members and the infamy which was in store for Great Britain, found himself unable to digest the Bill. His duty to the country was to vote against it. But the wretched law of his Parliamentary being compelled him to decline that duty and place his resignation in the hands of the caucus under the form of accepting the Chiltern Hundreds. No one doubts that many a Gladstonian has voted for the Home Rule Bill under the same influence and against his sense of duty to the country. An imperious idol of the caucus and impersonation of its tyranny can indulge his autocratic temper by trampling on the liberty and majesty of what was once the foremost assembly in the world. It does not appear that the Conservative members feel themselves much more independent than the Radicals. If they did, their leader would hardly have failed to make use of a majority of a hundred for the purpose of redressing the balance of the constitution and providing safeguards against revolutionary violence. Nor would he and his colleagues have been fain to bid against their antagonists for popularity by paying tribute to socialistic Radicalism, which they did with the usual effect of blackmail.

The Septennial Act still preserves to Members of the House of Commons a small measure of independence for the first year or two of the Septennial term. It is to be repealed, the duration of Parliaments is to be reduced, and the last spark of a legislative independence offensive to the caucus is to be extinguished. A faint remnant of the principle that taxation and representation go together is left in the plurality of votes. This is to be swept away, and one man, one vote, is to be the rule.

But the most effective institution of a conservative kind yet left is the non-payment of members. This also is marked for abolition, and the Bill which abolishes it will probably receive the involuntary votes of Members of Parliament who abhor it in their hearts, knowing well that it will thrust them from their seats. In theory, the system of payment enables lowly merit to take the place to which the public voice calls it, but which poverty prevents it from taking; in fact, it is a direct incentive to men by no means of merit to engage in politics, the noblest of all callings but the vilest of all trades. The country will presently be in the hands of professional politicians, drawn from a class which prefers living upon the public to honest labour. These men, giving their lives to their trade, will oust men of principle, who, having no personal objects to gain, will grow weary of the incessant struggle while they will be disgusted with the task of flattering crowds and with the debasing tyranny of the "machine." Statesmanship already shows the influence of the stump, the incessant exactions of which leave a public man no leisure for rest or thought, and force him to be always committing himself, probably beyond his convictions, in his efforts to excite the crowd. Peel as well as Pitt would have been petrified by an invitation to speak at any election but his own. Pitt is believed to have made only two political speeches out of Parliament in his life, and one of these was a single sentence. A minister could then spend his vacations in maturing his measures, and he could keep his own counsels till the time came for disclosing them to Parliament. All public men had time for study and reflection. With the enlargement of the constituencies and the extension of the popular element in government, the change became to some extent inevitable. It has its consequences all the same.

The falling off in the character of the House of Commons is apparent to all. A deliberative assembly, in the proper sense of the term, it can hardly be said ever to have been; for it has always been at once too partisan and too large. On any party question a debate has hardly been more worthy of the name of a deliberation than the exchange of fire between two regiments in a battle. But now the House has lost, with independence, order and dignity. Language, which half a century ago would have been utterly fatal to the man who used it, or could have been prevented from being fatal to him only by the most complete apology, is now used with impunity; and if the Speaker compels its withdrawal, is withdrawn in a style which amounts to a repetition of the outrage. Irish manners are uncontrolled.

It is strange to see a society intellectual, refined, luxurious even to excess, and ever inventing new refinements and new luxuries, yet all the time sedulously removing the barriers which protect it from a political deluge. Talleyrand said that the great motive power in the French Revolution was vanity. Vanity is at work here too. Vanity it is that makes M. Jourdain play the demagogue. But the chief element of disturbance is the madness of the party game, which that of the gambling-table itself does not surpass. Party politics, in fact, partake very much of the excitement of the Turf and are sustained a good deal by the same spirit. Paley thought that the money which he paid in taxes for the support of Parliamentary government with its lively scenes could not have been spent in any way which would have afforded him more fun. If it were only money that this sport cost!

The elective system has revealed its fatal weakness. The theory is that the electors choose, and that they will choose the best man to the measure of their lights. There might be some agreement between the theory and the fact when the electors met in the county court or in the town hall, held, it may be supposed, some sort of a conference, and voted under the guidance of their local leaders, whose influence probably was healthy upon the whole. But now, there is no meeting, there can be no conference, no personal communication or concerted action of any sort among the electors in a large constituency. These particles of political power are as the grains in a sand-heap, which cannot combine or co-operate, though they may be blown in the same direction by the wind. What is to bring them together? What is to designate the candidates for them when they cannot designate for themselves? What is to consolidate the votes of a sufficient number of them to constitute a majority and form a basis for a government? The practical answer is, organised party. So inevitable does this expedient appear, and so thoroughly are we inured to it, that some political philosophers have begun to represent the division into two parties as seated in human nature, every child being, as the comic opera has it, "born a little Conservative or a little Liberal." One writer, assuming party to be an ordinance of nature, fancies that he has discovered its law, which is that of alternate ascendancy, with a change at each general election; so that at each election the party whose turn it is in the course of nature to be beaten will have, for the maintenance of the system, knowingly to fight a hopeless battle. These philosophers do not observe that you might as well try to bisect a wave as humanity, that the shades of temperament are numberless, that the same man is conservative on some subjects, liberal on others, that political temperament varies with age, old men being generally conservative, but also varies with circumstance, your young aristocrat being the most violent conservative of all. Nor do they observe that this system, which they suppose to be a universal necessity of human nature, is in truth a recent product of British politics or of the politics of nations which have followed the leading of England. Factions of course there were, with the usual consequences of faction, at Athens, in Rome, and in the Italian Republics. But this system of government by two parties, perpetually contending for the offices of State, and each trying to make government by the other impossible is a modern British institution. By the hypothesis both parties are necessary to the system. Why, then, should each of them be always denouncing and trying to exterminate the other? Party may be moral, and a good citizen may to a certain extent be a partisan, so long as there is an organic question of sufficient importance to dwarf all other questions and justify submission to party discipline till the paramount object is attained. But when there is no organic question, what is there to make party moral? What is to hold a party together, no principle being at stake ? It can hardly be expected that merely for the purpose of keeping up a system the members of the community, when there is nothing really to divide them, will range themselves artificially into two political armies carrying on an objectless and senseless yet venomous war with each other.

The answer is, the Machine; and this must have workers and payment for workers, in other words, entail corruption in some form, and must bring with it a political morality notoriously, almost avowedly, inferior to the morality of ordinary life, so that you will have the lowest principles of action in the highest sphere. But party is now everywhere in a state of disintegration, brought on by the increased restlessness of intelligence, the multiplication of political sects, the clash of special interests, and the enhanced activity of individual ambition, for which there are not enough prizes or bribes. In Germany, in France, in every Parliamentary country, there is now a multiplicity of parties which is making party government impossible. Even in the British Parliament there are now five parties, the Conservatives, the Liberal-Unionists, the Gladstonian Liberals, the Radicals, and the Irish, while the Irish party is internally split into Parnellites and anti-Parnellites. Bismarck made Parliamentary government possible in Germany by his personal ascendancy, and by accepting or buying support wherever he could find it. In France, the instability has been alarming. In Italy, disintegration went to such a length that the leaders of adverse parties had to come to an understanding, and make an arrangement for the purpose of averting Parliamentary anarchy. In Australia, governments have been ephemeral to a comical degree. In England, the newly enfranchised and ignorant masses being led by a name, the only thing they can understand, there is just now a strong demagogic leadership, which, however, to sustain it requires largesses of destruction. In Canada, there is a stability of corruption. But these are accidents. The general tendency is towards the dissolution of party and of the government that rests on it. Foresight and continuity of policy are impossible under these conditions. At the same time a fatal facility is given to every selfish interest and every fanatical sect of compassing its pet object by playing upon the balance of party and thus forcing the nation to do its will. Of this the Silver Bill, forced upon Congress by the votes of the Silver States, is one example; another is the anti-national and degrading homage paid to the Irish vote.

The truth is that the system of party and cabinet government, with all the political philosophy which it has generated, is the peculiar growth of the political situation in England consequent upon the Revolution of 1688. Even in the time of Charles II., though there were Tories and Whigs, there does not seem to have been party organisation; what was a cabinet in germ was dubbed as a cabal. The parties for a time were dynastic, the struggle between the Stuart and Hanoverian lines having been transferred from the field of battle to the political field, and thus each of them had a bond, moral after its fashion, or at all events superseding the ordinary obligation to follow conviction on particular questions. Afterwards, when the dynastic struggle had subsided, the parties, especially that of the great Whig houses, were closely identified with family connection, and with the struggles of different sections of the aristocracy for power and place. The players in the game were all born members of a political and social circle, owing allegiance to its interests and traditions. The popular element was very small and the scope for demagogism very narrow. Cabal and corruption there might be, and there were on a scandalous scale, but there was not the slightest danger of Parliamentary anarchy or of revolution. The country was in the hands of a single class, that of the landed aristocracy and gentry.

Let the upholders of party government trace the course of this Irish Question. Let them trace the process by which a proud and mighty nation has been compelled to surrender to a contemptible conspiracy, and dragged to the brink, not only of dismemberment, but of self-degradation so deep as that of allowing Ireland with a Parliament of her own to send eighty members to the British Parliament as a garrison of coercion for the purpose of combating British policy in the Irish interest and keeping the subservient allies of the Irish in power.

A petty rebellion broke out in Ireland, the last of a series since the Union all equally weak. Had it taken the field, it would have ended like that of Smith O'Brien, in a cabbage garden. Instead of taking the field, it chose Parliament as the scene of its operations, used votes in place of pikes, and tried to wreck the House of Commons by obstruction, while its agrarian wing, which alone was strong, entered on a campaign of organised outrage in Ireland. Had the House of Commons not been faction-stricken and caucus-ridden, the attempt to wreck it by obstruction would have been at once put down, if necessary by the expulsion of the conspirators. The Liberal government did its duty as far as a party government can. It procured the necessary powers for the Irish executive, and had it been patriotically supported, or even treated with forbearance, it would in time have suppressed rebellion, leaving such agrarian questions as needed settlement to be settled by remedial legislation. But the Conservative party, then in opposition, had for many years been led on the principle enunciated in an article entitled "Elijah's Mantle," which appeared in the *Fortnightly Review* on the occasion of the unveiling of a statue of Lord Beaconsfield:

" Possibly the character of Lord Beaconsfield was also, to some extent, imperfectly appreciated by Lord Salisbury, to whom, for some reason or other, an unknown master of the ceremonies had reserved the very secondary function of moving a vote of thanks to Sir Stafford Northcote for having unveiled the statue. Speaking to the delegates of the various Conservative associations on the eve of the ceremony, Lord Salisbury condemned in forcible language ' the temptation' which, he said, ' was strong to many politicians to attempt to gain the victory by bringing into the lobby men whose principles were divergent, and whose combined forces therefore could not lead to any wholesome victory.' Excellent moralizing, very suitable to the digestions of the country delegates, but one of those puritanical theories which party leaders are prone to preach on a platform, which has never guided for any length of time the action of politicians in the House of Commons, and which, whenever apparently put into practice, invariably results in weak and inane proceedings. Discriminations between wholesome and unwholesome victories are idle and unpractical. Obtain the victory, know how to follow it up, leave the wholesomeness or unwholesomeness to critics. Lord Salisbury, when he used the words quoted above, must have forgotten that a few hours later he was going to take part in unveiling the statue of a statesman whose whole political life was absolutely at variance with Lord Salisbury's maxim. The condemnation of a particular method of gaining political victories was in reality a condemnation of the political career of the Earl of Beaconsfield." *Fortnightly Review*, May, 1883.[1]

The conscious heir of Elijah's mantle had a precedent, at once exact and memorable, for the design which he now formed and induced his party to adopt, in the very manœuvre by which Elijah himself had originally climbed to power. In 1846 the Ministry of Robert Peel was thrown out, his party was broken up, and the way was cleared for the rise of Mr. Disraeli to leadership by a coalition of the Protectionist Conservatives with the Whigs, Radicals, and Irish against an Irish Coercion Bill. By this, and a series of applications of the same strategy, continued for thirty years, the character of the Conservative party, once the party at all events of honour, had been reconstructed on strategical principles, and was ready for Elisha's manipulation. As in 1846, the Conservatives virtually coalesced with the rebel Irish, and by the united vote the Liberal government was thrown out, the author of the scheme, when the division was announced, jumping upon the benches and waving his handkerchief in frantic joy. Of the Conservative party, the head was a marquess with everything to lift him above the vile and vulgar influences of faction. Yet he was too much under the yoke of party to say, when he was approached with a strategical proposal, that while he was a Conservative and would gladly see power in Conservative hands, he was above all things an English nobleman, and would never sanction an attempt to overthrow the Queen's Government when it was struggling with rebellion. Then followed the abandonment of the Act for the protection of life and property in Ireland, and the Maamtrasna debate with the speeches of Lord Randoph Churchill and Sir Michael Hicks-

---

[1] See Lord Malmesbury's *Memoirs*, i., 424.

Beach, condemned even by the most honourable organs of their own party. Let us be just and remember the share which the Conservative party as well as the Gladstonian party has had in bringing all this disaster and disgrace on the country.

A dissolution of Parliament ensued. Up to this time the Liberal leader had treated the Irish movement as rebellion, had denounced its leader as "wading through rapine to dismemberment," had himself announced the arrest of Parnell to an applauding multitude at Guild Hall, had imprisoned him and scores of his followers without trial under the Crimes Act, had been willing to part with three members of the Cabinet rather than that the Crimes Act should not be renewed. He went to the country asking for a majority which would enable him to settle the Irish question independently of Mr. Parnell and his followers. This the Irish prevented by voting with the Conservatives, exemplifying thereby the fell power of unscrupulous minorities under the party system. Finding then that he had lost power, and that he could only regain it by aid of the Irish vote, the Liberal leader at once threw himself into the arms of the rebels. He who had been half a century in public life, had been often as Cabinet Minister responsible for Irish measures, and had himself disestablished the Irish Church, pretended that up to this time he had been ignorant of the Irish question, ignorant of the leading facts of Irish history, and that a new light had now dawned upon his mind. He declared that when he threw Parnell and his followers into gaol he had not understood what Mr. Parnell's objects were. He put forth for the edification of the faithful a history of the previous workings of his own mind, showing that it had long been tending towards Home Rule; an avowal which implied that he had been all the time committing the nation, and allowing his Home Secretary to rise at his side night after night to pledge himself, to a policy which in his heart he at least suspected to be wrong. In concert with the rebel leaders, now transformed from inmates of his gaols into his privy counsellors and his masters, he framed a measure virtually for the repeal of the Union; that Union of which he had been wont to speak as the grand achievement of Pitt, the one effectual guarantee of peace between religious factions in Ireland, but which he now denounced as a masterpiece of fraud and iniquity, using in his transports of rhetorical fury even coarser terms. That the new light which dawned upon the leader's mind at the moment when he found the Parnellite vote indispensable to him should have dawned at the same moment on the minds of his followers passes ordinary belief. Bright, who did not speak at random, averred that there were not twenty members of the Liberal party outside the Irish section really in favour of their leader's Bill, which was as much as to say that the mass voted under the lash of party against their consciences for that which they must have known was ruinous to their country. So much for the aphorism that party is a kind of patriotism. Beaten by the vote of the independent section of his followers, and maddened by defeat, the Liberal leader now broke all bounds and gave the restraints of patriotism to the winds. He who owed all to culture and the support of the cultivated, appealed to the lowest and the worst passions of the multitude, the jealous hatred of the "masses" for the "classes," of the ignorant for those better educated than themselves. He recklessly falsified history to prove that intelligence had always been the enemy of justice. He fanned the cold ashes of provincial antipathy in Scotland and Wales as well as in Ireland. To inflame Irish rebellion, he revived and exaggerated the evil memories of Irish history. He abetted resistance to law in Ireland, bidding an excitable and savage race "remember Mitchelstown." Because England had voted against him, he, the son of a Liverpool merchant, bred at Eton and Oxford, having sat almost all his life for English constituencies, renounced the name of Englishman, traduced England in a foreign press, welcomed the calumnies of her foreign assailants. He allied himself morally with declared enemies of the realm, the Fenians of the United States. A Conservative more than half his life, who, if the place had been open, might, as some thought, have been leading the Conservative party, he put himself at the head of revolutionary radicalism and dallied with all the spirits of confiscation and destruction. He who had upheld Church establishment on the highest principles, held out disestablishment as a bribe to get votes for his Irish policy. At last, after solemnly pledging himself never to consent to the retention of an Irish representation in the British Parliament when Ireland had a Parliament of her own, he concerted with his Irish confederates a scheme for the retention of eighty Irish members in their joint interest. The Lords having rejected a Bill from a leading provision of which members of the Cabinet in that House allowed it to be seen in debate that they dissented, he now threatens them with destruction. But as he knows that an appeal from their verdict to the nation on the simple issue of Home Rule would result in his defeat, he puts off his appeal till he shall have had time to inflame and confuse the mind of the people by a number of revolutionary proposals, hoping thus to force through his Irish measure on false issues. This policy is in effect avowed by his partisans without shame. How much of this treatment do the upholders of party government think that any country can bear?

The present situation also betrays the tendency to demagogic despotism inherent in the system of universal suffrage with large and ignorant masses. Incapable of self-guidance, the masses blindly follow a leader about whom many of them know nothing but his name, but who they have been taught to believe is the man of the people. The result is a state of things far from identical with genuine liberty. "Old Hickory," the idol of the American populace, in the hour of his ascendancy was enabled to trample on real freedom in the United States much as a "G. O. M." is now enabled to trample on real freedom in Great Britain. American admirers of Mr. Gladstone, looking on at the scene, admit that he has hardly any supporters among the upper or middle classes, that is, in the classes of intelligence, the influence of which it thus appears may be eliminated from government when the uninformed multitude finds a man after its heart.

As it is in national, so it is in municipal affairs. Here, also, for large constituencies, the elective system seems to break down. In former ages the city was a social and political unit; the citizens knew each other, they met in the town hall or in their guilds; the great merchants, who now live apart in suburban villas, lived within the walls in daily intercourse with their fellow-citizens, exercised their natural leadership, sought and held municipal office. A city now has no unity. It is merely a densely peopled district requiring a special ad-ministration. There is no mutual intelligence. A man does not know his next-door neighbour. Sometimes in London he does not know his next-door neighbour's name. Conference for the purpose of an elective choice is no longer possible. In the case of such a city as London or New York, the very idea of it is absurd. Some one there must be, as in the case of a political constituency, to designate the candidates and combine the votes. Who is it to be? The answer is, the ward politician, who designates himself, or is designated by Tammany as the candidate, and organises the constituency or has Tammany to organise it for him. He, like the professional politician of the larger sphere, into whom in fact he will presently develop, devotes himself to the calling in which he finds his interest, an interest too often like that which was found in the municipal affairs of New York by William Tweed. He has his organisation always on foot. If in an access of municipal patriotism you attempt to oust him, responding to the cry which everlastingly goes up for the election of better men, you find yourself an amateur opposed to a professional, a casual interloper contending with the regular master of the field. He knows all about the constituency, especially the more corruptible or gullible part of it, while you know nothing. His forces are always on foot. Yours have to be set on foot with infinite trouble and no small cost. It is hardly possible even to start a movement for the improvement of elections. The great merchants will have nothing to do with municipal reform; they cannot afford to leave their business, they utterly refuse themselves to hold the offices,

they shrink with aversion from an acrimonious and often dirty
struggle. When the corruption or misgovernment becomes
insufferable, as it did at New York in the time of Tweed,
there is a spasm of reform. This passes away, you slide
back into the old hands, and city government runs once more
in its groove. We see what has happened in New York,
where, not many years after the exposure and overthrow of
Tweed, there were scandals of the same kind, though in magni-
tude less portentous. Men of the class of ward politicians, if
they are not paid, will find some way of paying themselves.
If there is not peculation there will be jobbery. Always
there will be waste arising from want of skill, foresight, or
system, and from the general character of the government,
which is political, when for municipalities it ought to be scientific. The first object of aldermen or city councillors is to
secure their own re-election. In the Middle Ages municipal
government had to do with franchises, with trade rules, with
the defence of city liberties against royal or feudal rapacity.
It had little or nothing to do with sanitary matters or education, and not much to do with police. The department of
education, if it is a municipal affair, will be found to lapse
into the same hands as the rest. Hence philosophic observers
of American institutions tell you, and every one on the continent repeats, that the great problem is city government.
American and Canadian cities are well governed in proportion
as the administration is not elective, but has by the good sense
of the people been made over to skilled officers or standing
commissions. The best governed city of all is Washington,
which, being in a Federal district, is in the hands of three commissioners appointed, like other Federal officers, by the President of the United States with the consent of the Senate.
There is a city debt, the bequest of a former régime. But
it is being reduced, and everybody seems satisfied with the
administration; indeed, this is one of the attractions to residence at Washington. In face of all this experience and of
the moral to which it points, the British Parliament bestows
on London, a province of brick and mortar without the slight-

est unity or power of collective choice, an elective government. Already the London Council seems to be highly demagogic, and likely to repel residence as much as Washington attracts it. Already it seems to be a paradise of municipal agitators; the city will be lucky if it does not presently become a paradise of Tweeds. Really good men may come forward and be elected at first, but experience shows that they will tire and that the future belongs to the ward politician.

The upshot is that if by government is meant anything possessed of authority or controlling power, Great Britain and the Empire are likely to be without a government. This is a case in which the politician most averse to speculative architecture and with least in him of Sieyès must admit that it is time to look over the building and see what repairs it needs. If the late Conservative government could have relied upon its men, this is what it might have done. But the task was renounced when the Prime Minister took the Foreign Office, and instead of giving his mind to political reconstruction gave it to diplomatic mysteries. What do the masses, whose votes decide the fate of an empire, care for diplomacy? What do they care even for finance? The chief effect of Mr. Goschen's brilliant achievements as Chancellor of the Exchequer in the mortal struggle which followed, was probably to turn against Mr. Goschen's cause a number of people with small incomes, whose dividends he had reduced by his conversion of the funds.

There are those who think no authority necessary. Anarchists, of course, think this, though it may be presumed that an anarchist, if you broke his head or stole his purse, would, provisionally, and all chimeras reserved, appeal to the police. But the extreme theory of self-government comes pretty nearly to the same thing. Its practical issue, as we have seen, is the government of the caucus, the "boss," and William Tweed, its tendency is to chronic revolution. Let government be so ordered, if possible, that our increased enlightenment, our advances in civilisation, our quickened sense of public interests, the elevation of our aims and hopes, all, in short, that makes us more worthy of the name of a community than were nations in the earlier stage of evolution, may tell on its character; without a government we can hardly do. The aim of the moderate Liberal is a government with real authority, national, not partisan, raised above the passions and delusions of the hour, stable enough to produce confidence, yet responsible and open to the influence of opinion, the free expression of which is the one clear gain of all these revolutions. Government of the people, Lincoln said, was never to perish from the earth. It was perishing when Lincoln spoke, and the government of the "boss" was taking its place.

What is this "people," the worship of which has succeeded to the worship of kings, and is too often not less abject or subversive of political virtue? On the lips of demagogues it means the masses without the classes, that is, without the education and intelligence. In the minds of the Jacobins it was a deity: they called it the divine people. In the minds of most of us it is a vague impersonation of the community abstracted from individual follies, cupidities, and infirmities. Nothing answers to this fancy. Let us have done with figments in which we can no longer afford to indulge. Ignorance a million times multiplied does not make knowledge, nor are politics so different from other subjects that without knowledge, and under the influence of passion, political questions are likely to be settled aright. A man no more forfeits freedom by availing himself of the guidance of statesmanship than he does by consulting a physician or engineer.

Few, even if they desire it, would deem it possible to restore hereditary monarchy as a political power. All things serve their purpose and have their day. Hereditary monarchy served a purpose which nothing else could serve; and apparently it has had its day. The new world, the leading shoot and the index of tendency, rejects it. In Europe, it can hardly be said to live otherwise than in form and name except in Russia, and in Germany, where, owing to the circumstances of federation, the part played in it by the monarch personally and the military character of the Empire, the Emperor retains power.   France, once its grandest seat, has to all appearances definitively abandoned it.   In Spain, formerly so intensely loyal, it was for a time overthrown, and appears now to be regarded as a stop gap and a respite.   In England, though it has lost all power, even the power of naming its own household, which was denied it by the loyal Peel, it has not lost hold on sentiment, particularly in the rural districts.   A man of ability, courage, and commanding character on the throne, coming forward at a crisis like the present, might appeal with effect to the heart of a nation.   But there is no use in looking for such qualities in kings at the present day.   Kings in the Middle Ages had to exert themselves in order to keep their crowns upon their heads, and were trained more or less in the school of practical duty, in spite of which they often succumbed to the temptations of a Court.   But a modern king is nursed in luxury and flattery, without the former correctives, responsibility, and need of exertion.   He is protected by an invisible fence from contact with rude realities.   Knowing that he will not be allowed to govern, but only to hold levées and lay first stones, he has no inducement to fit himself for government.   Public duty can be little more than a name to him.   You have no right to expect of him more than that he will be a respectable and harmless sybarite, and you have not much reason to complain if he is a George IV.   Ask a Minister of any Court how often he has found the Court willing to sacrifice its personal convenience or even its fancies to the public service.   Think how, during the last two centuries, British royalty has discharged the very easy, gracious, and useful duty of visiting Ireland.   Not one man in twenty, or perhaps in a hundred, will work hard or practise self-denial unless he is compelled.

The House of Lords is now the only hereditary chamber left in Europe, though in some others there lingers an hereditary element.   It is the last leaf on that tree, and it has hung so long because its power has been so small and its Order, having no social privileges so offensive as those of the French Noblesse, has, compared with the French Noblesse, given little umbrage. At this juncture destiny has been kind to it. It has the honour of standing between the nation and dismemberment, and it will receive the support of wise friends of union, whatever they may think of it as an institution for the future. Nor does freedom suffer more disparagement from the interposition of an hereditary Peerage than from the uncontrolled conviction of a dictator. The despot of the Closure has received a check. Law in its resistance to lawless violence has found for the moment a bulwark in the House of Lords. It is pleasant, too, while the House of Commons is cringing to the caucus and its idol, to see something like independence elsewhere. Yet few, looking at the course which things have been taking in Europe, can believe that a privileged order is destined to be the sheet anchor of the State in the future, or even that it will long be allowed to exist. What has been said of hereditary kingship is true also of an hereditary Peerage. It is not an object of rational hatred; it may be an object of historical gratitude. It was an organising force, perhaps the only available force of the kind, at a time when, there being no central administration strong enough to hold society together, the only mode of preserving order was territorial delegation. Nor could anything else well have curbed the lawless aggrandisement of kings. In those days the Baron was local ruler, judge, and captain. His life was one of exertion and of peril. Historians even think that the lives of the nobility were shortened by their troubles as well as by the sword. But there is nothing now to prevent an hereditary Peer from sinking into sybaritism, and into sybaritism, for the most part decent and qualified, but sometimes unqualified and scandalous, hereditary Peers sink. They cannot be got even to attend in their own house. The number of Peers present at important debates hardly equals that of a dinner-party, though during the session, which is also the season, there must be hundreds of them in town. Their wise leaders have always been lecturing them on this subject; but in vain. Nor can it be denied that the House of Lords, besides representing a privileged Order in an age when privilege is condemned, represents too exclusively a special interest, that of the proprietors of land. This disqualifies it from acting as an impartial court of legislative revision. In fact it has never played that part, but always the part of an organ of the landed interest indiscriminately opposed to change. Delay, by whatever opposition caused, always affords time for reconsideration; but in no other sense can it be said that the House of Lords has given expression to the sober second thought of the nation. It cannot claim and it does not possess the national confidence on that ground. Moreover, the authority of the Peers rests on their entailed estates; a landless Peerage would be weak indeed; and entailed estates are visibly threatened by the advance of social and economical democracy. That the House of Lords will have to be mended or ended is the general conviction, alike of those who look forward to the revolution with glee, and of those who tremble at the thought of being left with a caucus-ridden and faction-stricken House of Commons.

Is the bi-cameral system to be retained? Its existence is an accident of British history, arising out of the division of the Barons into the greater, who sat in the Great Council, and the lesser Barons, who did not, and who formed a gentry which cast in its lot with the Commons, while the Clergy drew apart to their own Convocation, preferring to be taxed there. In the French States-General and in other Mediæval Parliaments, there was a chamber for each Order. Chance, however, often chooses well. The weakest point of the bi-cameral system is that, to form the Senate, it is necessary to take the experience and the mature wisdom out of the popular house, which needs their control, and to put them into a house by themselves where they are in danger of being discredited as the experience and wisdom of greybeards who are behind the age, and estranged from the feelings and wishes of the people. We have seen the rock upon which Cromwell's experiment split. Again, there is always danger of a dead-lock. In the United States, where the Senate is really co-ordinate with the House of Representatives, as often as the majorities of the two Houses belong to different parties, dead-lock ensues, and legislation on important matters is in abeyance. There is also danger of diminishing the sense of responsibility in the lower House, members of which will give a popular vote for a measure which they disapprove, trusting that the measure will be thrown out by the Senate. This has notoriously happened in the United States, and is happening now in England, where it is known that not a few of those who voted for Mr. Gladstone's Bill condemned it in private, and would scarcely have been able to stifle conscience had they not felt sure that the measure would be thrown out by the House of Lords. It would be easy, without a second chamber, to provide safeguards against legislative precipitancy by regulating the procedure, or by giving a suspensive veto to a certain proportion of the House. But the bi-cameral system is in possession. It is in possession not only of all the constitutional laws and forms, and of the Palace at Westminster, but of the national mind, and Lincoln's advice not to swap horses when crossing a stream has double force when the stream is so heady.

How to reorganise the House of Lords, however, is a question the solution of which must be left to those who, believing in the bi-cameral system, have deeply studied the problem of construction. A partition between the hereditary and the life principle does not seem likely to be successful, even if public opinion were to allow the hereditary principle to be retained. The new cloth would fret the old garment. The two elements would hardly amalgamate, and there would be a continual and dangerous contrast between their votes. As often as a popular measure was thrown out by hereditary votes, the cry of hereditary legislation would again be raised. What is wanted is a settlement in which the mind of the nation may repose, not a mere rectification of collisions. There might be something to be said for election by the House of Commons, or, to put it in constitutional phrase, designation by the vote of the House of Commons for appointment by the Crown. This would be likely to keep the two Houses in tolerable harmony.

It might be combined with membership of right for Ministers or ex-Ministers of State, and others holding or having held high posts or commands. There would of course be provisions for removal in case of infirmity or non-attendance. But the problem, it must be repeated, is one for the bi-cameralist to solve.

Another problem to be solved is that of getting the Commons to consent to any reform of the House of Lords. The Commons would feel, evidently they do feel, that in reforming and thereby strengthening the House of Lords they were parting with power. It would be difficult to devise a Bill which in their present mood they would pass. The question arises whether the House of Lords can possibly do anything to reform itself by resolution, as it abolished proxies; or by understanding, without formal resolution, as it excludes its lay members from voting on legal questions, which in the O'Connell case some of them were inclined, and, it must be said, had great temptation to do. Could they, not legally, yet by moral force reduce themselves practically to something like a Senate which would command the respect at least of the anti-revolutionary portion of the country, or, at all events, rid themselves of scandals?

Still, if we take institutions as they are, and look in this spirit at the case of the House of Commons, the objects in view will be to redeem it from the condition of a voting machine worked by the caucus, to prevent it from becoming, as violent men try to make it, a mere organ of revolution, and to restore to it the character of a council of the nation. The only guarantee for independence, saving with heroic souls, is a certain security of tenure. Let each member hold for the term of seven years certain, or whatever the term is to be, from the day of his election, unless he takes office under the Crown; . in which case, perhaps, a sentiment rooted, though rather obsolete, would still require him to go to his constituents for re-election. It would be found that the House, to which many men are elected late in life, changed fully as fast as national opinion, especially if the killing length of the sessions and the killing lateness of the hours are maintained. But it would always have in it a certain number of men tolerably free to vote according to their convictions. Its existence would be continuous, and there would not be, as there now is, an anomalous interval. between dissolution and re-election, when, the supreme power being now vested in the House of Commons, that power is for a time in abeyance.

Such a change would involve the abandonment of the prerogative, vested nominally in the Crown, really in the party leader, of penal dissolution. This is the relic of a time when government was really in the Crown and Parliament was called to advise the Crown and grant taxes. It became irrational when supreme power vested in Parliament. Still it was till lately exercised with some measure and in accordance with some principle lodged in the breasts of hereditary or trained statesmen. It is now used as a card in the hands of a leader of faction, who dissolves Parliament to bring on an election, when his local wire-pullers tell him that the chances are in his favour. Thus the tenure of a member of Parliament is not for a legal term, but during the pleasure of a leader of a dominant faction, and he votes always under peril of dissolution as well as under the dictation of the caucus. The abuse of this prerogative in the colonies, where politicians are totally unrestrained by unwritten principle or tradition, shows what may be expected in England. On the last occasion in Canada, the Dominion Parliament was dissolved on a false pretext which was exposed upon the spot, simply because the party leader thought that the wind at that moment was in his favour. A middle course would be to leave the prerogative of dissolution, but provide that it shall be exercised only on the advice of the Privy Council, a body the composition of which, by the way, pretty well fulfils the ideal of a Senate.

There would be an end also of general elections. These, again, are a survival, and in surviving have totally changed their nature. They were originally a summons to the people to send up representatives of their counties and boroughs to inform the Crown about local needs, and vote the subsidies.

Each of them is now an enormous faction fight, the prizes of which are the offices of State and the control of the national policy. Each of them is a civil war without arms, and excites the same anti-social and anti-national passions which civil war itself excites, sometimes with results hardly less grave. A false and dangerous stimulus is given to innovation, because each of the parties, especially the party of movement, has to allure support by promises which in the excitement of the game become reckless, as well as by denunciation of its opponent. The Newcastle programme, drawn up to gain votes, raises issues which together would be enough to bring on revolution. In America, civil war ensued upon a presidential election, which corresponds to a general election in England, and was its natural result. No country can bear forever these convulsions, which grow more violent as the suffrage is extended, and more frequent as the exercise of the prerogative of dissolution becomes more unrestrained.

The plebiscite, where it can be used, as it well might be in the case of any amendment to the constitution, has the immense advantage of submitting a single and definite question to the vote, clear of all alien issues, and as clear as possible of personal and local influence. It might be that the people would decide in favour of woman suffrage; but they could not be worried or coaxed into voting for it as some individual members of a legislature are; nor would they, like party leaders, succumb to the fear of offending and estranging a coming vote.

A parliament which is sovereign, having unlimited power of legislation on all subjects, has over a parliament bound by a written constitution, like the American Congress, the advantage of a greater freedom of adaptation and national development; though it would not be necessary to copy the extreme rigidity of the American safeguards. But the present course of events in England seems to indicate that in a democratic republic a written constitution may be indispensable. Without it there may be a perpetual danger of a revolutionary exercise of the legislative power by any ephemeral faction in the moment of its ascendancy. For something of the kind the radical "bugle" is now being sounded, and if this prospect is pleasant for political sportsmen, every man of sense will know what is in store for the nation.

To reascend the slope of democratic concession is not less difficult, under the elective system with the parties bidding against each other for votes, than the descent is easy. To very extended male suffrage you have already come. To universal male suffrage, with one man, one vote, you are visibly coming. To universal suffrage, male and female, you are very likely to come. With universal suffrage, male and female, and without a written constitution, or any check whatever except the "throne," upon the exercise of sovereign power by the "will" of such a "people," you may look forward to interesting times. In the end, perhaps, by a convulsive effort of society to escape from confusion, the truncheon may revert to the Protector's hand. But in the meantime what may happen to a highly commercial nation, most sensitively organised, in which a moment of confusion means widespread distress? It is surely irrational to assert that any man has a right to a vote, that is, to a share of political power, whether he is capable or whether he is incapable of using it for the general good and his own. It has been truly said that if such a right exists, it must exist in every human being, in the Hottentot as well as in the civilised man. To fix a standard of age is to fix a standard of fitness, and to fix a standard of fitness is to bar ignorance and irresponsibility as well as nonage. The right which every one has is that of qualifying himself for the exercise of political power, if he can. Audiences of workingmen, however democratic, seemed never to resent the assertion that political power was a trust, and that a man ought to qualify himself and give the State some guarantee for its exercise. A property qualification as evidence of a stake in the country may be obsolete, or at least practically no longer feasible, though there is surely still some sense in the axiom that representation and taxation should go together, while the experience of American and colonial democracy at least seems to show that unless representation and taxation do go together, expenditure is likely to be free. But property qualification as a test of industry, frugality, and responsibility can never be obsolete till communism reigns and property is no more. Still less can it be said by any one but a Jacobin that an educational qualification is obsolete, or that while on every subject but politics, ignorance is fatal, a man is fit to decide by his vote the question of Home Rule who hardly knows on which side of England Ireland lies. If it is our duty to educate our masters, it is the duty of our masters to get themselves educated, and to give proof that they have had schooling sufficient to be capable of understanding at least what the political questions mean. Nor is there any reason, except the tyrannical exigencies of party, why the suffrage should be thrust by a self-acting system of registration upon the man who does not care enough for it or for public questions to take the trouble of putting himself upon the Register. An educational qualification, which there are simple methods of ascertaining, and personal application for the vote as a guarantee for a spark of civic duty are surely no more than the commonwealth has a right to require.

After all, what is a vote? That is a question which socialistic radicalism, if it goes to the length of dismemberment and rapine, may force people to ask themselves in earnest. Is the right of majorities divine? Are people bound in conscience to allow themselves to be voted to perdition when the real force is on their side and they might save themselves, if they chose, by the strong hand? Nobody pretends to believe that a majority is infallible; or even that it is a very strong guarantee for wisdom, truth, and justice. If any one did, the history of opinion would rise up in judgment against him. By agreeing to count heads, men avoided decision by force, the only arbitrator in that primitive state of things of which the Polish *liberum veto* was a relic. Counting heads was not as weighing brains; still it was an invaluable invention, and communities owe it, if not invariable wisdom, unbroken peace, freedom at least from physical violence. Decision by count of heads is an institution as worthy of profound respect, as sacred, if you will, as utility can make it. But utility cannot give a title higher than itself, and if in nine hundred and ninety-nine cases out of a thousand it is right for those who think they have the real force upon their side to yield for the sake of peace and order to the more numerous yet weaker party, in the thousandth case it may not be right. A vote is, in a vast number of instances, an artificial power which strength concedes to weakness, and which places weakness politically on a level with strength. If weakness abuses the artificial power beyond a certain limit, strength would appear to be morally at liberty to assert itself. People are not bound to fold their arms in tame submission when they can prevent the cruel indulgence of class hatred, public rapine, or the dismemberment of the nation, any more than they are bound to fold their arms in tame submission when the tyranny of a despot becomes insufferable. There are international situations, though few, out of which the only exit is war. There are domestic situations, far fewer still, out of which, as Mirabeau saw, the only exit is civil war or the display of a determination to face civil war rather than suffer the extremity of wrong. A majority, conscious that its power is artificial, and that the real strength is on the other side, will almost always decline the conflict and refrain from further aggression. If it does not, the national destiny at all events will be decided, not by demagogic appeals to passion and the love of plunder, or by the craft of Old Parliamentary Hands, but by the genuine force and manhood of the nation.

THE EMPIRE.

THE EMPIRE.

The name Empire stirs in the British heart a sentiment of pride which the writer thoroughly shares, but which, unless it is kept within the bounds of fact and policy, may be the precursor of a fall. When the House of Commons has passed a bill for the severance of the British Islands from each other, to discuss the advantages and disadvantages of remote dependencies can hardly be deemed an insult to the national honour.

Freeman did us a service in making us think what we meant by "Empire." The vague use of the name is practically delusive and perilous. British Empire in India is empire in the true sense of the term, since Hindustan is governed with imperial sway. So, in their way, are the military dependencies such as Malta and Gibraltar. But the self-governed colonies are not empire at all. The reasons for retaining the three classes of possessions are totally different, as are the rules of dealing with them. The West India Islands, again, a set of extinct slave plantations, are a case by themselves. No plan or systematic policy has governed this motley accumulation of possessions. England has had no Will of Peter the Great. The only pervading agency, besides the aggressive energy of the race, fruitful of splendid adventurers, has been the maritime superiority which enabled and induced England, while she had not the means of putting a great land force on European battle-fields, to extend her acquisitions by sea at the expense of less maritime rivals. Cases essentially different, common sense requires to be differently treated, and as to all cases, common sense says that change of circumstance ought to be taken into account. But in approaching the question of Empire from a rational point of view, and essaying to test the value of its several elements, we are met at once by the cry of "prestige." Give up anything, we are told, and you ruin the prestige of that Empire on which the sun never sets. What is prestige? Etymologically, a conjuring trick. Actually, a sham force. Is it possible that there can be anything really valuable in a sham? Will not your enemy see through it as well as yourself? Wooden guns may be of use till it is found out that they are wooden, after which they are hardly worth defending. Dependencies widely scattered which you have no adequate force to guard must be military weakness, of which your enemy cannot fail to be aware. Your enemy, in fact, is aware of it, and acts in all his dealings with you upon the knowledge that you are vulnerable in all parts of the globe. England deems herself the happy nation that has no frontier. She has a frontier in India of vast extent, menaced, as is supposed, by the greatest military power in the world, to say nothing of the neighbourhood, on the other side, of China, which may some day become military. In Canada she has a frontier of three thousand miles perfectly open to the attack of a nation of sixty-five millions, which the other day had a million of men in arms, and can at any moment throw an irresistible force across the line. The primacy of the sea remains to her. Supremacy is no longer hers, as it was at the time when the navies of France and Spain had fallen into decrepitude and that of Russia was but just born; or again, when Duncan had crushed the navy of Holland at Camperdown, and when Nelson had crushed the navies of France and Spain at Trafalgar. Steam, too, has changed the aspect of naval affairs. Hoche would now be sure of his landing in Bantry Bay. Nor, till the fearful experiment of a naval war with ironclads has been tried, can we tell how far the pre-eminence of the British sailor will be affected by the change from the *Victory* to the turret and the ram. A Frenchman, though inferior to a Briton in close action or in boarding, may behind his iron wall show as much intelligence in handling a machine.

There is surely no disparagement in saying that England's real strength was always in herself. It was in her race

of men, her position good for commerce with both hemi-
spheres, her coal and iron, the spirit of her free institutions.
Opponents of territorial aggrandisement are always taxed
with insularity. What is it that makes British policy insular? Cromwell's policy was not insular, nor was that of the
statesmen of Elizabeth. What compelled England to stand
aloof, lending no help but protocols, while Italy was struggling for independence? What would compel her to stand
aloof if Russia and France should set on Germany and overturn the balance of power in Europe with the ultimate humiliation of Great Britain herself in view? What but those
dispersed possessions which she knows herself to be unable
to defend?

Thirty years ago the question arose of ceding the Ionian
Islands to Greece. They were useless to England as possessions. Their people, though well treated, were fractious, and
were always giving trouble. Not only did they bring no
strength, but in case of war with a Mediterranean Power,
either they must have been abandoned with disgrace, or a force
which could not have been spared must have been shut up in
them and would probably have been lost. Yet the cry was
raised at once that cession would be a betrayal of weakness,
and would be fatal to Imperial prestige. The Islands were
ceded, nevertheless, and by Lord Palmerston, the Minister of
aggrandisement, whose ambition it was to make the name of
Englishman as formidable as that of Roman had been of old.
Did Great Britain thereby lose a particle of real strength or
of genuine reputation? Did she not rid herself of weakness
and gain reputation for wisdom? Of the present generation,
perhaps few are conscious that England was ever possessed of
the Ionian Islands, any more than they know that the King
of England was once King of Corsica, and for good reasons
resigned that Crown.

Spanish historians begin the reign of Philip II. with the
resounding roll of the kingdoms, provinces, colonies, and fortresses of which he was lord in all parts of the globe. "He
possessed in Europe the kingdoms of Castile, Aragon, and

Navarre, those of Naples and Sicily, Milan, Sardinia, Roussillon, the Balearic Islands, the Low Countries, and Franche Comté; on the western coast of Africa he held the Canaries, Cape Verd, Oran, and Tunis; in Asia he held the Philippines and a part of the Moluccas; in the New World he held the immense kingdoms of Mexico, Peru, and Chili, and the provinces conquered in the last years of Charles V., besides Cuba, Hispaniola, and other islands and possessions. His marriage with the Queen of England had placed in his hands the power and resources of that kingdom. So that it might well be said that the sun never set in the dominions of the King of Spain, and that at the least movement of that nation the whole world trembled." We now know what relation all these possessions and titles bore to real strength and to the sources of a genuine prosperity. How does the refusal to examine rationally the Imperial policy of Great Britain on the ground that you detract from her prestige, differ from the blind pride that went before the fall of Spain? Suppose some bold man at the Council Board of Philip II. had said that Spain in grasping the globe was losing Spain, would he not have forfeited his head? Yet would not his voice have been that of true patriotism and real greatness? Spain was at the height of her "prestige" when Drake, seeing her impotence, went into Cadiz and singed the Spaniard's beard. The policy of real strength must be the patriotic policy; the policy of real weakness, however colossal, must be that which a true patriot would discard. This will not be a mere truism till it is accepted as the truth.

The British Empire in India is an Empire in the true sense of the word, and the noblest the world has seen, though the Roman Empire had the honour of being the mould in which modern Europe was cast. Never had there been such an attempt to make conquest the servant of civilisation. About keeping India there is no question. England has a real duty there, she has undertaken a great work and stands pledged before the world to perform it. She has vast interests and investments. Her departure would consign Hindustan to the sanguinary and plundering anarchy from which her advent rescued it. The Hindu and the Mahomedan, between whom she with difficulty keeps the peace, would again grapple in murderous strife, while Mahrattas and Pindarees would recommence their raids. The "cultivated baboo," who, owing his being to the Empire, sometimes rails against it, would be the first to perish, crushed like an egg-shell amidst the warring elements which its withdrawal would let loose.

No moral compunction need be felt in retaining this conquest. It is a monument not of British rapacity but of British superiority, especially at sea. England was only one of four competitors for the prize. Portugal came first, but she was too small to retain so distant an Empire, and at the critical moment she fell into the paralysing grasp of Spain. Holland had, as has been remarked, the advantage of undivided devotion to the aims of commerce, while England was divided between those of commerce and those of territorial aristocracy; but she, again, was too small, and she also was crippled at the critical moment, being attacked by France, who thus unwittingly played the game of England. France herself was the most formidable rival, and by the hand of Dupleix she had all but grasped the prize. But being less maritime than England, she was less capable of securing the sea base essential to the tenure of an Empire formed, unlike preceding Empires, unless we except the Carthaginian and Spanish, by extension not from a territorial centre, but from a sea base. The navy of France once overpowered, her access by sea once barred, her military force was useless. Her government also was corrupt, was swayed by harlots, was weak yet despotic, and meddled mischievously with the French East India Company while the British East India Company had political power to back it and a comparatively free hand.[1] The British had also the great advantage over Catholic powers of religious toleration. The Portuguese brought the Inquisition with them to Goa and proclaimed a war of extermination against paganism. The

---

[1] See Sir Alfred Lyall's *The Rise of the British Dominion in India.*

religion of the Englishman was political. If he persecuted Papists or Dissenters, it was on political grounds. He was willing, like the Roman, to respect the religions or superstitions of other races so long as they did not rebel against his rule. He carried this so far as to own Juggernaut and swear by the sun, moon, and earth to the observance of a treaty. Far from seeking to convert the heathen by force, he looked, in the early days of the Empire, with little complacency even on voluntary conversion. When to these advantages are added the qualities of the race, the schooling of its institutions, and the appearance on the scene of such men as Clive, Hastings, and Wellesley, British dominion in India is seen to be no accident.

Still less can the Empire be said to be the fruit of a settled policy of aggrandisement. An act of Parliament in 1793 declared that "to pursue schemes of conquest and extension of dominion in India are measures repugnant to the wish, the honour, and the policy of this nation." Both on the part of the government and on that of the Company there was a desire to restrain extension and keep out of native embroilments which sometimes went the length of pusillanimity and desertion of allies. The pioneers of British lordship over India were Clive and Hastings. But the idea of lordship dates only from the proconsulate of Wellesley, who, after his Imperial achievements, wrote to his chief in England that he did not know whether he would be praised or hanged for what he had done. The invasion of Scinde by the hot-headed Napier was an aggression, and was generally condemned. Against the annexation of Oude protests were raised, but it was justified by the necessity of putting an end to the misgovernment of the native dynasty, which became insufferable and the responsibility for which rested on the protecting power. With these exceptions, it may be said that from the repulse of Surajah Dowlah's attack on Calcutta to the repulse of the Sikh invasion, which was totally unprovoked, British Empire in India has been acquired by defensive war. By no moderate or timorous counsels could the march of destiny be stayed. Threatened by the French and Dutch as well as by the anarchy around it, the Company could not help taking arms. In the chaos of devastation, plunder, and massacre which followed the fall of the Mogul Empire, a power at once of force and of order could not help gaining ground. The fragments of the shattered structure were sure to gravitate towards the only centre of reorganisation. No other power was left save those of the Mahrattas, not rulers, but raiders, with the fell Pindarees in their train, of the Sultans of Mysore, mere barbaric conquerors, and of the militant sect of Sikhs beyond the Sutlej, who would have waged against the Mahomedans a war of extermination. Our title has been force, but it has not been rapine, which was the chief title of the chief native dynasties and powers.

No national feeling has been trampled on. Hindustan has never been a nation. It is a vast expanse of social tissue of which the cell is the village community, while the pervading influences are religion and caste. The great movements have been religious and not political: Buddhism, which asserted spiritual equality against caste, Vishnuism, a liberal and philanthropic reform of Hinduism and Sikhism, a Hindu schism which gave birth to a military sect. Government had always been sheer despotism. For centuries it had been the despotism of conquerors who descended from the mountains of the north upon the languid population of the plains, and would probably have repeated their inroads if the British had not come upon the scene. Conquest might also have resumed its desolating march from the mountain home of the Mahratta, who was already levying his blackmail far and wide, or from the table-land of Mysore. The Moguls were foreigners as well as the British. Their court and government were foreign, they were the heads of a dominant race, alien to the Hindu in blood and religion, and sometimes persecuting, for though Akbar might be tolerant, not so was Aurungzebe. Caste itself was probably the result of the conquest in remote antiquity by an Aryan race of the pre-Aryan races, whose remains are found under various names — Bheels, Kols, Sonds, Meenas —

in the corners and crannies of Hindustan, and who have no connection or fellowship with either Hindu or Mahomedan, while the British have brought them law, humanity, and the rudiments of civilisation. What domination can be more oppressive than caste? What insolence of the haughtiest of conquerors can match the self-exaltation of the Brahmin in the sacred books of the Hindus? What degradation of the most despised of subject races can match the degradation of the Sudra?

Between the second and third visits of Clive to India, there was a period of scandalous intrigue and corruption, attended with robbery and oppression of the natives. At that time the Company's servants, being very poorly paid, were tempted to pay themselves by foul means, while the political power, which by force of circumstances they had irregularly acquired, being yet unrecognised, was not coupled with responsibility. Clive applied the sure antidote to corruption by giving good and regular pay. He coupled responsibility with power by obtaining a legal grant of the province from the Emperor at Delhi. The memorable proconsulate of Warren Hastings, though beneficent, and felt by the natives to be beneficent, on the whole, as well as marked by consummate genius for government and diplomacy, was not untainted by contact with oriental statecraft, or by the cravings of a commercial company for gain which Hastings was compelled to satisfy. But the crimes ascribed to Hastings and Impey are the ravings of Burke, inspired by generous but riotous fancy, combined with the malignity of Francis. Thanks to Sir James Stephen,[1] we know that the judicial murder of Nuncomar is a fiction. Thanks to Sir John Strachey,[2] we know that the Rohilla charge was far less grave than it was believed to be; that the Rohillas, instead of being an agricultural people with a tinge of poetry, were a body of Afghan freebooters with no calling but that of arms who had imposed their yoke

---

[1] *The Story of Nuncomar and the Impeachment of Sir Elijah Impey.* By Sir James Fitzjames Stephen, K. C. S. I., 2 vols.

[2] *Hastings and the Rohilla War.* By Sir John Strachey, G. C. S. I.

on the Hindu population, that they were not exterminated, and that Hastings reproved instead of encouraging the atrocities of his native ally. It is scandalous that such a tissue of false-hoods as Macaulay's "Essay on Hastings" should be still in everybody's hand, should be read in India, and be used in schools. That he flung the head of Hastings to his enemies, probably under the sinister influence of Dundas, is one of the worst blots on the character of Pitt. From the time when the Company ceased to be commercial, and as a political power was brought under Imperial control, crime ceased, though from ignorance of the land and people, blunders, notably in land settlements and in the judicial department, continued to be made.

The conquest of India was no accident, yet was it most marvellous. The native armies enormously outnumbered the British; Plassey was won by four thousand men against sixty thousand; the arms were equal; the natives had sometimes been trained by European officers; the British soldier had to fight and march, sometimes to make forced marches in pursuit of a nimble enemy, beneath the Indian sun, without the palliatives which he has now. Most Englishmen still know little of the achievements or the heroes. They have heard the names of Clive and Lake, Wellington and Havelock, but not those of Pattinson and Pottinger. That story remains yet to be worthily told. The grandest scene perhaps is the last, the struggle with the Sikhs. Nothing can appeal to the imagination more than the night of Ferozeshah, with Lord Hardinge, who, nobly loyal to duty, had sunk the Governor-General in the soldier, moving over the field to brace his troops for the renewal of the mortal conflict on the morrow. A striking part of the history is the devotion of the Sepoys, which seems to show that the Englishman is not so utterly incapable, as is supposed, of winning the hearts of other races. Sikhs and Goorkhas received, after a tough conflict with them, as worthy brethren in arms, became the most faithful soldiers of the Empire, and helped to save it in the Mutiny.

Great have been the feats of war; fully as great have been the feats of civilisation, such as were performed among the Bheels by Outram, among the Mairs by Dixon, among the Khonds, steeped in human sacrifice, by MacPherson; above all, by John Lawrence in the Punjaub. The devout belief of such a man as John Lawrence in the goodness of his work, was strong proof that the work was good. He could hardly have thought as he did that the Empire was upheld and blessed by God, if it had been a kingdom of the devil. In Lawrence, too, and in his compeers, we have a type with which the world can hardly afford to part, of the public servant whose character has been formed by duty, not by party or quest of votes. We might prize the Indian civil service, if it were for this alone.

To the conquered the Empire has given peace, peace unbroken, saving by the Mutiny, for forty years, under which population has so increased that the Empire is in some districts oppressed by the results of its own beneficence. It has given vast growth of trade. It has given railways, canals, and bridges, the fruits of a public expenditure not less liberal than that of the Mogul Emperors, and untithed by the pride and folly which built a mausoleum over a tooth. It has given facilities of distribution which mitigate famine. It has given education, which, if not widely diffused, is diffused enough to open the leading Hindu minds to western civilisation, and of a stationary to make, in prospect at least, a progressive race. It has given medical science and some notion of sanitary reform. It has given redemption from suttee, human sacrifice, female infanticide, slavery; the hope of redemption from infant marriage, if philanthropy will be circumspect; and perhaps the hope of ultimate redemption from caste, which seems to be yielding in some measure to the railway. It has given release from the cruelty, the corruption, and the extortion of oriental despotism. It has given a system of taxation regular, not predatory, and moderate compared with that of the Mogul or with the Mahratta blackmail. It has given good faith as the rule of statesmanship in place of eastern perfidy. It has given, above all, in place of lawless power, law, the realm of which advances with the British flag, with the Anglo-Saxon race. That cannot be an Empire of mere force which in a population of two hundred and eighty millions rests on a British army of seventy thousand men. Metternich, who said that you could do anything with bayonets but sit upon them, would find here no exception to his rule. Of the civil administration it may safely be said that, whether it is the cheapest or not, the most beneficent or not, it is the purest in the world. Its purity is secured by good pay, and by the bracing exigencies of a service always arduous and seldom free from peril. Since the establishment of the Empire there has been no rising against British rule except in the wake of mutiny.

What is the condition of the Hindu peasant? Some reformers say that he is the most miserable of mankind. On the other hand, Dr. Birdwood, a high authority, says, "for leagues and leagues round the cities of Poona and Sattara there stretch the cultivated fields. . . . Glad with the dawn, the men come forth to their work, and glad in their work they stand all through the noontide, singing at the well, or shouting as they reap or plough ; and when the stillness and the dew of evening fall upon the land like the blessing and the peace of God, the merry-hearted men gather with their cattle, in long winding lanes to their villages again. . . . Thus day follows day and the year is crowned with gladness."[1] In some districts, evidently, the check of war being removed, population, in spite of child-marriage and filth, has increased too fast, and the unwelcome discovery of Malthus is once more confirmed. Everywhere the Hindu peasant has little. In his climate he can do with little, perhaps hardly cares for more. As he does not and cannot work hard, his production cannot be large. His harvest, whatever it is, he reaps. It is not reaped, nor is he butchered or tortured, by Mahrattas or Pindarees. Nothing can be taken from him or be done to him except by course of law.

---

[1] *Industrial Arts of India.* Quoted by Sir R. Temple in his *India in 1880*, p. 103.

Of the progress of Christianity in India, it is difficult to speak. The government of the Company feared to encourage the missionary, and almost disavowed Christianity. The Queen's government is bolder. It has discovered that the Brahmin is not an enemy of theological discussion, though he is jealously tenacious of caste. It is Christian while it is strictly tolerant. John Lawrence was emphatically both. It would seem that some impression has been made on the Hindus, on the Mahomedans none. The great obstacle to the spread of Christianity in India is the failure of belief in it at home. Strange to say, the West is now receiving a faith from the East; for the mind of philosophic Europe, perplexed with theological doubt, seems inclined to accept something like Buddhism as an anodine, if not as a creed.

It is said, and it would not be hard to believe, that the natives prefer native rule with all its evils to that of the stranger. One answer is that, if they did, there would probably be more migration to the native States, which still cover nearly half a million of square miles, with a population of fifty-five millions, proving by their existence that the rapacity of the conqueror is not boundless. The rulers of all these trust, and, since the recognition of adoption and the restoration of Mysore to its native dynasty, have had the best reason to trust, the good faith of the Empire. When Russian invasion threatens, they all come forward with offers of aid. Their subjects perhaps may have some reason to question the beneficence of a protectorate which guarantees misgovernment, till it passes all bounds, against the rough eastern remedy of dynastic revolution. Still the average may be an improvement, since eastern misgovernment did not seldom pass all bounds.

The press, native as well as European, is free; free enough, at all events, to criticise even with violence the acts of government. Lord Hastings, as Governor-General, declared freedom of publication "the natural right of his fellow-subjects, to be narrowed only by urgent cause assigned," affirming that "it was salutary for supreme authority, even when most pure, to look to the control of public opinion." The Hindu who in an

American periodical denounces the tyranny of the British in India, shows by that very act and by the freedom of his language that the tyranny is not extreme.[1]

We must not gloss over the hideous Mutiny or its still more hideous repression. A mutiny, it seems, it was, and nothing more, having its sources in the insolence of a pampered soldiery, paucity of European officers, consequent laxity of discipline, and, at last, that suspicion of an assault on caste which had caused the Vellore and other mutinies before it. Its horrors cancelled many a glorious page of the history, while it added such pages as those of the defence of Lucknow and the capture of the vast and strongly walled Delhi by an army of three thousand men. The fiendish passions of a dominant race, rage mingling with panic, were excited to the highest pitch. Lord Elgin was there; in his diary he says:

"It is a terrible business, however, this living amongst inferior races. I have seldom from man or woman, since I came to the East, heard a sentence which was reconcilable with the hypothesis that Christianity had ever come into the world. Detestation, contempt, ferocity, vengeance, whether Chinamen or Indians be the object. There are some three or four hundred servants in this house. When one first passes by their *salaaming*, one feels a little awkward. But the feeling soon wears off, and one moves among them with perfect indifference, treating them not as dogs, because in that case one would whistle to them and pat them, but as machines with which one can have no communion or sympathy. Of course, those who can speak the language are somewhat more *en rapport* with the natives, but very slightly so, I take it. When the passions of fear and hatred are engrafted on this indifference, the result is frightful; an absolute callousness as to the sufferings of the objects of those passions, which must be witnessed to be understood and believed."

The next entry is:

". . . tells me that yesterday at dinner the fact that government had removed some commissioners, who, not content with hanging all the rebels they could lay their hands on, had been insulting them by destroying their caste, telling them that after death they should be cast to the

---

[1] See "English Rule in India," by Amrita Lal Roy, in the *North American Review*, April, 1886.

dogs to be devoured, etc., was mentioned. A reverend gentleman could not understand the conduct of government; could not see that there was any impropriety in torturing men's souls; seemed to think that a good deal might be said in favour of bodily torture as well! These are your teachers, O Israel! Imagine what the pupils become under such leading!"[1]

But the terrorism of this clergyman and his compeers, as well as that of sentimentalists in England, and the atrocities of butchers like Hodson of Hodson's Horse, were in some measure redeemed by the mixture of clemency with firmness in Canning and Lord Lawrence.

Of Lord Elgin's words, part was true only of the period of the Mutiny; part remains true. British dominion in India is and ever must be that of the stranger. Between the ruling and the subject race a great gulf is fixed. The Moguls came from abroad, but they made India their home. The Englishman, incapable of acclimatisation, can only be a sojourner. He is more so than ever, since he is no longer severed by a six months' voyage from his own country. His rule is feared, respected, perhaps regarded with gratitude; but it can never be loved. Nothing, says a writer on India, is sooner forgotten than a British triumph, or longer remembered than a British reverse. It is implied that what the people remember longest is that which pleased them most. Association in government and the judiciary has probably been carried nearly as far as it can be without abdication. There it must stop. Social fusion there appears to be none. It would be barred by caste on the one side, as well as by pride on the other. Professor Monier Williams wondered why certain Pandits always called on him very early in the morning. He found that they wanted time for purification after contact with the unclean. Nor can it be expected that the demeanour of the lower members, at all events, of the dominant race towards the subject race should be free from haughtiness. It has probably not improved since the personal connection of the European with India has

---

[1] *Letters and Journals of James, Eighth Earl of Elgin.* Edited by Theodore Walrond, pp. 199, 200.

been loosened. Officials of the old school whose time had been passed in India, however strong their prejudices, never spoke of the natives, at least of those of the higher class, with disrespect. Nor can we suppose that an imported civilisation will equal in value or vitality one of natural growth. Whatever there was of peculiarly native excellence could hardly fail to suffer in the process. Manchester goods there may be in plenty; but where these fill the market there will no longer be the products, some of them marvellous, of native taste and skill; there will no longer be the joy of the native workman over his exquisite work. Buildings there may be of utility, better than mosques or mausoleums; but there will be no Pearl Mosque or Taj Mahal. Perhaps to the Oriental, the pageantry of his native dynasty made up in some measure for oppression.

The process of lifting a race not more than half civilised to a high plane of civilisation, is costly as well as difficult. India, though gorgeous, is poor. She is poor because the power of work and the rate of production are low. Yet the administration is expected to come up to the standard and fulfil the ideals of the wealthiest of European nations. How can it dispense with the salt tax, which no doubt is oppressive, or with the opium duty, which scandalises, though perhaps it is only the spirit duty of Hindustan? Hard, too, it must be to infuse the western spirit of justice and probity into native policemen and officials of the low class. Home opinion exacts of the Indian government an administration up to a mark higher than has been reached by half the countries of Europe, while home philanthropy demands of it the abandonment of its revenue from opium.

As soon as the Company became military and political, it was of necessity brought under the control of the Home Government. An empire could not be left outside the Empire with separate powers of peace and war. This was the first step. The second was to divest the Company entirely of the commercial character which vitiated and enfeebled political action. The Mutiny brought the end of the Company's rule.

The army on which its authority rested had gone to pieces and the Empire passed to the Crown. Yet the incorporation of a vast and despotic Empire with a free commonwealth was regarded with misgiving both by some who feared the influence of the Empire on the commonwealth, and by some who feared the influence of the commonwealth on the Empire.

The Company discouraged the settlement of Europeans in India. By the Queen's government it is encouraged. Besides being an Empire, India is now a considerable British colony, though the settlers are birds of passage. It will be more clearly seen in time how the presence of a European community with its Magna Charta will consist with the administration of an Empire necessarily autocratic. Community of danger is a strong curb on dissention, yet it may not always prevail.

What does the Indian Empire bring to Great Britain? Not tribute, except in the shape of the pensions and savings of the civil servants. It brings a large trade, though no monopoly, England having opened the ports of India to the world. Of military force it brings so much as is indicated by that somewhat theatrical appearance of a Sikh corps in the Mediterranean which bespoke lack of British troops rather than the availability of Sepoys for European wars; and by the employment the other day of a Sikh corps in Egypt. No one supposes that the Sepoys generally could be used on western fields. A British army of seventy thousand is maintained by India, but in case of war could not be withdrawn. The material value of the possession is, after all, secondary to its moral value as a field of achievement, which, though the days of romantic enterprise as well as those of fabulous gains are over, is still, for a young man of capacity and courage, about the finest in the world. The competitive system has thrown it open to all, not without some risk, perhaps, to the nerve and muscle as well as to the corporate unity of the service, yet, it seems, with good results; so at least thought John Lawrence. The place of family or social connection as a bond of corporate unity has perhaps been supplied by partnership in responsibility and possible peril. On the debit side of the material account must be set down the danger and difficulty of maintaining so distant a possession in time of maritime war; enmity with Russia and the Crimean war; the necessity of occupying Egypt at the risk of embroilment with France; the general effect of this vast liability on British diplomacy, and on the influence of England in her own circle of nations. What is the real danger on the side of Russia, apart from mere guard-room talk, it is for those who have read the genuine Will of Peter the Great to say. In the game of Empire, Russia has the great advantage of keeping her own counsels. The extension of her Asiatic dominions has been as natural as the extension of our own; and there seems no reason why, each Empire having reached its limit, the two should not rest amicably side by side. From subduing and annexing barbarous tribes, it is a wide step to invading a civilised power. Our fatal expedition to Afghanistan in 1840 is a warning against rushing to meet imaginary danger. Russia will be unfriendly and will no doubt menace the Indian Empire by way of diversion as long as England persists in barring her way to an open sea. But why should England persist in barring Russia's way to an open sea? Why should Russia be more dangerous to England in the Mediterranean than the other Mediterranean powers? Why should she not rather, if England can keep on good terms with her, help to balance those powers? It is for statesmen, not for a student, to say.

What may be fermenting in the dark depths of the Hindu mind, few, it seems, pretend to tell. At times there is a ruffling of the surface which bespeaks some agitation below. Yet danger of a serious kind from internal insurrection there appears to be none so long as the army is faithful and while the people remain so intersected by differences of race, religion, and language, so totally disunited, and so incapable of organising rebellion as they are. The uniting influence of the Empire itself is, perhaps, so far as things on the spot are concerned, the greatest, though a very remote danger. There is now no dynasty or standard of any kind round which insurrection on a large scale could rally, and the government will take care never to tread on caste; if it is left alone, it will take care to keep rash hands off the Zenana. The Mahomedans, whom we thrust from power, no doubt are sullen; but they are a small minority; they are hated, as constant broils show, by the Hindu; and sullenness is not insurrection. The cloud of Wahabi fanaticism seems to have passed away.

A greater danger, and one far more imminent than Russian invasion or Hindu insurrection, is British democracy, if it meddles with Indian government, as meddle with Indian government it almost certainly will, indeed is already beginning to do; while Hindu politicians are joining hands with it by presenting themselves as candidates for Radical constituencies in England. The shadow cast some years ago by demagogic Vice-Royalty has been lingering since. That a dependent Empire should be governed on demagogic principles is impossible, and the impossibility cannot fail soon to appear. A conquest, however clement and beneficent the conqueror, is a conquest, and if it is to be held at all, it must be held as it was won.

"There are, of course," says Sir Edwin Arnold, in pleading for the retention of India, "many collateral considerations which ought to move the popular mind; such as commercial benefit, colonial advantage, and national prestige; but these are weak in comparison with the force which ought to be exercised upon the general imagination by the sublime duty laid upon Great Britain, if ever any duty was sublime, by the visible decree of Providence itself." The clearest of the inducements to retain India, perhaps, is the duty.

Egypt, occupied by Great Britain, may be regarded as an annex to India, to which Egypt controls, or is thought to control, the present access. As a possession in itself, its value is partly a tradition of the past, like that of Rome, once the capital of a Mediterranean Empire rather than of Italy, that of Constantinople, once the link between the Empires of the east and west, or that of Cyprus, once in a peopled angle of those waters. In the infancy of agriculture, the mud of the

Nile, which produced without human effort, was priceless. Egypt, however, like Hindustan, is a field not only of ambition or profit, but of beneficent achievement. Impartial Americans have borne the strongest testimony to the improvement made by British rule in the condition of the Egyptian people. For the first time since the Pharaohs, the Fellaheen see the face of Justice. The price is the jealous enmity of France, who, for some reason, imagines that Egypt is hers.

British Empire has been won by the great adventurers of whom Clive was a type. Nor is the breed extinct. Gordon was a specimen of it, as under a religious guise and in the missionary sphere was Livingstone. Unlike the Spanish adventurers, who conquered and wasted Mexico and Peru, these men are organisers and pioneers of civilisation, owing their ascendancy not to the arquebus, but to character and mind. There may be fresh fields for them in Africa, and possibly, when the Turkish Empire comes to its end, in the provinces now subject to its rule. They may redeem by their exploits in distant oceans the reign of political degeneracy which seems to have set in at home. But they will do well to remember Khartoum, and trust to themselves alone.

As to the military dependencies, such as Malta and Gibraltar, all that a civilian can have to say is that their occupation and retention ought surely to be regulated by sound military reasons and not by empty pride. A general would not be thought great who persisted in holding a useless and untenable post because he had once occupied it. The coaling stations are necessary in an age of steam, but they were not necessary before the age of steam, and it would be folly to cling to them if steam were superseded by some new motor. Weakness can never be shown by wisdom. Nor can the memory of any glorious exploit be cancelled or dimmed by abandonment of the spot which happened to be its scene. We are not the less proud, or proud with a less reason, of the defence of Torres Vedras or of Hougoumont because the lines of

Torres Vedras and the farm of Hougoumont are no longer in our hands. Elliot's defence of Gibraltar would not be the less memorable or the less inspiring if policy had led the British government under the treaty which followed to restore Gibraltar to Spain.

Is it the policy of Great Britain, as once it was, to dominate in the Mediterranean? Is such a policy any longer possible, since the growth of other Mediterranean navies, French, Spanish, and Italian, since the change which steam has made in naval warfare, and since the unification of French power effected by the railway and the telegraph between Brest and Toulon? In case of war with France and Russia combined, would there be naval forces disposable for command of the Mediterranean? What is the practical object of this policy? Is it safe access to the Suez Canal? Could that route be used in time of war? Would not international law close the Canal against belligerents? Would not the Canal itself be easily obstructed by an enemy? Could convoy be afforded for trade through the Mediterranean? Would not it be necessary to resort to the route by the Cape of Good Hope? In that case, would not military expenditure be wiser at the Cape of Good Hope? If Great Britain means permanently to hold Egypt, there is conclusive reason for the retention of her rule over the Mediterranean. But does she intend permanently to hold Egypt, or merely to accomplish her mission of reform and then depart?

If command of the Mediterranean is to be retained, no question will arise about the retention of Malta. Malta, it seems, with the requisite works and with a sufficient garrison, is deemed by military men impregnable, while as it belongs by nature to nobody, geographically or ethnologically, it is an invidious possession, and by its occupation no enmity is incurred. Far different is the case of Gibraltar, the price of retaining which is the perpetual enmity of Spain. The parallel of a Spanish flag flying on the Isle of Portland is hackneyed, but it is just. Great Britain poured out blood and money to rescue Spain from Napoleon. Yet the feeling of the

Spaniards now is better towards France than towards Great Britain. When Cobden expressed to a Spanish friend his surprise at this, the Spaniard's answer was, "We have got rid of the French, of you we have not got rid." The sight of a foreign flag on his fortress can hardly be made more agreeable to the Spaniard by the recollection that England took Gibraltar, not in international war, but when she was acting as the ally of her candidate for the Crown of Spain. Again and again in the days of her decrepitude, Spain, passionately desiring to recover her great fortress, dragged her half-paralysed limbs to the attack. Nothing else led her to join the league against Great Britain at the time of the American war; for the colonists were her enemies in America, and she was as far as possible from seeking their aggrandisement or sympathising with their republican aspirations. Gibraltar alone it was that sent the Spanish fleet to join the combined armament by which the British flag was chased down the Channel. Up to the last and greatest of the three sieges, the cession of Gibraltar as a post more dangerous than profitable was always in the thoughts of British statesmen. It was contemplated by Stanhope, by Shelburne, even by Chatham. But Elliot's famous defence, coming as it did with Rodney's victory to redeem the humiliation of defeat in America, gave the rock such a hold on English sentiment that thenceforth those who talked of ceding it spoke with a halter round their necks. Shelburne mooted the question in negotiating for peace with America; but he at once drew upon him the denunciation of Fox, who on that single occasion acted the part of patriot. A recital of Fox's arguments and those of Burke, who followed in the same strain, is enough to show how circumstances and the objects of policy have changed. "A sagacious Ministry," said Fox, "would always employ Gibraltar in dividing France from France, Spain from Spain, and the one nation from the other." This possession it was, according to Fox, which gave us respect in the eyes of nations, and the means of obliging them by protection. "If we gave it up to Spain, the Mediterranean would become a pool which they could navigate at their pleasure and without control. As the States of Europe bordering on the Mediterranean would no longer look to England for the free navigation of the sea, it would no longer be in her power to be useful, and we could expect no alliances." It is due to Fox and Burke to remember that Gibraltar, if it was not the sole title of England to the respect of nations, or her only hope of obtaining allies, was the only British stronghold in the Mediterranean, Minorca having been lost, and Malta being not yet ours. The question was again mooted thirty years ago, when the change in the military value of Gibraltar, owing to steam and the improvements of artillery, was just beginning to appear, and when the cession would have thoroughly won the heart of Spain. But discussion was still branded as treason. Now a naval writer in the *Fortnightly Review* proclaims the military decadence of the fortress, which he says can no longer shelter a fleet lying under it; while as a mere post by itself it would be worthless, and its garrison would be wasted, since it does not, as most Englishmen fondly believe, command the strait. Nor does it any longer retain its equivocal value as a dépôt of contraband trade. Apparently it does nothing which is not better done by Malta without offence to anybody's feelings or flag. When it comes to a question of bargain with Spain, we have to remember that during the last quarter of a century the post has been losing strength and value, and that of this the Spaniards must be aware. We are told that they have a plan of siege ready, and are confident of success. An exchange for Ceuta is proposed and seems natural. But Ceuta would be of use, like Malta, only for the purpose of commanding the Mediterranean. Another suggestion is that Spain should cede to England the Canaries as a field for emigration. That England is becoming over-crowded, and needs an outlet for population fully as much as a fortress, is too certain. But after all the greatest object, not merely of sentiment but of policy, is the friendship of Spain, who is now taking her place again among the nations.

Heligoland has been ceded at last. The retention of it

after the fall of the Napoleonic Empire and the continental system on which its value as a post depended, was an instance of the tendency to cling to everything on which the flag has once been set up, however useless it may have become. Fortunately the power to which Heligoland belonged was friendly, or cession might have been attended with disgrace.

To come to the colonial dependencies. It is of colonial dependencies that we speak, not of colonies, the value of which no man contests any more than the necessity of migration. Greece had colonies which were not dependencies and were bound to the mother country only by a filial tie. England herself was a colony of Friesland or some district of North Germany, though she was not under the Frisian Colonial Office. The founders of New England and other British colonies were as fit for independent self-government as any Greek, and independent they would have been from the beginning, had it not been for the twin superstitions : Discovery which made a European king sovereign over every shore discovered by his subjects; and Personal Allegiance which made the emigrant indefeasibly a subject of the realm in which he had been born. To these beliefs is traceable the relation of colonial dependence with its natural consequences, incessant friction, rupture when the colony grew strong, and the American Revolution. There is nothing of which an Englishman has more reason to be proud than the colonies; there are few things of which he has less reason to be proud than the Colonial Office.

To the colonial dependencies so large a measure of self-government has, after a long course of altercation, ending in Canada with a rebellion, been conceded, and to such a shadow has the supremacy of the Imperial Kingdom over them been reduced, that the other day a colonial governor, to pay a compliment to his colony, denied that it was a dependency at all. But a community which receives a governor from an Imperial country, whose constitution is imposed upon it by the Act of an Imperial Parliament, which has not the power of amending its constitution, which has not the power of peace and war, of making treaties, or of supreme justice, play with language as you will, is a dependency. It has and can have no place among the nations.

Of what use, then, are colonial dependencies now to the Imperial country? This is a distinct and reasonable question apart from the question of sentiment, which nobody would wish to disregard. Fiscally, the colonies have gone out of the Empire. They have asserted and have freely used the power of levying not only duties, but protective duties, on British goods. A Canadian politician, who poses as the organ of Canadian loyalty in England, in Canada receives credit as the author of a protective duty for the exclusion of British iron. There is something almost humiliating in the position of Great Britain, bound as she is to protect the trade of colonies which are waging a tariff war against her. If they were independent she might negotiate commercial treaties with them, or supposing she thought fit to adopt that policy, force their ports open by retaliation. Formerly the colonies were prized for the monopoly of their trade and markets, the right of the mother country to which was, as we know, asserted by Chatham in emphatic terms. Trade, we are still told, follows the flag. Trade follows profit wherever it is to be found. Colonies, before they have manufactures, import from the mother country, not because she is their mother, but because she makes the articles they want. How can trade follow the flag when the flag no longer makes it free? When colonists propose an Imperial zollverein, the answer is, that the colonial trade which the zollverein would foster is small compared with the foreign and Indian trade which it would impair. The returns show that for the five years 1886–90 England's imports from foreign countries averaged 77.1 per cent of her total imports, whilst her imports from the colonies including India averaged 22.9 per cent. Her exports to foreign countries amounted to 70.5 per cent of her whole export trade, and her exports to the colonies to 29.5. It is not true, as often alleged, that her trade with the colonies is advancing very much faster than her trade with foreign countries. For the five years 1856–60 her imports from and exports to foreign countries averaged 77.5 and 77.1 per cent respectively of her total import and export trade; and her imports from and exports to the colonies 22.5 and 28.9 respectively. Nor, in spite of the security apparently afforded by Imperial jurisdiction, does British capital seem to find a field for investment more in the colonies than in foreign countries. Whether investors under the flag are exempt from loss, the stockholders of Australian banks, and of Canadian railways, those of the Chignecto Railway among others, can tell. The Chignecto case is notable because political connection was probably part of the inducement.

But the colonies, we are told, though they lay protective duties on the mother country's goods, do not discriminate against her. That there was to be no discrimination against the mother country was the cry raised by Canadian Protectionists when they wished to stave off Commercial Union with the United States. Commercial Union would have done Great Britain no harm. It would have added to the value of her $650,000,000 of investments much more than it took away from the amount of her exports. But the fact seems to be that Canada does discriminate against the mother country in favour of the United States by her tariff as a whole, if not on specific articles, to the amount of at least 4 per cent in the aggregate.[1]

[1] The Toronto *Globe* gives a table compiled from the official returns, which discloses the actual *ad valorem* paid in 1892, in cases where specific or mixed specific and *ad valorem* duties are imposed. It appears that specific duties are aimed at cheap goods, to which the protected Canadian industries are most hostile, and, British goods being cheap, they suffer.

Iron rivets or bolts from Great Britain	64	Bar iron from Great Britain	38¾
Iron rivets or bolts from United States	42	Bar iron from United States	27¼
Sewing machines from Great Britain	40	Boiler iron from Great Britain	41
Sewing machines from United States	83½	Boiler iron from United States	23¼
Nails and spikes, average	40	Cast iron vessels from Great Britain	82
Railway fish plates, Great Britain	41	Cast iron vessels from United States	30
Railway fish plates, United States	30¼	Cast iron pipe from Great Britain	52
Rolled iron or steel angles, Great Britain	45¾	Cast iron pipe from United States	43¾
Rolled iron or steel angles, United States	29¾	Cut tacks and brads from Great Britain	133¼
Iron or steel screws, Great Britain	64	Cut tacks and brads from United States	39
Iron or steel screws, United States	37	Cut tacks and brads, over 16 oz. per M, Great Britain	43¾
Skates from Great Britain and United States	48	Cut tacks and brads, over 16 oz. per M, United States	30½
Skates from Germany	62		

That the colonies are sources of military strength, or could help England in time of war, few would maintain. They are always being exhorted to arm themselves, which they will not do so long as they feel that they have a claim upon Great Britain for protection. Australia sent a regiment to Suakim, but it seems she will not do the like again. Canada distinctly declined to follow the example, Conservative journals being most emphatic in protesting, to avert suspicion, that there was no intention of the kind. She sent a party of Voya-

Wrought iron tubes, Great Britain and United States	50
Wire fencing (barbed) from Great Britain	40
Wire fencing (barbed) from United States	43
Wire fencing (Buckthorn) from United States	31
Wire fencing (Buckthorn) from Germany	45
Wrought iron or steel nuts, bolts, Great Britain	55
Wrought iron or steel nuts, bolts, United States	41
Steel ingots, slabs, etc., Great Britain	39
Steel ingots, slabs, etc., United States	25
Chopping axes	33
Picks, sledges, etc., Great Britain	36½
Picks, sledges, etc., United States	38
Stereotype plates, average rate	119
Plated cutlery from Great Britain	50½
Plated cutlery from United States	43⅝
Lead pipe from Great Britain	46
Lead pipe from United States	28
Lead shot from Great Britain	40
Lead shot from United States	29
Show cases from Great Britain	76
Show cases from United States	52
Cotton shirts, from Great Britain (per cent)	48
Cotton shirts from United States	44
Cotton shirts from other countries	41
Cotton stockings from Great Britain	42
Cotton stockings from United States	41
Cotton stockings from other countries	43
Winceys from Great Britain	38¾
Cuffs from Great Britain	62½
Cuffs from United States	48½
Cuffs from other countries	69½
Linen shirts	41
Glass bottles	38½
Waterproof clothing	34
2 and 3 pronged forks	45½
4 and 6 pronged forks, Great Britain	53½
4 and 6 pronged forks, United States	52
Hoes from Great Britain	52
Hoes from United States	47
Garden rakes	50½
Scythes from Great Britain	49½
Scythes from United States	48½
Spades and shovels from Great Britain	44½
Spades and shovels from United States	42½
Axles from Great Britain	61
Axles from United States	44½
Fire engines, average	35
Forgings of iron and steel, Great Britain	37
Forgings of iron and steel, United States	35
Hoop or band iron from Great Britain	47
Hoop or band iron from United States	28½
Iron in slabs, blooms, etc., Great Britain	58
Iron in slabs, blooms, etc., United States	42
Iron bridges from Great Britain	42
Iron bridges from United States	37
Pig and scrap iron, Great Britain	34
Pig and scrap iron, United States	20½
Blankets from Great Britain	55
Blankets from United States	37
Blankets from other countries	31
Cashmeres from Great Britain	34
Cashmeres from United States	26
Cloths from Great Britain	33
Cloths from United States	28
Cloths from Germany	32
Coatings from Great Britain	36
Coatings from United States	27
Coatings from other countries	29
Meltons from Great Britain	38
Tweeds, Great Britain and United States	32
Felt cloth from Great Britain	30
Felt cloth from United States	29
Horse collar cloth, Great Britain	41
Flannels from Great Britain	34
Flannels from United States	31
Woollen socks from Great Britain	39
Woollen socks from United States	38
Woollen socks from Germany	41
Knitting yarn, Great Britain and United States	33
Knitting yarn from Germany	35
Woollen cloaks from Great Britain	32
Woollen cloaks from United States	29
Coats, vests, etc., from Great Britain	34
Coats, vests, etc., from United States	30
Shirts, drawers, etc., from Great Britain	38
Shirts, drawers, etc., from United States	32
Horse clothing, shaped, Great Britain	42
Horse clothing, shaped, United States	33
All other clothing, Great Britain	32
All other clothing, United States	29
Woollen carpets, Great Britain	37
Woollen carpets, United States	38
Woollen carpets, other countries	24
Vinegar from Great Britain	65
Vinegar from United States	67
Vinegar from France	81

geurs at British cost. Her arming against France would be vetoed by the French Canadians who control her legislature, and whose hearts would be on the French side. The French would in fact refuse to pay for any British armaments whatever. To defend the three thousand miles of open frontier, including a chain of great lakes, the colony has an army of four companies of regular infantry, two squadrons of regular cavalry, a small force of artillery, and a militia numbering about 38,000, of which about half are drilled for a fortnight in each year.

Emigration returns which show 152,000 to the United States against 27,000 to the North American colonies are a conclusive answer to any allegation that the colonial dependencies are necessary as new homes. That political connection may sometimes misdirect emigration, those who have seen the Skye Crofter settlements in Manitoba will be inclined to suspect. There are now nearly a million of Canadians in the United States. The object of the emigrant in leaving his home is to better his condition, and he goes where this will most surely be done. If he feels any other attraction, it is to the place whither his friends and relatives have gone before him.

To the colony, what is the use of dependence? Does it really give military protection? Could Great Britain, in case of war with a maritime power, afford fleets and armies for her distant possessions? From Canada, we are told plainly, she would have at once to withdraw. So says Lord Sherbrooke, who tells us that Lord Palmerston agreed with him; and it is understood that the War Office is of much the same mind. Yet protection may fairly be demanded, since it is through the connection with Great Britain, and the liability to be involved as dependencies in her quarrels, that the colonies are in danger of attack. Australia and Canada the other day might have been involved in a war between Great Britain and France about Siam. They may any day be involved in a quarrel about Afghanistan, Egypt, or some African territory in which they have not the remotest interest. Their trade may be cut up, possibly they may be exposed to invasion, which, as militia never stand against regulars, they would hardly be prepared to meet. The sole danger of Canada arises from the connection. Since the extinction of slavery the people of the United States have had no thought of territorial aggrandisement; they have shrunk even from natural extension. Canada, were she independent, might sleep in perfect safety "under the gigantic shadow of her rapacious neighbour." Nobody can doubt this who knows the American people. While Canada is exposed to danger by the connection, Great Britain hardly dares to stand erect when she deals with the American Republic, because her North American dependencies are a pledge in the adversary's hands. In almost all negotiations the impotence of Great Britain on the American continent has been felt. In each dispute about boundaries, Canada has been obliged to give way. She has complained, but what else could she expect? British diplomacy has done its best, but diplomacy is little without cannon.

Commercially the colonies may be thought to have an advantage in a special facility of borrowing, though Spain, Turkey, Mexico, the Argentine Republic, have been able to borrow from England on a liberal scale. But it may be doubted whether facility of borrowing, if it is apparently a blessing, is not really a curse in disguise.

Is any political advantage derived ·by the colonies from dependence? Is it possible that a salutary tutelage should be exercised by a democracy in Europe over a democracy in America or at the antipodes, its equal in intelligence, its equal in power of self-government, and placed in circumstances widely different? The idea is ludicrous. What does one Englishman in ten thousand know or care about Australian affairs; what does Parliament know or care about them? Does not a colonial question clear the House? The Constitution imposed by Parliament on Canada twenty years ago has disclosed serious defects. The Senate, especially, has proved a dead failure or worse. Yet the Constitution is practically riveted on the Colony because Parliament could never be got to attend to amendments. Thus the political development of the

Colony, instead of being aided by the supposed tutelage, is impeded in the most important respect. All the machinery of British Parliamentary government the colonies in common with many independent nations have. The spirit of British statesmanship you cannot impart, unless you send out British statesmen instinct with it in virtue of their peculiar training and traditions. The game of colonial faction will not give birth to it; perhaps its life may not be long in the mother country herself. Whether the standard of political morality in a colony is raised by the connection, recent disclosures in Canada too clearly show, though the government having barred the door against inquiry, only a part, probably, of the truth has come to light. Any one of those disclosures would have been the ruin of a politician in the United States. Mr. Edward Blake complains of "lowered standards of public virtue, deathlike apathy of public opinion, debauched constituencies, and increased dependence on the public chest." Government has been unblushingly corrupt. Subsidies to railways and local works have been notoriously used for the purpose of influencing elections. No President of the United States, as a candidate for re-election, would have dared to assemble the protected manufacturers in the parlour of a hotel, assess them to his election fund, and pledge to them the fiscal policy of the country.

A Governor is now politically a cipher. He holds a petty court, and bids champagne flow under his roof, receives civic addresses, and makes flattering replies; but he has lost all power, not only of initiation, but of salutary control. His name serves only to cloak and dignify the acts of colonial politicians. It makes the people put up with things against which public self-respect even at a low ebb might revolt. Parliament in Canada was dissolved the other day for the convenience of the Minister, who wanted to snap a verdict, on the pretence that a popular mandate was required for negotiations respecting the tariff which were on foot with the government of the United States. The pretence was false, and the falsehood was at once exposed by the American Secretary of State, who declared that no negotiations whatever were on foot.   In the fraud thus practised on the people, the representative of the Crown, who can hardly have failed to know the truth, was constrained constitutionally to bear a part.   In the noted case of the Pacific Railway scandals, while public morality was struggling, perhaps for the last time, with corruption, the weight of the Governor-General's authority was actually cast into the wrong scale.   By the advice of the accused Ministers, which he deemed it his constitutional duty to take, he transferred the inquiry from Parliament, which was seised of it, to a Royal Commission appointed by the Ministers themselves, whose object manifestly was to evade justice, as they would probably have succeeded in doing had not public indignation been too strong.

Nor does the political connection form anything in the way of social character which a man of sense would value, or from which a man of sense would not turn away.   There is no need of using harsh words in order to suggest to what colonial worship of a coronet must lead.   The tendency at present is to revive the system of colonial titles.   Anybody can guess what titles and title-hunting in colonial society must beget.   The accolade does not confer chivalry.   In the Pacific Railway scandal, out of four men implicated, three were knights at the time, the fourth was afterwards knighted, and as a knight got into other scrapes of the same kind.   A knight pays with a place in a government department a printer who has stolen proofs from his office for the use of the party at an election. A baronet employs without shame, for a political purpose, private letters, the property of other persons, which he cannot have obtained in an honourable way.   Few can believe it possible to plant aristocracy in the New World.   Pitt tried it and utterly failed.   An hereditary peerage is clearly impossible without entailed estates; you would have a marquess blacking shoes.   Even a baronetcy is a temptation to provide an estate for its heirs at the public cost.   The tendency of the whole system is to breed subjects for a colonial Thackeray. By the good sense of the Canadian people it is regarded with aversion, and if it depended on their vote, it would come to an end. As to any influence of titles or of the political connection generally on social manners, all that need be said is that the manners of honest industry are good enough if they are let alone, and that the character of the English gentleman is highly susceptible of imitation on its bad side.

Nationality exalts and saves. To the self-respect of a nation appeals are seldom made wholly in vain. Appeals are not made in vain to the self-respect of the people of the United States. Americans outside the political ring are ambitious of being great citizens; for that name they will work hard, and, if they have wealth, spend it freely. The natural ambition of a colonist who has made a fortune is to get a title, go to Court, have his wife presented, and gain a footing in the aristocratic society of the Imperial country. His affections and aspirations do not centre in the colony. Not seldom he leaves it during a great part of the year, sometimes wholly, for London. He must, if he is made a Peer. In public munificence, the dependency, even when allowance is made for the difference of wealth, will not bear comparison with the nation. Deadlift efforts may be made to cultivate national spirit in dependencies. Like all efforts to cultivate artificial sentiment, they will be made in vain. If England is to be the mother of free nations, the nations must be free.

To repeat the words of an old and long forgotten work, "The great migrations by which the earth has been peopled have at the same time unfolded the great scenes of history, and carried man through the successive phases of social and political existence. Old England has failed to shake off feudalism; but the founders of New England left it behind, and planted a realm beyond its sway. The knell of privilege tolled when they, at the foundation of their State, bound themselves in a voluntary covenant to 'render due obedience to just and equal laws framed for the general good.' They from the first renounced the Norman law of primogeniture in succession to land, and returned to the old Saxon law of just division, under the name of gavelkind. When hereditary aristocracy offered itself in the person of certain Puritan Peers, who wished to retain their privilege in New England, they calmly but firmly put it away. From the State Church they were hunted and persecuted exiles; and if they did not reach at a bound the doctrine, then unknown, of perfect religious liberty, they reached it, and then embraced it without reserve, while intolerance still reigned at home. By the issue of their enterprise, victorious though chequered, man has undoubtedly been taught that he may not only exist, but prosper, without many things which at home it would be treason to think unnecessary to his existence. It is a change, and a great change; one to be regarded neither with childish exultation nor with childish fear, but with manly reverence and solicitude, as the opening of a new page in the book of Providence, full of mighty import to mankind. But what, in the course of time, has not changed, except that essence of religion and morality for which all the rest was made? The grandest forms of history have waxed old and passed away. The English aristocracy has been grand and beneficent in its hour, but why should it think that it is the expiring effort of creative power, and the last birth of time? We bear, and may long bear, from motives higher perhaps than the public good, the decrepitude of feudalism here; but why are we bound, or how can we hope, to propagate it in a free world?" [1]

The case of Canada is not to be confounded with those of Australia and South Africa. Australia lies in an ocean of her own, without great neighbours nearer than China, or fear of collision, save possibly with European interlopers in her sphere. South Africa has no neighbours except the Boers and the savages. The Canadian Dominion, as a glance at the map — the physical and economical, not the political map — will show, is the northern rim, broken by three wide gaps, of a continent of which the inhabitants are a people of the same race, language, religion, and institutions, with whom its peo-

---

[1] *The Empire*, 1863, pp. 143–4.

ple, severed only by an obsolete quarrel, are rapidly blending, and would unite if nature had her way. In the United States is Canada's natural market for buying as well as selling, the market which her productions are always struggling to enter through every opening in the tariff wall, for exclusion from which no distant market either in England or elsewhere can compensate her, the want of which brings on her commercial atrophy and drives the flower of her youth by thousands and tens of thousands over the line. Her own market, as a whole, is not large, and it is broken into four, between which there is hardly any natural trade, and little has been forced even by the most stringent system of protection. The demand for aid for settlement may have awakened England to the fact that the Canadian North-West remains unpeopled. It remains unpeopled while the neighbouring States of the Union are peopled, because it is cut off from the continent to which it belongs by a fiscal and political line.

There is an especial danger in the retention of Canada, both to the Imperial country and to the colony. Canada, British Canada at least (and England cannot be too often reminded that there is a French Canada as well as a British), with her Governor-General's Court and her mimic aristocracy of Baronets and Knights, presents herself as a political outpost of monarchical and aristocratic England on the territory of American democracy. In this spirit her fervent loyalists act, all the more because they cannot help feeling that nature is drawing together the two sections of the English race on the continent, and that only by cultivating antagonism can the attraction be countervailed. Safe, as they think, under the shield of England, and not being called upon even to pay the expense of their own diplomacy, they indulge in a spirited bearing towards the United States. Thus are bred disputes, of one of which arbitration may fail to dispose. At the last election the government distinctly appealed to anti-American feeling, and its leaders made anti-American speeches which they afterwards tried to soften, but which had been faithfully taken down; while their less responsible followers, going greater lengths, insulted the American name and flag. Suppose, to use the illustration once more, Scotland were an American possession and an outpost of American Anglophobia.

A reunion of the Anglo-Saxon race in a political or diplomatic sense there can hardly be. The race is too widely scattered, the circumstances of its members differ too widely, some of them are too much mixed with other races, for any combination of that kind. How could Great Britain confederate, even in the loosest way, with the United States? Where would the centre of such a union be, and what would be its objects? If the object were merely to keep the peace among the members of the confederacy, that might be done in a simpler way; if to impose the will of the confederacy upon the world, the world would rise against the confederacy. This is a day-dream. But there is nothing visionary in the hope of a moral reunion of the race, in which would be buried the old quarrel with all its miserable traces, including that subserviency to a people alien to the Anglo-Saxon mission of law, into which partly by their dissensions both sections have been brought. England was bound, after the American Revolution, to keep her flag flying over the loyalists who had settled in Canada as well as over the French Catholics who had taken her side. This duty has been done ; and if Canada, situated as she is commercially as well as geographically, and with a solid French nationality in the midst of her, is capable of being and desires to be an independent nation, from American aggression, once more, she has nothing to fear. The Americans have territory enough; though they cannot fail to see the advantages of a united continent, they are too wise to incorporate disaffection. They know that if they wish to put pressure on Canada, they might do it without giving England a pretext for drawing her sword by stopping the bonding system, depriving Canada of winter ports, excluding her products from their markets, and laying a hostile hand upon her railways, including the Canadian Pacific, which, though Englishmen seem to be unaware of the fact, runs through the State of Maine. Let England, then, fairly weigh the advantages and disadvantages of this possession both to herself and to the dependency, and let her not be beguiled by official reports or by those of Governors-General who do not live in the castle of truth. It was to such sources that England and her government continued to trust for information while the current of events was drawing them towards the American Revolution.

Sentiment, apart from utility, nobody would disparage; but apart from utility it cannot long subsist. Nor is loyalty, however loud, or even sincere, worth much unless it is attested by self-sacrifice. A Canadian Parliament, a Conservative Minister leading the way, voted sympathy with Home Rule. This was done, as a leading Conservative confessed on the platform the other day, because, an election being near, it was necessary to capture the Irish Catholic vote. Judge whether these men are likely to pour out their blood without stint for British connection; see at least, first, whether they are ready to pour out a little money or to reduce their duties on your goods. "Loyalty," said Cobden, "is an ironical term to apply to people who neither pay our taxes nor obey our laws, nor hold themselves liable to fight our battles, who would repudiate our right to the sovereignty over an acre of their territory, and who claim the right of imposing their own customs duties even to the exclusion of our manufactures."[1]

---

[1] Cobden visited Canada and the United States more than once, and when the Confederation Act was on the stocks wrote as follows to a friend : "I cannot see what substantial interest the British people have in the connection to compensate them for guaranteeing three or four millions of North Americans living in Canada against another community of Americans living in their neighborhood. We are told indeed of the loyalty of the Canadians, but this is an ironical term to apply to people who neither pay our taxes, nor obey our laws, nor hold themselves liable to fight our battles, who would repudiate our right to the sovereignty over an acre of their territory, and who claim the right of imposing their own customs duties even to the exclusion of our manufactures. We are two peoples to all intents and purposes, and it is a perilous delusion to both parties to attempt to keep up a sham connection and dependence, which will snap asunder if it should ever be put to the strain of stern reality. It is all very well for our Cockney newspapers to talk of

Nothing can be more kindly than the feeling of ordinary Canadians, who seek no titles and have no railways to vend, towards the mother country; but it does not prevent them from thinking of their own interest first, or from freely exchanging the British for the American flag whenever their interest calls them to the other side of the line. Every one who has lived in the United States knows that there is many an American of the better class whose heart has turned to Old England. The affection of these men is undeniably genuine, and would perhaps stand as severe a test as the loyalty of the dependency. That the love of colonists other than those whose special interests or aspirations are bound up with the present system would be loosened by the dissolution of the political tie, there is not the slightest reason for believing. It has not been lessened by the reduction of the tie to a mere thread; why should it be loosened by the dissolution? Race, history, literature, depend not on political connection. The Governor-Generalship as a channel of British influence on the Canadian mind would be well exchanged for the free importation of British books.

This question of the relation of the colonies cannot be set

defending Canada at all hazards. It would be just as possible for the United States to sustain Yorkshire in a war with England as for us to enable Canada to contend against the United States. It is simply an impossibility. Nor must we forget that the only serious danger of a quarrel between the two neighbors arises from the connection of Canada with this country. In my opinion, it is for the interest of both that we should, as speedily as possible, sever the political thread by which we are as communities connected, and leave the individuals on both sides to cultivate the relations of commerce and friendly intercourse as with other nations. I have felt an interest in this Confederation scheme because I thought it was a step in the direction of an amicable separation. I am afraid from the last telegrams that there may be a difficulty either in your province or in Lower Canada in carrying out the project. Whatever may be the wish of the colonies will meet with the concurrence of our Government and Parliament. We have recognized their right to control their own fate even to the point of asserting their independence whenever they think fit, and which we know to be only a question of time." — Morley's *Life of Cobden*, Vol. II., pp. 470, 471.

aside as unpractical. It may at any moment present itself in the most practical form; for a maritime war would at once reveal the inability of England to protect her distant dependencies and the inability of the dependencies to defend their own trade. At some time it must come, for nobody believes that Australia and Canada can forever remain in a state of dependence. Nobody imagines that the American colonies which are now the United States, even if there had been no quarrel with George III., could have remained to the present day dependencies of Great Britain. "There is a period," said Lord Blatchford, "in the life of distant nations, however close their original connection, at which each must pursue its own course, whether in domestic or foreign politics, unembarrassed by the other's leading. And the arrival of that period depends upon growth. Every increase of colonial wealth, or number, or intelligence, or organisation, is in one sense a step towards disintegration. The Confederation of Canada was therefore such a step." The opinion of Sir G. Cornewall Lewis in his "Government of Dependencies," though, like all his opinions, cautiously worded, is easy to read. Even Lord Beaconsfield told Lord Malmesbury in confidence that the colonies would be independent in a few years, nor did he shrink from saying that they were a millstone round the neck of England in the meantime.[1] If the question must come, then, why not face it? Because British governments are ephemeral, and in the perpetual faction fight have enough to do to-day without thinking of to-morrow. Probably, therefore, the end will come in the form of a crash or shock of some kind. But discussion will at least teach statesmanship to interpret the event and deal wisely with it when it comes.

The West India Islands are lovely, romantic, steeped in historic memories. But as a British possession they are almost penal. Profit or strength from them Great Britain derives no more. In case of a maritime war, they would be a real burden to her. But she is bound to sustain what remains of a white

---

[1] See Lord Malmesbury's *Memoirs of an Ex-Minister*, Vol. I., p. 344.

race, and to keep peace between the races, so that there may be no more Jamaica massacres. This penalty she pays for her share in the gains of slavery, gains which themselves were losses, for the West Indian slave-owners corrupted her society and her politics. Peace, it is to be feared, can be kept between whites and blacks only by a power superior to both of them, and it would be probably better for the Islands if they were dependencies outright, and ruled by Imperial governors, provided the governors were strong men and impartial, not febrile partisans like Governor Eyre. Negro democracy, after a pretty long trial in Haiti, seems to be a total failure, even when due allowance is made for the inauspicious circumstances of its birth. The Americans do not want to incorporate barbarous populations which would send corrupt elements to Congress, nor do they want to annex islands for the defence of which they would have to keep a large fleet.

There is an impression that the question of the colonial system and of the Empire generally was mooted some time ago by the Manchester school, and that the mercenary ideas of the school prevailed for a time, but were presently discarded, while Imperialism resumed its generous sway. Opinion is a plant not only of slow, but of fitful growth. The Manchester movement, as it is styled, swept away military occupation. Before that time there had been large bodies of British troops in the colonies, and, as a consequence, a series of Maori and Kaffir wars. The movement got rid of the useless and troublesome protectorate of the Ionian Islands. It gave a general impulse to colonial emancipation, which has constantly advanced since that time. Almost every question has been determined in favour of colonial self-government, till at last the colonies stand upon the brink of independence. Canada is now even claiming diplomatic independence in the matter of commercial treaties, which she proposes to make for herself under the name and on the responsibility of the British Foreign Office. She has half emancipated herself judicially from the Privy Council by the creation of her own Supreme Court.

She begins to be rather restless under the military command of generals sent from England. At this point there is a natural recoil, as there is sure to be at any parting, however inevitable, at the breaking of any tie, familiar, though it may be obsolete. Moreover, there are classes whose interests and aspirations are bound up with the system. There are the circle of Colonial Governors and the candidates for Imperial titles. Another reactionary influence of a subtle kind is felt. Home Rulers find in fervent Imperialism a set-off against their separatism at home. They promise themselves and their country an ampler union as compensation for dismemberment. Hence the movement in favour of Imperial Federation. On this subject the writer can only repeat what he has said in another work, which, being on a special question, may not have met the eye of the reader of this book.[1]

"It was probably the sight of the tie visibly weakening and of the approach of colonial independence that gave birth, by a recoil, to Imperial Federation. But the movement has been strangely reinforced from another source. Home Rulers, who under that specious name would surrender Ireland to the Parnellites, think to salve their own patriotism and reconcile the nation to their policy by saying that in breaking up the United Kingdom they are but providing raw materials for a far ampler and grander union. In the case of the late Mr. Forster, the only statesman who has very seriously embraced the project, something might be due to the Nemesis of imagination in the breast of a Quaker.

"The Imperial Federationists refuse to tell us their plan. They bid our bosoms dilate with trustful enthusiasm for arrangements which are yet to be revealed. They say it is not yet time for the disclosure. Not yet time, when the last strand of political connection is worn almost to the last thread, and when every day the sentiment opposed to centralisation is implanting itself more deeply in colonial hearts! While we are bidden to wait patiently for the tide, the tide is running

---

[1] *Canada and the Canadian Question*, pp. 296–309.

strongly the other way. Now Newfoundland claims the right of making her own commercial agreements with the United States independently of other colonies. Disintegration, surely, is on the point of being complete.

"At least we may be told of whom the Confederation is to consist. Are the negroes of the West Indies to be included? Is Quashee to vote on Imperial policy? But above all, what is to be done with India? Is it, as a Colonial Federationist of thoroughgoing democratic tendencies demanded the other day, to be taken into Federation and enfranchised? If it is, the Hindu will outvote us five to one, and what he will do with us only those who have fathomed the Oriental mystery can pretend to say. Is it to remain a dependency? If it is, to whom is it to belong? To a Federation of democratic communities scattered over the globe, some of which, like Canada, have no interest in it whatever? Its fate as an Empire would then be sealed, if it is not sealed already by the progress of democracy in Great Britain. Or is it to belong to England alone? In that case one member of the Confederacy will have an Empire apart five times as large as the rest of the Confederation, requiring separate armaments and a diplomacy of its own. How would the American Confederation work if one State held South America as an Empire? Some have suggested that Hindustan should be represented by the British residents in India alone. If it were, woe to the Hindu!

"Again, the object of the Association surely must be known. Every Association of a practical kind must have a definite object to hold it together. The objects which naturally suggest themselves are common armaments and a common tariff. But Canada, as we have seen, refuses to contribute to common armaments, and Australia, though she sent a regiment to the Soudan, now apparently repents of having done it. Great Britain is a war power; the colonists, like the Americans, are essentially unmilitary, and here would be the beginning of troubles. As to the tariff, the Canadian Protectionists, who make use of Imperial Federation as a stalking-horse in their struggle against free trade with the United States, are always careful to say that they do not mean to resign their right of laying protective duties on British goods. Victoria also seems wedded to her Protective system. What remains but improvement of postal communication and a Colonial Exhibition, neither of which surely calls for a political combination unprecedented in history?

"Unprecedented in history the combination would be. The Roman Empire, the thought of which and of its *Civis Romanus sum*, is always hovering before our minds, was vast, but it was all in a ring-fence. Moreover, it had its world to itself, no rival powers being interposed between Rome and her Provinces. It was an Empire in the proper sense of the term. Its members were all alike in strict subordination to its head. The head determined the policy without question, and danger to unity from divided counsels there was none. We confuse our minds, as was said before, by an improper use of the term Empire. The name applies to India, but to nothing else connected with Great Britain unless it be the fortresses and Crown Colonies. Our self-governed colonies are not members of an Empire, but free communities virtually independent of the mother country, which for the purpose of Confederation would be called upon to resign a portion of their independence. Of the Spanish Empire it is needless to speak. Its name is an omen of disaster and a warning against the blind ambition which mistakes combination for union and colossal weakness for power. After all, the Roman Empire itself fell, and partly because the life was drawn from the members to the head.

"The Achæan League, the Swiss Bund, the Union of the Netherlands, the American Union, all were perfectly natural combinations, not only suggested but commanded by a common peril. In three out of the four cases the communities which entered into the compact were kindred in all respects; in the case of the Swiss Bund they were equal. In the case of the Confederation now proposed, they would be neither kindred nor equal; and fasten the people of the British Islands, those of self-governed colonies, the Hindu, the African, and the

Kaffir together with what legislative clamps you will, you cannot produce the unity of political character and sentiment which is essential to community of counsels, much more to national union.

"Steam and telegraph, we are told, have annihilated distance. They have not annihilated the parish steeple. They have not carried the thoughts of the ordinary citizen beyond the circle of his own life and work. They have not qualified a common farmer, tradesman, ploughman, or artisan to direct the politics of a world-wide State. How much does an ordinary Canadian know or care about Australia, an ordinary Australian about Canada, or an ordinary Englishman, Scotchman, or Irishman about either? The feeling of all the colonists towards the mother country, when you appeal to it, is thoroughly kind, as is that of the mother country towards the colonies. But Canadian notions of British politics are hazy, and still more hazy are British notions of the politics of Canada. When John Sandfield Macdonald, the Prime Minister of Ontario, died, his death was chronicled by British journals as that of Sir John A. Macdonald, the Prime Minister of the Dominion.

"The different Provinces of Canada cannot be made to sink their local interests in that of the Dominion. How much less could all the colonies be made to sink their local interests in that of the Imperial Federation!

"About India Englishmen know more, because their interest in it is so great; but Canadians know nothing. The framers of these vast political schemes, having their own eyes fixed on the political firmament, forget that the eyes of men in general are fixed on the path they tread. The suffrage of the Federation ought to be limited to far-reaching and imaginative minds.

"A grand idea may be at the same time practical. The idea of a United Continent of North America, securing free trade and intercourse over a vast area, with external safety and internal peace, is no less practical than it is grand. The benefits of such a union would be always present to the mind of the least instructed citizen. The sentiment connected with it would be a foundation on which the political architect could build. Imperial Federation, to the mass of the people comprised in it, would be a mere name conveying with it no definite sense of benefit on which anything could be built.

"To press this receding vision a little closer, what would be the relation of the Federal Government to the British monarchy? Would the same Queen be sovereign of both? Would she have two sets of advisers? Suppose they should advise her different ways! Would she appoint, as she does now, the heads of all the other members of the Federation? It would hardly do to let the President of the United States appoint all the State Governors. How would the Supreme Court be constituted? Such an authority would certainly be needed to interpret the Constitution, and the British monarchy would have to be a suitor before it. How would the decrees of the Federal Government be enforced, say, in case of refusal to send the war contingent? How, again, would the representation in the Federal Parliament be apportioned? If by population, the representation of the British Islands would so outnumber the rest that the rest would deem their representation practically a nullity, and jealousy and cabals would at once arise. The very number, too, would be a difficulty. If Great Britain had members in proportion to St. Helena and Fiji, the Parliament would have to meet on Salisbury Plain. These are not questions of detail, nor do they attach only to a particular scheme; they are fundamental, and attach to every scheme that can be conceived.

"The Parliament of Great Britain must cease to be a Sovereign Power. The Imperial Congress itself would not be a Sovereign Power. Like the Congress of the United States, it would be subject to the Federal Constitution, and would have so much authority only as that Constitution assigned it. The Sovereign Power would be the people of the Empire at large, and a curious Sovereign they would be.

"The same person could not be the head at once of a Federation and of one of the communities included in it, any more than the same person could be President of the United States and Governor of the State of New York. Her Majesty would have to choose between the British and the Pan-Britannic Crown.

"Canada is a Confederation in herself. Movements are on foot for a Confederation of the Australian Colonies and of those of South Africa. A Confederation of the West India Islands has also been proposed. We should thus have a striking novelty in political architecture in the shape of a Confederation of Confederations. But it seems certain that New Zealand would not, and that some isolated colonies could not, join any Federation, in which case the members of the Central Parliament would represent partly Federations, partly single communities. Strange, apparently, would be the complication of fealties, obligations, and sentiments which would hence arise.

"This Union, so complex in its machinery, with its members scattered over the world, and distracted by interests as wide apart as the shores of its members, Home Rulers think they could maintain, while they bid us despair of maintaining the Parliamentary Union of Ireland with Great Britain.

"Even to assemble the Constituent Convention would be no easy task. The governments, British and Colonial, are all party governments and all liable to constant change. The delegate trusted by one party would not have the confidence of the other, and before the Convention could proceed to business somebody's credentials would be withdrawn. We have seen in the case of Canadian Confederation how Nova Scotia, New Brunswick, and Prince Edward Island flew off from the agreement at which their delegates had arrived. In truth there would probably be a general falling away as soon as payment for Imperial armaments came into view.

"The Federation would be nothing if not diplomatic. But whose diplomacy is to prevail? That of Great Britain, a European Power and at the same time Mistress of India? That of Australia, with her Eastern relations and her Chinese question? Or that of Canada, bound up with the American

Continent, indifferent to everything in Europe or Asia, and concerned only with her relation to the United States? Australia, we have been told, already betrays her intention of breaking away from England should British policy ever take a line adverse to her special interests in the East, and such a line British policy must take if the special interests of Australia are ever to lead her into a conflict with the Chinese.

"Switzerland, the Netherlands, and the United States, all federated under the pressure of necessity, which, stern and manifest as it was, had yet scarcely the power to overcome the centralised forces. To do the work of that necessity there ought at least to be an equally strong desire. But what proof have we of the existence of such a desire? Australia, far from being eager, seems to be adverse; in some of her cities the missionary of Imperial Federation can scarcely find an audience. From South Africa comes no audible response. In British Canada the movement has no apparent strength except what it derives from an alliance with Protectionism, which, as has already been said, repudiates a commercial union of the Empire and insists on maintaining its separate tariff. To the French Nationalists of Quebec anything that would bind their country closer to Great Britain is odious, and they were recently disposed to receive a Governor-General coldly because they suspected him of favouring such a policy. In Great Britain itself the movement shows no sign of strength. For several years, under Lord Beaconsfield, Imperialism had everything its own way, yet not a step was taken towards Federation. This was the grand opportunity; but Federationists failed to grasp it by the forelock. Nothing has been done to this hour beyond holding a meeting of colonists, absolutely without authority, which dined, wined, and talked about postal communications, all power of dealing with the great question having been expressly withheld. Lord Beaconsfield's successor in the Tory leadership has plainly declined to commit himself to the project. We seem to be a long way from a spontaneous and overwhelming vote, nothing short of which would suffice.

"The approach to centralisation at once sets all the centrifugal forces in action; it did this even in the American Federation, so that the project narrowly escaped wreck; and miscarriage would beget, instead of closer union, discord, estrangement, and perhaps rupture. Let us bear in mind the warning example of the rupture with the American colonies.

"What is the real motive for encountering all the difficulties and perils of this more than gigantic undertaking, for running laboriously counter to the recent course of colonial history, as well as to the natural tendencies of our race, and for taking the political heart and brain, as it were, out of each of these free communities and transferring them to London? We are told that the Federal Empire would impose peace upon the world. This assumes that dispersion is strength, and that Great Britain would be made more formidable in war by being bound up with unwarlike communities. But suppose it true; surely the appearance of a world-wide power, grasping all the waterways and all the points of maritime vantage, instead of propagating peace, would, like an alarm gun, call the nations to battle? The way to make peace on earth is to promote the coming not of an exclusive military league but of the Parliament of Man, the moral Parliament of Man at least, by enlarging the action of international law and repressing the ambitious passions to which, however philanthropic may be our professions, Imperialism really appeals.

"If no distinct object can be assigned, if no definite plan can be produced, if the projectors are conscious that there is no practical step on which they can venture, surely the project ought to be frankly laid aside and no longer allowed to darken counsel, hide from us the real facts of the situation, and prevent the colonies from advancing on the true path.

"There is a federation which is feasible, and, to those who do not measure grandeur by physical force or extension, at least as grand as that of which the Imperialist dreams. It is the moral federation of the whole English-speaking race throughout the world, including all those millions of men speaking the English language in the United States, and parted from the rest only a century ago by a wretched quarrel, whom Imperial Federation would leave out of its pale. Nothing is needed to bring this about but the voluntary retirement of England as a political power from a shadowy Dominion in a sphere which is not hers.

"Unless all present appearances on the political horizon are delusive, the time is at hand when the upheaval of the labour world, and the social problems which are coming into view, will give politicians more serious and substantial matter for thought than the airy fabric of Imperial Federation.

"The old project of giving the colonies representation in the Imperial Parliament appears to have been laid aside. The objections urged against it by Burke on the ground of distance have been to a great extent removed by steam, though it might even now be difficult to call together a world-wide Parliament in time of maritime war. But the objection still decisive is that the colonies would not put their affairs into the hands of an Assembly in which their representation would be overwhelmingly outnumbered. Nor could they trust representatives domiciled in London who, under the influence of London society, would be apt to become more British than the British themselves. These new countries, which have such difficulty in finding suitable men for their own legislatures, would have difficulty in finding men to represent them at Westminster at all. They might have to fall back on expatriated men of wealth, in whom, as representatives of colonial sentiment, very little confidence could be placed. Supposing that the members for the colonies remained colonial, and tried to make up for their lack of numbers at Westminster by combining among themselves and log-rolling, they might become a serious addition to the distractions of the British Parliament, which assuredly need no increase.

"Let it be taken as certain and irreversible that the colonies will not part with any portion of their self-government. If a scheme can be devised by which they can be governed by an Assembly at Westminster without any loss to them of self-government it may, supposing it be presented to them in an intelligible and practical form, stand a chance of consideration at their hands.

"A crumb of comfort has just fallen to the advocates of Imperial Federation in the shape of a peerage conferred on a colonist. This is hailed as representation of the colonies in the British Parliament. The number of such Peers must always be very small, while the House in which they sit is not.that of power but that from which power has departed. But who can less represent colonial sentiment than a millionnaire transplanted to Mayfair? A millionnaire, to be made a Peer a man must be, and to have made money out of the Colony rather than to have done service in it will be the indispensable qualification for the honour. In particular cases the two qualifications may no doubt be combined; but the general fruits of the practice are likely to be false ambition and enhanced desire of gain.

"The Imperial Federationists seem now to be splitting into sections with different policies and organs. Apart from the advocates of an Imperial Parliament, whose confidence seems to be failing, stand the advocates of a military league on one hand and of a fiscal league on the other, or, if the German words are preferred, of a Kriegsverein and a Zollverein. The advocates of a Kriegsverein have had their answer, so far as Canada is concerned, from the Canadian Commissioner, who tells them that liberty of transit over Canadian roads, at the regular rates, will be Canada's contribution. They are now confronted by fact. The advocates of a Zollverein will find themselves confronted by fact as soon as they choose to put to the protected manufacturer of Canada the question whether he is willing, in consideration of Imperial discrimination in her favour, to reduce the import duties on British goods. Had the apostle of fiscal Imperialism, who fancies that he has all Canada in his favour, mooted that point before an audience at Toronto or Montreal, a chill would at once have come over the assembly.

"The latest scheme is that proposed by the Canadian Commissioner, who suggests that to cement the Imperial fabric he and his two fellow Commissioners from Australia and South Africa should be made Privy Councillors and members at once of the Imperial and the Colonial Cabinet. He at the same time lauds the practice of making Colonial Peers. It is to be feared that among these Commissioners only one would be found capable of thus mentally bestriding the ocean and sharing at once the councils of two Cabinets, perhaps belonging to opposite parties and having different ends in view. The scheme has found as yet but one adherent."

As war is the peril of Empire, a paper on the subject of the Empire is hardly complete without a word as to the probabilities of war. Is the tendency to war declining? Are the hopes of the Peace Society on the eve or near the eve of being fulfilled? More men are under arms in Europe than ever were under arms before. There can be no doubt that in the course of history the war spirit has on the whole grown weaker. It plainly recedes before the advance of civilisation. An Assyrian or Persian king made his annual war as regularly as a king of France his annual hunt; and the same was the habit of the Turkish Sultans while their Empire was strong. War in the eyes of a Greek or Roman was the highest of occupations, and Plato's ideal citizens are warriors. Industry was the lot and badge of the slave. War is now not normal but exceptional. Of late there has been a distinct growth of moral sentiment against the use of the sword. Charles V. told a young soldier who pined for action that he loved peace no more than the youth himself. At a much later day Chatham avowed himself "a lover of honourable war;" and in the writings of Burke will be found a general recognition of success in war as a test of national happiness and greatness. Peace sentiment is of course confined to the domain of moral civilisation; it does not prevail among the Turks, or among the people of South America; nor does it prevail in its moral form among the Chinese, though they have an industrial antipathy to arms and the military profession. It can scarcely be said that religion has done much to quell the spirit of war. The Polytheistic religion of the ancients encouraged it by identifying the god with the victory and aggrandisement of the tribe. The books which embody the tribal religion of the Jew incited him to wage internecine war with the neighbouring tribes, and Christian believers in the authority of the Old Testament have thence learned to fight the battles of the Lord. The Gospel is in principle against war, yet does not expressly condemn it; but, on the contrary, recognises the soldier's calling as lawful, and by likening the Christian's fight to that of the warrior seems to imply that there is nothing in the warrior's fight repugnant to Christian sentiment. It is needless to say that Christianity has not persuaded nations to turn the other cheek to the smiter. National churches have lapsed into something very like tribalism in this respect. They have assumed that the Lord of Hosts went forth with the national army to battle. They have sung *Te Deum*, hung up trophies in their churches, and blessed standards, to say nothing of the part played by the clergy as trumpeters of religious war.

The tendency of democracy appears to be against war. Rome, though a Republic, was not a democracy, but an aristocracy ending in an Empire. Athens, which has been often cited as an example of military ambition in a democracy, was a slave-owning State. The Italian Republics were born into a world of feudal war; but they presently showed their tendency by hiring mercenaries to do the fighting on their behalf. If the motive power here was industry rather than democracy, the two commonly go together, and it is only under democracy that industry rules the State. The case of revolutionary France was manifestly abnormal. Even under the Convention she was a Dictatorate rather than a democracy, and the forces which her masters wielded were inherited by them from the military monarchy, while the supplies were raised by confiscation. Among the South American States there has been constant fighting; but they are democratic in form only, in reality they are dictatorates, power passing usually by violence from hand to hand. The American democracy made the greatest war since those of Napoleon. But this was a war of self-preservation, and no disposition was shown to make use of the vast armaments on foot at its close. The American army was rapidly reduced to its regular number, which was twenty-five thousand, for a total community of sixty-five millions, barely sufficient to fight the Indians and secure domestic order; while of the navy, an American wit has said that it could be run down by a coal barge. The strongest case on the other side is that of France, where universal suffrage has so far not made the government less military or led to reduction of armaments; though it might have been suspected that the peasantry who have groaned under the conscription would at once have voted it down. But the Bonapartes, following the Bourbons, have so filled France with military spirit, and obedience to military command is so ingrained, that a change was likely to take time. Democracy is humane, as its criminal code proves; for no one would set down the French Reign of Terror as democratic. Its humanity is connected with its equality, which makes all lives of the same value, and forbids the common people to be treated as food for powder. With a military despot like Napoleon, or a high and cold aristocracy, the slaughter of peasants goes for nothing. For the same reason democratic wars are expensive, popular sentiment requiring that good provision shall be made not only for the general but for all alike. The American War of Secession was enormously expensive to the democratic North, which supplied its armies lavishly, gave large bounties for enlistment, and is now paying in pensions an annual sum equal to the total cost of a great European army. The slave-owning aristocracy of the South could raise its forces by sheer conscription, and force them to fight without pay and sometimes without food.

Of the old causes of war, some may be said to have died out so far as the civilised world is concerned. No civilised government would now set out, like Sennacherib or Xerxes, on an unprovoked career of territorial conquest. No civilised government, or government pretending to be civilised, except perhaps that of a Bonaparte, would even commit such territorial aggression as was committed by Louis XIV. Frederick the Great, at all events, set up a legal claim to Silesia. The last great exception to this improvement of sentiment, a tremendous exception certainly, were the conquests of Napoleon, especially his piratical invasion of Spain. Napoleon was not a child of moral civilisation; he was a child of Corsican brigandage and barbarism, whose military genius, called into play by the wars of the Revolution, made him for a time almost master of the civilised world. His influence did not end with his fall. He had evoked a spirit of militarism which, like his ascendancy, may be regarded as an accident of history and destined to pass away. Russia, among other characteristics of a backward civilisation, may still be capable of a war of sheer conquest. But her ambition points in one direction, that of Constantinople, and seeks at least to reconcile itself with morality by pleading the decadence of Turkey and the duty of rescuing from oppression the Slav and Christian subjects of the Porte. The fear, real or affected, of Russian ambition it was which, by bringing on the Crimean war, broke the spell, which Europe had begun to hope would be lasting, of the forty years' peace. Of the religious wars which desolated Europe in the sixteenth and seventeenth centuries we shall hear no more. Faith is now too weak for Catholic leagues as for crusades. By the middle of the seventeenth century the conflict had lost much of its religious character and become political or territorial. Presently we have the Pope himself as an Italian Prince on the same side with Protestant Powers. Dynastic wars may also be considered as numbered with the past. So may the commercial wars which owed their origin to the monopolist fallacies of the last century. On the other hand, we have recently had wars of national revival and reconstruction: the war between Austria and Germany, which attended the restoration of German unity, and the war between Germany and France, which the French jealousy of the restored unity of Germany entailed. There may yet be more trouble of this kind in the Austrian Empire, in the Turkish Empire, and possibly in Scandinavia, in Poland, and the Baltic Provinces of Russia. The thirst of France for glory seems still unslaked, and to it has been added a thirst for revenge. The break-up of the Turkish Empire and a scramble for its spoils are always in prospect. A new set of disputes is also arising out of rival claims to fields for colonisation in Africa. Similar disputes may arise about other waste places of the earth, as Europe becomes overcrowded and the need of outlets grows. Though religious revolution as a source of war has lost its force, it seems not impossible that social revolution may take its place. The wars to which social revolution would lead would be likely, it is true, to be civil rather than international. But it is conceivable that some military power born of social revolution, like the Spanish Intransigentes or the French Communists, may get hold of a government and imitate the crusading fury of the Jacobins. Nor, while we scan the horizon of the civilised world, ought it to be forgotten that there is a world outside, of which China is the greatest power, still uncivilised, which may give birth to military force, and arm itself with the weapons of civilisation. This would be a sufficient reason against universal disarmament, such as the Peace Society preaches, even if we could dispense with the soldier as an upholder of order and an example of discipline amidst a general dissolution of authority.

The enormous armaments which the European Powers now have on foot appear to make war at some time certain, since it would seem that the tension must at last become insufferable, and that somebody must break. On the other hand, the very apprehension of conflict with forces so vast and engines of war so destructive acts as a strong deterrent and may prevail over international hatred and other incentives to war till financial deficit enforces reduction. The change in the mode of warfare from embattled hosts to long-range projectiles, and from fleets such as fought at Trafalgar to turrets and rams, is probably in favour of peace; not only because it

makes war more dreadful by increasing its destructiveness
(which may be doubted), but because by taking away the
pomp, pride, and circumstance of the battle-field, it robs war
and the soldier's trade of much of their hold upon the imagination. Waterloo or Trafalgar must have been a superb and
enthralling sight. Cannæ and Actium must have been still
more so. But Sedan, as painted by Zola, has nothing in it
superb or enthralling. It is a prosaic scene of scientific
butchery. As to the "plumed troop" of Life Guards, it is
now of no more use than the Beefeaters, and is probably
maintained upon the same grounds.

By the introduction of the new and long-range weapons a
new advantage has apparently been given to the defence over
the attack. This is in favour of the invaded, and against the
invader. It does not seem, however, that the change of
weapons has diminished the ascendancy of discipline; fighting
as a skirmisher needing even more discipline than fighting in
line or in column. The hope of political enthusiasts, that
long-range rifles will be the death of standing armies is, therefore, not likely to be fulfilled.

Arbitration has now been so often employed and with so
much success, as to raise very high the hopes of its advocates.
Yet apparently there are still limits to its operation. Resolute ambition or fierce passion would hardly yield to it. Nor
can it be expected that the strong will always forego its prerogative and allow every question to be settled by a tribunal
before which they would stand on a level with the weak.

WOMAN SUFFRAGE.

WOMAN SUFFRAGE.

IT is not necessary, in entering upon this question, to dilate on its sentimental side. Nothing can add force or tenderness to the names of wife and home. Suffice it to say, that man cannot withhold from woman anything that is good for her, or give her anything that is bad for her, without injuring himself and their children in the same measure.

Shall man make over to woman half of the sovereign power which has hitherto been his, and which, if he chooses, he can keep? This is the question broadly stated. Woman, in making the demand, shows confidence in man's affection. The rule by which the question is to be settled is the joint interest which the two sexes have in good government, not any abstract claim of right. For an abstract claim of right there appears to be no foundation. Power which is natural carries with it right, though it is subject to the restraints of conscience. Weakness cannot be said to have a right to artificial power, though the concession of such power within reasonable limits may be not only kind but wise, just, and beneficial to humanity and civilisation. That to which every member of a community, whether man, woman, or child, whether white or black, whether above or below the age of twenty-one, has a right, is the largest attainable measure of good government. If this or any other political change would be conducive to good government, the whole community has a right to it; if it would not, the whole community, including the women, or those, whoever they may be, whom it is proposed to enfranchise, have a right to a refusal of the change. The number of women who have spontaneously asked for the change appears to be small; and its smallness is important as an index of woman's feeling respecting her own interest. But were the number larger, it would still be incumbent on the present holders of power before abdicating to consider whether in the common interest their abdication was to be desired.

As to the equality of the sexes, no question is necessarily raised; they may be perfectly equal though their spheres are different, that of the man being public life, that of the woman the home. Nor is there any occasion for pitting male or female gifts or qualities together. Supposing woman even to be superior, it does not follow that the field of her superiority is public life.

That the tendency of civilisation has been to elevate woman is true. But elevation is a different thing from assimilation to man. We are told, not so much by women, perhaps, as by their champions, that the time for protection and chivalry has past and the time for justice has come. But it is not made evident that bare justice, which regulates the relations between man and man, would suit the relation between man and woman, or that chivalry and protection on the one side, with the corresponding recognition of them on the other, do not in this case constitute justice.

The movement in favour of woman suffrage is part of a general attempt to change the relations between the sexes, to set woman free from what hitherto have been considered the limitations of her sex, and make her the competitor instead of the helpmate of man. Women are making their way into the male professions, including that of law, into the dissecting-room, in company with the male students, into male places of education, and even into the smoking-room. Some of them have taken to riding astride.[1] The Revolt of woman, as one of the leaders called it, is part of the ferment of a revolutionary age in which the foundations of authority are shaken by the decay of the old beliefs on which public order as well as personal morality has hitherto rested, and by the political disturbance which has accompanied the final deca-

[1] See Mrs. E. Lynn Linton, on women as social insurgents, in the *Nineteenth Century* of October, 1891.

dence of the hereditary principle of government and the advent of democracy.

One of the features of a revolutionary era is the prevalence of a feeble facility of abdication. The holders of power, however natural and legitimate it may be, are too ready to resign it on the first demand. They do not take time to consider whether their power is rightful or not, whether it has or has not on the whole been used for good, whether, if in any case it has not been used for good, they cannot amend their course, or whether it is likely to be better employed by those to whom they are called upon to transfer it. The nerves of authority are shaken by the failure of conviction. It is an inevitable consequence of the demagogic system that every demand for the suffrage, reasonable or unreasonable, should prevail as soon as it shows strength, because the politician is afraid by opposition to make an enemy of the coming vote.

It is evident that sexual revolution must have its limitations if the human race is to continue. There are some landmarks of nature which cannot be removed, and the females of every species must be the organs of its perpetuation. Women must bear and nurse children; and if they do this, it is impossible that they should compete with men in occupations which demand complete devotion as well as superior strength of muscle or brain. There appears to be a tendency among the leaders of the Revolt of woman to disparage matrimony as a bondage, and the rearing of children as an aim too low for an intellectual being. Such ideas are not likely to spread widely, or they would threaten the life of the race. They prevail chiefly in the highly educated and sentimental classes, not in the homes of labour. If it is a question of right, children have their rights as well as women. They have not less right to motherly care than they and their mother have to being fed by the husband's labour.

At present the demand in England is only for the enfranchisement of spinsters and widows. But this limitation, while it betrays a consciousness that there would be danger to the peace and order of the family, is understood to be merely a stroke of tactics.   Widow and spinster suffrage is the thin edge of the wedge.   From the political point of view there would be manifest absurdity and wrong in making marriage politically penal, and excluding from the franchise the very women who are commonly held to be best discharging the duties of their sex, and would be likely to be its fairest representatives.   Already the thoroughgoing section of the party repudiates the limitation.   The spinster and widow vote would be an irresistible lever whenever political parties were nearly balanced.   When the suffrage had been conceded to all women, as the women slightly outnumber the men, and many of the men, sailors, for example, or men employed on railways, or in itinerant callings, could not go to the poll, the woman's vote would preponderate, and government, if it was in unison with the votes, would be more female than male. Nor is it by the leaders and chief authors of the movement intended that we should stop here.   The woman of the political platform does not limit her ambition to a vote.   She wants to sit in Parliament or in Congress.   When she gains her first point she will have practically established her claim to the next; those who are qualified to give a mandate, she will say, are qualified to bear it; those who are qualified to decide principles of legislation are qualified to legislate; those who are qualified to dictate a policy are qualified to carry it into effect.   It might shock our prejudices at first to see a woman taking part in Parliamentary debate.   It shocks our prejudices at first to see her taking part in a faction fight, mounting the pulpit, or thundering from a platform, as well as to see her in half male attire, or riding in man's fashion. Established sentiment and old ideas of delicacy have been already set aside.   The female aspirant to a seat in Parliament or Congress, and to a place in the Cabinet will have, therefore, little difficulty in proving her claim.   She will have no difficulty whatever in enforcing it.   That, the woman's vote will do for her.   A tenth part of the woman's vote would do it for her if the parties were nearly balanced and the politicians were alarmed.   Politics under the party system are one demagogic auction, and an inevitable slide down hill. In the United States, where all qualifications for the suffrage other than that of simple citizenship have been abolished or practically nullified, female suffrage, like male suffrage, would no doubt be universal. That the change thus presents itself at once in its full extent may partly account for the general conservatism of the American people on this subject. But there is also the safeguard of the special process which is required in the States as well as in the Federation for amendments of the Constitution, and which enforces the submission of the question to a constituency beyond the range of the arts and influences to which individual legislators are apt to yield.

Political power has hitherto been exercised by the male sex; not because man has been a tyrannical usurper and has brutally thrust his weaker partner out of her rights, but in the course of nature, because man alone could uphold government and enforce the law. Let the edifice of law be as moral and as intellectual as you will, its foundation is the force of the community, and the force of the community is male. Women have not yet thought of claiming the employment of policemen, soldiers, or any function for which force is required. This fundamental fact may be hidden from sight for the moment by the clouds of emotional rhetoric, but it will assert itself in the end. Laws passed by the woman's vote will be felt to have no force behind them. Women are the great prohibitionists, having only too strong inducements, many of them, to support any supposed antidote to drunkenness, and not seeing that the taste of a man engaged in heavy labour and exposed to the weather for the stimulus of wine or beer may be as natural as the taste of his home-keeping partner for tea. With woman suffrage we should certainly have prohibition. Prohibitionists advocate woman suffrage on that account. Behind prohibition of strong drinks begins to loom prohibition of tobacco. We have had proposals from women to extend capital punishment to cases of outrage on their sex. Would the stronger sex obey such laws when it was known that they were enacted by the weak? Would it obey any laws manifestly carried by the female vote in the interest of the women against that of the men? If it would not, the result would be contempt for the law and anarchy, which would not be likely to enure to the advantage of the weak. Man would be tempted to resist woman's government when it galled him, not only by the consciousness of his strength, but by his pride, which would make itself heard in the end, though its voice for a time might be stifled by sentimental declamation. "In muscle," says the Report of Mr. Blair's Committee of the United States Senate in 1889, "woman is inferior to man. But muscle has nothing to do with legislation or government. In intellect she is man's equal, in character she is, by his own admission, his superior and constitutes the angelic portion of humanity." We have seen reason for thinking that muscle has something to do, if not with the acts of legislatures or governments, with that which gives those acts their force.

In Dahomey there are female warriors. There may have been Amazons in primitive times. But in the civilised world the duty of defending the country in war falls on the male sex alone, and it would seem that there ought to be some connection between that duty and political power. To this it is answered that not all men perform the duty, and that women as well as men contribute as taxpayers to the support of the army. In some countries, as in Germany, all men of military age are, and in every country they ought to be, liable to military service. But everywhere the responsibility rests on the men, who would have to meet the necessity if it arose. That some men are old or disqualified for arms signifies nothing; political rules must be general and disregard exceptional cases. That the women, or such of them as have property of their own, contribute to the expense of the army, is an argument hardly in point unless it is used to found a claim for exemption from contribution, any more than the argument which has also been used that they give their husbands and sons to the military service of the State. The question is about the qualities of the sex. At the same time it would be a mistake to think that female rulers have been averse from war, and that if the power were in female hands war would be no more. Women are apt to be warlike because their responsibility is less. In the Southern States at the time of Secession no partisans of the war were fiercer than the women. Few male rulers have been more bellicose than Catherine of Russia, Elizabeth Queen of Spain (the Termagant, as she was called), Maria Theresa of Austria, Madame de Pompadour, and the Empress Eugénie. Nor is it unlikely that female sentiment might be in favour of some war when male sentiment or prudence was against it. French women might have voted for a crusade in aid of the Pope. English women might have voted for armed intervention in favour of the Queen of Naples, whose heroism touched their imaginations at the time. Would the men obey? Would they shoulder their muskets and march or bid the army march? They would not; and here again law and government would break down.

Besides, the transfer of power from the military to the unmilitary sex involves a change in the character of a nation. It involves, in short, national emasculation. What would be the fate of a community in some dire extremity if it were largely ruled by its women? Philanthropy, theosophy, and utopianism have not yet triumphed. This is the age of Bismarck, of the Franco-Prussian war, of the War of Secession. How would the North have fared in its conflict with the South if, at each turn of the wavering and desperate struggle, it had been swayed by the emotions of its women? One of the ladies whose evidence was taken before Mr. Blair's Committee, admitted that, in the days of force, when women needed the protection of man, male government may have been justifiable; but these, she said, were piping times of peace. Piping times of peace, when America is paying the pension list of an enormous war and Europe has millions of men in arms! Woman does not in civilised countries need the protection of the individual man except as policeman or escort. But she does need, or may at any time need, the armed protection of the male sex as a whole.

We have had successive extensions of that which is called liberty, but ought, if we would think clearly, to be called political power; for a man may have liberty without a vote and a vote without liberty. But hitherto the changes, though some of them have been blind and dangerous enough, have imperilled only the State. The change now proposed vitally affects the family, which, until the Socialists have their way, will be of fully as much consequence to us as the State. It is easy to draw ideal pictures of husband and wife agreeing to differ on political questions, going at elections to opposite committee-rooms, perhaps speaking on opposite platforms, voting on opposite sides, and then returning to a blissful hearth, with harmony and affection unimpaired. This ideal might be realised in the case of such a couple as Mr. and Mrs. John Stuart Mill. But what are the effects of a faction fight on the tempers of ordinary humanity? Would unbroken harmony now prevail between a Unionist husband and a Gladstonian wife? Hitherto the family has been a unit represented in the State by its head, and whatever storms may have raged in the commonwealth, the peace and order of the home have remained usually undisturbed. A change which throws the family into the political caldron calls surely for special consideration. In political and economical discussion our attention is commonly turned to wealth, education, or some factor of our being which is increased or diminished by government or legislation. We seldom think so distinctly as we ought how large a measure of happiness as well as of excellence depends upon affection. A man who prized his home would probably say that if it was thought fit that his wife should have the vote instead of himself, she might have it, but that he protested against any proposal to give the family more than one vote.

Caution is the more necessary since it is clear that party has laid hold of this question. Each party, or a section of each party in England, fancies that it would gain by the change. Some Conservatives believe that the nature of woman is conservative, and that she would vote under the influence of traditional sentiment, perhaps also under that of her priest. The late leader of the Conservatives in England was in favour of enfranchising the women, as he was in favour of enfranchising the proletariat, with the same expectation of votes. But Conservatives who play this game should remember that the conservative woman as a rule is probably feminine and likely to stay at home, while the radical woman is pretty sure to go forth rejoicing to the fray. Nor would the clerical influence be all on one side. Every Catholic Irishwoman would be brought to the poll by the priest. Assuredly the female character is not unsusceptible of revolutionary violence. France saw the Mænads of the Revolution, and has had her Louise Michel. In New York a·female enthusiast has just been inciting the destitute to armed violence and public rapine. However this may be, when party lays its hand on the home, those who care for the home more than for party receive a warning to be on their guard.

Previous extensions of the suffrage have been to an unrepresented class, and a class which might plead that its special interest would suffer by want of representation, though possibly in some cases those interests were likely to suffer as much by the influence of enfranchised ignorance on government as by any class bias. But women are not a class, they are a sex. Their class interests throughout the scale are identical with those of the man, and effectually represented by the male vote. It would probably be impossible to devise a case in which a legislature dealing with female interests in regard to property, taxation, or any other subject, could be misled by motives of class. If property held by women is taxed without being represented, so is that held by men, in the United States absolutely, and in England, saving only the trifling amount of property still required as a qualification for the suffrage.

Have women as a sex any wrongs which male legislatures cannot be expected to redress, so that in order to obtain redress it is necessary that there shall be an abdication by man of the sovereign power? If there are, whether in England or the United States, let them be named. Named hitherto they

have not been. The law regarding the property of married
women has been so far reformed in the interests of the wife,
that, instead of being unduly favourable to the husband, it
seems rather inspired by mistrust of him. The practice is
still more so. It is becoming the custom to tie up a woman's
property, on marriage, so that she shall not be able, even if she
is so inclined, to make provision for her husband, in case he
survives her, in old age, and save him from the necessity of
receiving alms from his own children. The lawyers naturally are active in the work which multiplies legal relations
and interests. About everything has been done which civil
legislation could do to impress the wife with the belief that
her interest and that of her husband are not only separate but
adverse; that she does not leave her father's home when she
is married; that her husband is not one flesh with her; and
that all her relations by blood are nearer to her, in interest at
all events, than the man on whose breast she lays her head.
Matrimonial superstition has been effectually rebuked by
enabling husband and wife to sue each other. The laws of
Massachusetts discriminate in favour of women by exempting
unmarried women of small estate from taxation; by allowing
women and not men to acquire a settlement without paying
a tax; by compelling husbands to support their wives, but
exempting the wife, even when rich, from supporting an indi-
gent husband; by making men liable for debts of wives, and
not *vice versa*.[1] Legal reformers are able to boast that they have
"emancipated woman from the domination of her husband."
They must not forget that the domination carries with it maintenance and protection which will not be given without return.
Make the marriage contract too onerous to one party, and that
party will some day begin to think of emancipation. If he
does he is the stronger. Nothing can alter that fact or its
practical significance in the long run. Of this the leaders of
the Revolt of Woman will do well to take note. That the
administration of the law has been unfavourable to women, few

[1] See *Minority Report* of Mr. Blair's Committee of the Senate of the
United States, February, 1889, p. 14.

will contend. In jury cases, at least, the difficulty is not for women to get justice against men, but for men to get justice against women. It is doubtful whether the introduction of women into the jury-box, for which woman-suffragists contend, could make juries more partial to women than they are. If it did, the failure of justice would be monstrous indeed. In criminal cases mercy has been shown to women. "Since I have been in Parliament," said John Bright, "I think I could specify nearly a score of instances in which the lives of women would be spared where the lives of men would be taken." Can it be believed that the efforts which have been made to save Mrs. Maybrick from punishment would have been made in favour of a husband convicted of the murder of his wife? There is no reason for this partiality except one, which implies a radical difference between the sexes and the willingness of the weaker sex to accept the protection of the stronger.

Does the grievance consist in any bar to the competition of women with men in the professions or trades? Such bars have by male legislation been largely removed. We have female doctors of medicine everywhere, and if their practice is limited, it is because women themselves in the graver cases seem still to put more confidence in men. Women are being admitted to the law. To their addressing themselves to the feelings of juries there seems to be an objection apart from delicacy, if justice is the object of courts. They have been admitted into male universities, we shall presently see with what effect on the masculine character of the system, while, in spite of the principle on which coeducation is based, female colleges are not yet thrown open to men. They have got the school-teacherships largely into their hands; with doubtful benefit, whatever theorists may say, to the characters and manners of the boys. Government clerkships and offices of all kinds are now filled with women, who are thus made independent of marriage, though this cannot be done without at the same time withdrawing employment from men who might have maintained women as their wives. It is complained that female workers are underpaid, and female claimants of the franchise say that if they had power, they would legislate so as to raise woman's wages. Legislation of this kind would require supplementary enactments forbidding employers and capital to go out of the trade. But are women underpaid? Are they paid less than the men when their work is of equal value? It may be that in some cases custom has been unjust to them, as it often is to male workers also. This time will redress. It is only the lighter trades that women can ply, and a needlewoman can hardly expect to be paid like an engine-driver or a stevedore. In some trades certain continuance is an element of value, and certain continuance is impossible for woman unless she renounces marriage. Fashionable dressmakers, female artists, singers, and actresses are not underpaid. The gains of prima donnas are enormous; their rapacity is notorious, and they stint without compunction the inferior performers of their own sex.

A proof of man's injustice to woman commonly cited was the difference made in the treatment of the two sexes in regard to infidelity. The law can hardly now be said to be unjust; that the social penalty should be the same in both cases is not to be expected, for the simple reason that the offence is not the same. The sin of the woman is a sin not only against her partner, but against the family, into which she brings an adulterine child. A pointsman and the man who tends a furnace may alike fall asleep at their posts without any difference in their moral guilt, but one lets a fire go out, the other wrecks a train. All the legislation and all the language on the subject of seduction assume that the blame rests entirely on the man, though there are cases in which he is more the seduced than the seducer, and in no case where the woman is grown up and is consenting can the guilt be wholly on one side.

Mr. Blair's Report indeed proclaims that "without the exercise of the natural and inalienable right of suffrage neither life, liberty, nor property can be secured." If by liberty is meant the exercise of political power, that part of the allegation is undeniably true. To say that neither life nor property can be secure without the suffrage would be to say that no security for life or property has existed in any country in Europe till within the last century, except in Switzerland and England, nor for the great majority of the people in England. To the ordinary observer it appears not only that the lives, liberties, and properties of American women are secure, but that they are more secure, if anything, than those of the men; and that the attitude of men in the United States toward women is rather that of subjection than that of domination. "Actual and practical slavery," which one of the ladies who gives evidence declares to be the condition of woman without the ballot, has certainly in the case of the American slave disguised itself in very deceptive forms. "No one," says another lady, "has denied to women the right of burial, and in that one sad necessity of human life they stand on an equal footing with men." Such language seems to mock our understandings. Comparisons of the condition of woman denied the suffrage with that of the Negro in the South, have often been made, and in this report we are told that the exclusion of women from a convention "constituted the startling revelation of a real subjection of woman to man world-wide and in many respects as complete and galling, when analysed and duly considered by its victims, as that of the Negro to his master." The Negro, nevertheless, would not have been sorry to change conditions. The papers the other day gave an account of a raid made upon a place where liquor was sold, by a party of women in masks, who beat the proprietor with clubs. Several such acts of violence on the part of women have been recorded; but they are committed apparently not only with impunity but with general approbation. Resistance to them appears to be proscribed. American women, also, seem to use the cowhide whenever they think fit to avenge their personal wrongs. These are not practices in which the Negro was allowed to indulge toward his master before emancipation, or in which he has even been allowed to indulge since. If the men of the United States were called to account for their treatment of the women, and the women at the same time for the performance of their special duty to the race, it seems doubtful, at least supposing that American writers on these subjects tell the truth, whether before an impartial tribunal judgment would go against the men.

Against wife-beating, or cruelty of any sort to wives, which is commonly confined to the dregs of the people, the law seems now severe enough; if it were more than severe enough it would be in danger of becoming a dead letter. Male brutality finds vent in bodily outrage, which can be reached by law. The bad wife can make her husband's home miserable by vexations which no law can reach. Many years ago an English clergyman was convicted of the murder of his wife, but his sentence was commuted when it was learned what his life had been. A man in England narrowly escaped imprisonment as a felon on a false charge of uttering base coin, cast on him by the machinations of a perfidious wife who wanted to live with her paramour. Law could have done nothing in the first case, practically could do nothing in the second. Children are less able to make their wrongs known than are women, yet cases not seldom come to light of cruel ill-treatment of children by women, especially by step-mothers. These cases, like those of wife-beating, are hideous. We punish the criminals when we can. But we do not propose to alter domestic relations. We trust, and in the immense majority of cases with reason, to affection, which is stronger than law. That affection is stronger than law is a fact often forgotten in dealing with these questions. It seems to be thought that the Statute Book is all. Nothing in the Statute Book, it has been truly said, prevents the most courteous of hosts from turning his guests out of his house at midnight in a storm.

That the man should exercise authority over his household will become unnatural and unjust when he ceases to be held responsible for the household. At present the State casts upon him the undivided responsibility. What the leaders of the woman's rights movement practically seek is, for the woman power without responsibility, for the man, responsibility without power. But this is an arrangement in which man, though he may be talked into it for the moment, is not likely in the end to acquiesce.

Is the marriage tie still too tight?[1] Is divorce not easy enough? One would think that divorce was easy enough in America, when in some States you have a divorce for every ten marriages, when a judge at Chicago can dissolve eight marriages in sixty-two minutes, when wedlock is beginning to be talked of as an experiment which may be terminated if it is not found pleasant to both sides.[2] Mormonism, if its polygamy is denounced, has matter for a retort. American legislatures themselves are beginning to recoil. In Great Britain divorce is not so easy, yet it is surely not too difficult if the marriage tie is to be preserved. The children, who cannot fail to suffer by the wreck of the family, are entitled to consideration as well as the parents. Society at large is entitled to consideration. Though marriages are made not in heaven but on earth, it may safely be said that the great majority of them are happy; at least that the partners are happier united than they would have been alone. But their success depends, in ordinary cases, on the permanence of the bond, which enforces restraint of temper and mutual accommodation. If divorce were always open, compatibility would be seldom found; the bond would be broken by the unscrupulous as often as matrimony failed to realise the dreams of courtship. It is easy to paint horrible pictures of unwilling union after mutual disappointment. Such things do happen, and very tragical and deplorable they are. The remedy is caution before marriage, not the virtual overthrow of an institution

---

[1] See Mona Caird's articles in the *Fortnightly* (Vol. liii) and *Westminster Reviews* (Vol. cxxx). See also Mill's *The Subjection of Woman*, Chap. ii.

[2] It seems that the largest number of divorces are found in the communities where the advocates of female suffrage are most numerous, and where the individuality of woman in relation to her husband, which such a doctrine inculcates, is greatest. The movement, therefore, or at least the tendencies, appear to be connected. See *Minority Report*, p. 10.

on which, so far as we can see, the order, purity, and happiness of society depend.[1]

Marriage may be described from one point of view as a restraint imposed upon the passions of the man for the benefit of the woman. Cold-blooded philosophers choose to speak of the sexual passion in man as brutal. Mighty it is; it is no more brutal than any other passion or appetite gratification of which is necessary to the preservation of life and the race. It is the physical basis of sentiments, the most beautiful and refined. At all events it is in most natures imperious. Were it not, man could hardly be induced to take on him the burden of wife and children. Being imperious, it will be gratified, if not by marriage, in other ways, and woman would not be the gainer by the change.

The matrimonial history of Shelley is instructive and full of warning because he was so highly refined, and raised so much above the animal passions of ordinary men. Shelley, as his admiring biographer frankly tells us, finding after some two years or more of marriage, that his Harriet "did not suit him," though she "had given no cause whatsoever for repudiation by breach or tangible neglect of wifely duty," cast her off in an "abrupt *de facto*" manner and took Mary to his arms. Mary, of course, was of the same opinion. "Shelley," says the biographer, "was an avowed opponent on principle to the formal and coercive tie of marriage; therefore in ceasing his marital connection with Harriet, and assuming a similar relation to Mary, he did nothing which he regarded as wrong, though as far as anything yet published goes, it must distinctly be said that he consulted his own option rather than Harriet's." The biographer asserts that Harriet, after the separation, connected herself with some other protector, a charge which, it is to be

[1] Reference cannot be made to this momentous subject without acknowledging the great service rendered to society by the Rev. Samuel W. Dike, LL.D., Corresponding Secretary of the United States National Divorce Reform League, whose laborious investigations have brought the facts before us.

presumed, he would not make without knowing it to be true, and the truth of which would not in any way mend the case. Legislation on these lines would suit some men better than any woman.[1] It did not suit poor Harriet.

It appears that in the series of legislative reforms which in the course of a century has been bringing Europe finally out of the feudal system, with its quasi-military relations, and with the vestiges of tribalism which lingered in it, into the system of modern society, the interests of both sexes have been embraced, and that of the female sex has had its full share. This, as the legislatures were male, seems to prove not only that men in legislating are unlikely to forget their wives, mothers, sisters, and daughters, but that women without votes can exercise great influence on legislation. The press is open to them, it is powerful, and not a few of them make use of it. The platform is open to as many of them as do not shrink from its publicity. They have access under the most favourable conditions to those by whom the law is made. That they have confidence in the justice and affection of men their present appeal, as has been said before, shows; for it is from man's free will that they must expect the cession of the suffrage: some of them, it is true, threaten society with a terrible vengeance if their petition is not heard, but they are powerless to give effect to their threats. They will renounce their present influence in grasping the vote. Let them appear as a separate interest in the political arena, and they will, like every other separate interest, awaken an antagonism which does not now exist.

The plain question then presents itself in the joint interest of the two sexes, whether the exercise of political power by women would be generally conducive to good government. If it would not, the concession, it must be repeated, would be a wrong done to the whole community. We know very well

---

[1] See Mr. William Michael Rossetti's *Memoir* prefixed to his edition of Shelley's Poetical Works, London: Moxon, 1870. I am aware that different versions have been given, but there can be no dispute about the main facts.

that in some gifts and qualities woman is superior to man. Suppose she is superior to him on the whole. Suppose, to adopt the somewhat amatory language of Mr. Blair's Committee, she is the angelic portion of humanity. It does not follow that she is political any more than man is maternal or adapted for housekeeping. Nor is the absence of political qualities a disgrace to her any more than the absence of maternal or housekeeping qualities is to him. Difference of spheres, the spheres being equal in importance, implies no disparagement. As a rule, it is in the affections and graces that woman is strong; and these, the affections at least, though they may be worth more than the practical qualities needed in politics, are not the practical qualities. But the training also is wanting. The political wisdom of men in general, to whatever it may amount, is formed by daily contact and collision with the world in which they have to gain their bread and which impresses upon them in its rough school caution, prudence, the necessity of compromise, the limitations of their will. Some of them are flighty enough after all, and the world just now is in no small peril from their flightiness. But their general tendency as a sex is to be commonplace and practical. Their life usually is more or less public, while that of woman is in the home. Moreover, they feel as a sex the full measure of responsibility in public action. This is not felt so strongly by their partners. If rash measures get the community into trouble, it is by the men that it must be got out again. To them it will fall to pull the waggon through the slough. The exception taken to female legislators, or Ministers of State, or judges, on account of the interruptions of the nursery might be met by appointing only spinsters or widows. But it would be impossible, without total change of sentiment, to hold the female legislator, minister, or judge to the full measure of male responsibility. If they were called to account they would plead their sex. We are told that ladies in New York objected to the appointment of education commissioners of their own sex on the ground that they were exempted from criticism by the gallantry of the men.

It is supposed that women would allay the angry strife of faction and refine its coarseness by imparting their gentleness, tenderness, and delicacy to public life. But is it not because they have been kept out of politics and generally out of the contentious arena that they have remained gentle, tender, and delicate? Weakness thrown into an exciting struggle usually shows itself, not by superior gentleness, but by loss of self-control. Of this, the crusade against the Contagious Diseases Act in England has given some proof. By the use which both the political parties in England have of late been making of women for electioneering purposes, they do not seem to have mitigated the fury of the fray.

"Corruption of male suffrage," says Mr. Blair's Report, "is already a well-nigh fatal disease." Would it be cured by throwing in the other sex? That women would be likely by taking part in public life to make it pure, that they are less prone than men to favouritism, jobbery, and corruption, is contrary to experience, which shows that they are prone to these minor vices while they are comparatively seldom guilty of the greater crimes.

In a paper prepared at the request of an association of women, which is cited in the Minority Report of the Senate Committee, Mr. Francis Parkman says of the female politician as she is and is likely to be in the United States:

"It is not woman's virtues that would be prominent or influential in the political arena, they would shun it by an invincible repulsion; and the opposite qualities would be drawn into it. The Washington lobby has given us some means of judging what we may expect from the woman 'inside politics.' If politics are to be purified by artfulness, effrontery, insensibility, a pushing self-assertion, and a glib tongue, then we may look for regeneration; for the typical female politician will be richly endowed with all these gifts.

"Thus accoutred for the conflict, she may fairly hope to have the better of her masculine antagonist. A woman has the inalienable right of attacking without being attacked in return. She may strike, but must not be struck either literally or figuratively. Most women refrain from abusing their privilege of non-combatants; but there are those in whom the sense of impunity breeds the cowardly courage of the virago.

"In reckoning the resources of the female politicians, there is one which can by no means be left out. None know better than woman the potency of feminine charms aided by feminine arts. The woman 'inside politics' will not fail to make use of an influence so subtle and so strong and of which the management is peculiarly suited to her talents. If — and the contingency is in the highest degree probable — she is not gifted with charms of her own, she will have no difficulty in finding and using others of her sex who are. If report is to be trusted, Delilah has already spread her snares for the Congressional Samson; and the power before which the wise fail and the mighty fall has been invoked against the sages and heroes of the Capitol. When 'woman' is fairly 'inside politics' the sensation press will reap a harvest of scandals more lucrative to itself than profitable to public morals. And as the zeal of one class of female reformers has been and no doubt will be largely directed to their grievances in matters of sex, we shall have shrill-tongued discussions of subjects which had far better be let alone.

"It may be said that the advocates of female suffrage do not look to political women for the purifying of politics, but to the votes of the sex at large. The two, however, cannot be separated. It should be remembered that the question is not of a limited and select female suffrage, but of a universal one. To limit would be impossible. It would seek the broadest areas and the lowest depths, and spread itself through the marshes and malarious pools of society."[1]

That some women are political and many men not, is as true as it is that some men are unmilitary and a few women are Amazons. But this does not alter the general fact; and it is upon general facts that political institutions must be founded.

Mill, appealing to history, bids us mark that so excellent a judge of practical ability as Charles V. set women to govern the Netherlands. Charles V. appointed women because he had no males in his family to appoint. It was in fact this failure of males in dynasties, combined with the superstition of hereditary right, that led to the introduction of what John Knox called "the monstrous regiment of women." Charles' experiment was not happy, since the result was the revolt of the Netherlands. Blanche of Castile, is also cited by Mill. She appears to have been a woman of masculine qualities, not to say a virago, to have held her excellent but rather weak-minded son in complete subjection, and to have

----

[1] *Minority Report*, p. 24.

governed with vigour and judgment as his vicegerent; but there are evidently two sides to her character; which of them prevailed on the whole, she is too remote from us to decide.

If we are to go to history, to history let us go; only remembering that the examples are those of queens regnant, or women placed by their circumstances in positions of power, and that they afford no certain indication of what women would be when they had climbed to power as demagogues after passing through the party mill.

In England, the women who have wielded power legally or practically have been Matilda, the claimant of the crown against Stephen, about whom we know little, but who seems to have injured her party by her arrogance; Eleanor, the jealous and intriguing Queen of Henry II., who secured the succession to her favourite John, and whose record is not fair; Isabella, the paramour of Mortimer, and with him guilty of the murder of Edward II.; Margaret, the Queen of Henry VI., whose violence and favouritism helped to bring on the War of the Roses; Mary, of whom it need only be said that she was probably not a bad woman, but misled by influences to which her sex is specially exposed; Elizabeth; Henrietta Maria, who by her feminine violence had, like Margaret of Anjou, no small share in plunging the country into civil war; and Queen Anne, who, under personal influences and at the instigation of a favourite waiting-woman, upset a great ministry and deprived the country of the fruits of a long war, while, had she lived longer, her fondness for her family would have probably led to an attempt to restore the Stuarts. The star is Elizabeth. But Elizabeth's reputation for anything but the arts of popularity in which she was supreme, has suffered terribly by the researches of Motley and other recent writers. Her deceitfulness, perfidy, and ingratitude to those who had served her and the country best, were pretty well known, as were her vanity and her coquetry. But her reputation for statesmanship is now greatly reduced, and it is clear that the country was saved not by her, but by itself; from the Armada it was saved in her despite. Mr. Froude, who set out as her fervent admirer, has in the end to say that her conduct in the transaction which preceded the sailing of the Armada "would alone suffice to disqualify Elizabeth from being cited as an example of the capacity of female sovereigns." And when the country was saved, whom did the queen select for the honour? Whom did she prefer on this and all other occasions above the great servants of the State? The good-looking but worthless Leicester, "infamed," as Burleigh said he was, "by the death of his wife." Her ungrateful persecution of the Puritans in the latter part of her reign sowed the wind from which her unhappy successors reaped the whirlwind. She had the good fortune to be the crowning figure of an heroic age, and her sex threw about her a romantic halo, the brightness of which was enhanced by the·calamities, partly her bequest, which ensued.

In France the more recent list is Catherine de Medici, whose name suffices; Anne of Austria, who was in the able hands of Mazarin; Madame de Maintenon, to whose female piety France owed the revocation of the Edict of Nantes, while to her tenderness for the Catholic Stuarts it owed a great war; Madame de Pompadour, whose name again suffices; Marie Antoinette, who, besides helping to dismiss Turgot and to complete the ruin of French finances by plunging France into the war of the American Revolution, did so much to bring on the crash of the French Revolution that her misdeeds were scarcely washed out by her tears. The story is closed by the influence, partly religious, partly dynastic and domestic, which, Frenchmen say, made the Franco-German war and finished the work by interfering with its conduct in the interest of the dynasty and deterring the Emperor and his army from falling back on Paris.

Isabella of Castile graced her crown and formed a noble queen of chivalry in the war against the Moors. As a ruler, she had Ferdinand at her side. That it was to her feminine instinct that the genius of Columbus was revealed, recent researches have made less certain than it is that her piety established the Inquisition in Castile, and that great numbers of persons were burned by it in her reign.

Monuments of a female influence over government more certainly beneficent were the crosses which Edward I. erected in memory of the Queen who seems to have softened his sternness with her love, while she displayed the beauty of affection on the throne. England also owes a debt of gratitude to Caroline of Brunswick, by whose unambitious support Walpole, the best statesman of an unheroic time, was kept in power. Nothing need be said about queens nominally regnant who have reigned but not governed, and whose influence has been happily exerted in the social sphere which all admit to be the realm of woman.

Mill has also stated that Begums have shone as rulers in India. He was in the India House and his authority is good, though he does not give the names. It is hardly credible that a woman brought up in a Zenana should be a great ruler, but she might be better than a hog or a tiger. Not all Begums have escaped the common influences of the Durbar. We have one, styled a heroine, making away successively with her father-in-law, her husband, and her son, because they stood in her way, enrolling cut-throats, and practising corruption as freely as any male.[1] The difference can hardly be such as to give us much assurance of safety in revolutionising the relations between the sexes.

The writer of this paper signed, in company with John Bright, John Stuart Mill's first petition in favour of suffrage for unmarried women. Mr. Bright, as well as the writer, was a good deal influenced by his respect and regard for Mill. Both of them afterwards changed their minds, and Bright spoke strongly against the measure. The writer found that the women of his acquaintance for whom he had most respect, and who seemed to him the best representatives of their sex, were opposed to the change, fearing that the position and privileges of women in general would be sacrificed to the ambition of a few.

Since that time Mill's Autobiography has appeared, and

---

[1] See C. Forjelt's *Our Real Danger in India*, p. 39.

has revealed the history of his extraordinary and almost portentous education, the singular circumstances of his marriage, his hallucination (for it surely can be called nothing else) as to the surpassing genius of his wife, and peculiarities of character and temperament such as could not fail to prevent him from fully appreciating the power of influences which, whatever our philosophy may say, reign and will continue to reign supreme over questions of this kind. To him marriage was a union of two philosophers in the pursuit of truth, and wedded life was intellectual intercourse. In his work on "The Subjection of Women" not only does he almost leave maternity out of sight, but sex and its influences seem hardly to be present to his mind. Of the distinctive excellence and beauty of the female character, or of the conditions essential to its preservation, it does not appear that he had formed any idea, though he dilates on the special qualities of the female understanding.

Mill has allowed us to see that his opinions as to the political position of women were formed early in his life, probably before he had studied history rationally, perhaps before the rational study of history had even come into existence. The consequence, with all deference to his great name be it said, is that his historical presentment of the case is fundamentally unsound. He and his disciples represent the lot of the woman as having always been determined by the will of the man, who, according to them, has willed that she should be the slave, and that he should be her master and tyrant. "Society, both in this [the case of marriage] and other cases, has preferred to attain its object by foul rather than by fair means; but this is the only case in which it has substantially persisted in them even to the present day." This is Mill's fundamental assumption; and from it, as every rational student of history is now aware, conclusions utterly erroneous as well as injurious to humanity must flow. The lot of the woman has not been determined by the will of the man, at least in any considerable degree. The lot both of the man and of the woman has been determined from age to age by circumstances over which the will of neither of them had much control, and which neither could be blamed for accepting or failing to reverse. Mill and his disciples assume that the man has always willed that he should himself enjoy political rights, and that the woman should be his slave; forgetting that it is only in a few countries that man does enjoy political rights, and that, even in those few countries, freedom is the birth almost of yesterday. It may probably be said that the number of men who have really and freely exercised the suffrage up to the present time is not very much greater than the number of those who have in different ages and in various ways laid down their lives or made personal sacrifices of other kinds in bringing elective government into existence.

In the early stages of civilisation the family was socially and legally, as well as politically, a unit. Its head represented the whole household before the tribe, the State, and all persons and bodies without; while within he exercised absolute power over all the members, male as well as female, over his sons as well as over his wife and daughters. On the death of the head of a family his eldest son stepped into his place, and became the representative and protector of the whole household, including the widow of the deceased chief. This system, long retained in conservative Rome, was there the source of the national respect for authority, and, by an expansion of feeling from the family to the community, of the patriotism which produced and sustained Roman greatness. But its traces lingered far down in history. It was not male tyranny that authorised a Tudor queen to send members of the royal household to the Tower by her personal authority as the mistress of the family, without regard to the common law against arbitrary imprisonment. Such a constitution was essential to the existence of the family in primitive times; without it the germs of nations and of humanity would have perished. To suppose that it was devised by the male sex for the gratification of their own tyrannical propensities, would be most absurd. It was at least as much a necessity to the primitive woman as it was to the primitive man. It is still a necessity to woman in the countries where the primitive type of society remains. What would be the fate of a female Bedouin if she were suddenly invested with Woman's Rights, and emancipated from the protection of her husband?

That the present relation of women to their husbands literally has its origin in slavery, and is a hideous relic of that system, is a theory which Mill sets forth in language such as, if it could sink into the hearts of those to whom it is addressed, might turn affection to bitterness, and divide every household against itself. Yet this theory is without historical foundation. It seems indeed like a figure of invective heedlessly converted into history. Even in the most primitive times, and those in which the subjection of the woman was most complete, the wife was clearly distinguished from the slave. The lot of Sarah is different from that of Hagar; the authority of Hector over Andromache is absolute, yet no one can confound her position with that of her handmaidens. The Roman matron who sent her slave to be crucified, the Southern matron who was the fierce supporter of slavery, were not themselves slaves. Whatever may now be obsolete in the relations of husband and wife is not a relic of slavery, but of primitive marriage, and may be regarded as at worst an arrangement once indispensable which has survived its hour. Where real slavery has existed, it has extended to both sexes, and it has ceased for both at the same time. Even the Oriental seclusion of women, perhaps the worst condition in which the sex has ever been, has its root not in the slave-owning propensity so much as in jealousy, a passion which, though extravagant and detestable in its excessive manifestation, is not without an element of affection. The most beautiful building in the East is that which Shah Jehan raised as the monument of a beloved wife. Is it possible that an American lady living in Paris on the fruits of her husband's toil at New York, or looking on while a porter at Saratoga toils beneath her colossal trunk, should deem herself or be deemed a slave?

If the calm and philosophic nature of Mill is ever betrayed into violence, it is in his denunciations of the present institution of marriage. He depicts it as a despotism full of mutual degradation, and fruitful of no virtues or affections except the debased virtues and the miserable affections of the master and the slave. The grossest and most degrading terms of Oriental slavery are used to designate the relations of husband and wife throughout the book. A husband who desires his wife's love is only seeking "to have in the woman most nearly connected with him, not a forced slave, but a willing one; not a slave merely, but a favourite." Husbands have, therefore, "put everything in practice to enslave the minds of their wives." If a wife is intensely attached to her husband, "exactly as much may be said of domestic slavery." "It is a part of the irony of life that the strongest feelings of devoted gratitude of which human nature seems to be susceptible are called forth in human beings towards those who, having the power entirely to crush their earthly existence, voluntarily refrain from using their power." Even children are only links in the chain of bondage. By the affections of women "are meant the only ones they are allowed to have, those to the men to whom they are connected, or to the children who constitute an additional and indefeasible tie between them and a man." The Jesuit is an object of sympathy because he is the enemy of the domestic tyrant, and it is assumed that the husband can have no motive but the love of undivided tyranny for objecting to being superseded by an intriguing interloper in his wife's affections. As though a wife would regard with complacency, say a female spiritualist, installed beside her hearth! Mill's book, written with his usual clearness and impressiveness, having been the manifesto, has remained the manual of the movement. It is therefore still necessary to deal with it, nor can there be anything invidious, as some of his admirers seem to have fancied, in reviewing it by the light of the Autobiography. For what purpose is the life of a philosopher published if it is not to enable us better to understand his works? The book might poison marriage if it were not read with a knowledge of the influence under which it was written. Mill himself seems at last to start from the picture which he has drawn and to be inclined to qualify it. But he does this faintly and too late.

If, in this most imperfect world, woman, through the changeful ages, has, like her partner, had much to undergo, and too often at her partner's hands, she has also had advantages which she would have been sorry to forfeit, and which she would be sorry to forfeit now. She has sat safe in her home while her partner was toiling, hunting, battling with the sea, fighting for her abroad. By her partner's labour and with peril of his life the earth has been subdued for her and made fit for her habitation. When she complains that she has been treated as a toy, does she mean that she has been wronged because man has taken most of the rough and hard work to himself? War has comparatively spared her; public justice has been lenient to her; in a shipwreck she has been put first into the boat, while the slave to whom she now likens herself has been thrown overboard to save the provisions. In civilised countries she is on all occasions served and considered first; special provisions are made for her comfort and convenience. Is this the lot of a slave, or of one even more miserable than a slave?

Sometimes woman has had man's hard work to do. But this has been mostly under circumstances of special need or of general barbarism, and the revulsion which any such employment of her causes, denotes her general immunity. The Red Indian used his mate as a beast of burden. But the Red Indian was a barbarian. Even he, however, might have pleaded special need. The hunter, by the product of whose chase the wigwam was fed, would have been spoiled, his powers of endurance would have been reduced, and the keenness of his sense would have been impaired by heavy domestic labour.

Marriage has risen in character with the general progress of civilisation from the primeval contract of force or purchase to a free contract, of a contract generally of love. Primeval practice was not regulated by the will of those generations, but by primeval circumstance, and the improvement of the marriage tie has come, as all other great improvements of human relations have come, in the course of secular evolution. It was something when the passions of the male were subjected to a regular and lasting bond of any kind. If women are now to be made independent of marriage, which appears to be the aim of some of their champions, they would be made independent of that in which the happiness of a creature formed for affection usually consists, although to determine them to embrace it, some natural pressure may be required. Perhaps many of them will owe their champions but scanty thanks in their old age.

The anomalies in the property law affecting married women, to which remedial legislation has recently been directed, are, like whatever is obsolete in the relations between the sexes generally, not deliberate iniquities, but survivals. They are relics of feudalism or of still more primitive institutions incorporated by feudalism; and while the system to which they belonged existed they were indispensable parts of it, and must have been so regarded by both sexes alike. Any one who is tolerably well informed ought to be ashamed to represent them as the contrivances of male injustice. It is not on one sex only that the relics of feudalism have borne hard.

The exclusion of women from professions is cited as another proof of constant and immemorial injustice. But what woman asked or wished to be admitted to a profession a hundred or even fifty years ago? What woman till quite recently would have been ready to renounce marriage and maternity in order that she might devote herself to law, medicine, or commercial pursuits? The demand is probably in some measure connected with an abnormal and possibly transient state of things. The expensiveness of living in a country where the fashion is set by millionnaires, combined with the overcrowded condition of the very callings to which women are demanding admission, has put extraordinary difficulties in the way of marriage. Many women are thus left without an object in life, and they naturally try to open for themselves some new career. The utmost sympathy is due to them, and every facility ought in justice to be afforded them; though unhappily the addition of fresh competitors for subsistence to a crowd in which some are already starving will be as far as possible from removing the real root of the evil, to say nothing of the risk which a woman must run in committing herself irrevocably to a precarious calling, and closing against herself the gate of domestic life. But the demand, as has already been said, is of yesterday, and probably in its serious form is as yet confined to the countries in which impediments to early marriage exist. It is not always easy to distinguish the serious demand from a passion for emulating the male sex which has undoubtedly taken possession of some women, as it took possession of the women under the Roman Empire, who began to play the gladiator when other excitements were exhausted, and which is hardly more respectable in women than the affectation of feminine tastes and habits would be in a man. With regard to the profession of law, indeed, so far as it is concerned with the administration of justice, there is, as was said before, and while human emotions retain their force always will be, a reason, independent of the question of demand, for excluding women, at least for excluding one of the two sexes. The influence of a pretty advocate appealing to a jury, perhaps in behalf of a client of her own sex, would not have seemed to Mill at all dangerous to the integrity of public justice; but most people, and especially those who have seen anything of sentimental causes in the United States, or even in more phlegmatic England, will probably be of a different opinion.

What has been said as to the professions is equally true of the universities, which were schools of the professions. A few years ago, what English girl would have consented to leave her home and mingle with male students? What English girl would have thought it possible that she could go through the whole of the medical course with male companions of her studies? Even now what is the amount of settled belief in "co-education"? What would be said to a young man who applied for admission in the name of that principle at the door of any female college? Without arraigning the past, those whose duty it is may consider with the deliberation which they deserve the two distinct questions, whether it is desirable that the education of both sexes shall be the same, and whether it is desirable that the young men and the young women of the wealthier classes shall be educated together in the same universities. Beneath the first probably lies the still deeper question whether it is good for humanity that woman, who has hitherto been the helpmate and the complement, should become, as the leaders of the Woman's Right movement evidently desire, the rival and competitor of man. Both she cannot be; and it is by no means clear that in deciding which she shall be the aspirations of the leaders of this movement coincide with the interests of the sex.

If the education of women has hitherto been defective, so has that of men. We are now going to do our best to improve both. Surely no accomplishment in the acquisition of which woman has been condemned to spend her time could well be less useful than that of writing Greek or Latin has been to the generality of male students. That the education of woman has hitherto been lighter than that of men is no proof that for the purposes of woman's destination it has been worse. Among other things, it is to be considered whether the children would be healthy if the brain of the mother, as well as that of the father, were severely tasked. That the comparative absence of works of creative genius among women is due entirely to the social tyranny which has excluded, or is supposed to have excluded, them from literary or scientific careers, cannot be said to be self-evident. The case of music, often cited, seems to suggest that there is another cause, and that the career of intellectual ambition is in most cases not likely to be happier than that of domestic affection, though this is no reason why the experiment should not be fairly tried. Perhaps the intellectual disabilities under which women have laboured, even in the past, have been somewhat overstated. If Shelley was a child to Mrs. Mill, as Mr. Mill says, no "social disabilities" hindered Mrs. Mill from publishing poems which would have eclipsed Shelley. The writer once heard an American lecturer of eminence confidently ascribe the licentiousness of English fiction in the early part of the last century to the exclusion of women from literary life. The lecturer forgot that the most popular novelist of that period, and certainly not the least licentious, was Mrs. Aphra Behn. This lady's name suggests the remark that as the relations of the sexes have been the most intimate conceivable, the action of character has been reciprocal, and the level of moral ideas and sentiments for both pretty much the same.

Mill, seeing that the man is the stronger, seems to assume that the relations between man and woman must always have been regulated by the law of the strongest. But strength is not tyranny. The protector must always be stronger than the person under his protection. A mother is overwhelmingly superior in strength to her infant child, and the child is completely at her mercy. The very highest conception that humanity has ever formed, whether it be founded in reality or not, is that of power losing itself in affection. St. Paul (who on any hypothesis as to his inspiration, is an authoritative expositor of the morality which became that of Christendom) affirms with perfect clearness the essential equality of the sexes and their necessary relations to each other as the two halves of humanity. Yet he no less distinctly ratifies the unity of the family, the authority of its head, and the female need of that headship; a need which, supposing it to be natural, has nothing in it more degrading than the need of protection.[1]

Subjection is a word of sinister import, and Mill, in adopting it, prejudices the question. Subordination, or obedience, where it is necessary, implies no disparagement. Nothing grates on ordinary feelings when Beatrice, in "Much Ado about Nothing," says that she "will tame her wild heart to the hand" of the man whom she is to wed. Not the soldier

____
[1] I *Cor.* xi. 7–12; *Eph.* 22–33; *Col.* iii. 18.

ouly, but most of us have some one whom we are bound to obey, and whom, it being necessary, we obey without humiliation. A head of the family there must be if there is not to be domestic anarchy. Children must know to whom their obedience is due. Mill proposes that the authority shall be divided between the husband and wife in the marriage contract, and that the subjects in which each is to be supreme shall be set out in a schedule; but he has not given us a draft of such a contract. In the whole of this movement of sexual revolution the family, though it may not, with any one but a Nihilist, be the object of intentional or conscious attack, is practically threatened with dissolution. One utopian reformer, as we have seen, proposes not only that the wife shall be made independent of the husband, but that the children shall be made independent of the parents.

"Enfranchise women," says Mr. Blair's Report, "or this Republic will steadily advance to the same destruction, the same ignoble and tragic catastrophe, which has engulfed the male republics of history." This seems to imply a new reading of history, according to which republics have owed their fall to their masculine character. The Greek republics were overwhelmed by the Macedonian monarchy, their surrender to which was assuredly not due to excess of masculine force. The Roman republic was converted by the vast extension of Roman conquest into a military empire. The city republicanism of the Middle Ages was crushed by the great monarchies. The short-lived Commonwealth of England owed its overthrow to causes which certainly had nothing to do with sex. The Swiss republic, the American republics, the French republic still live, so do several constitutional monarchies, including Great Britain and her colonies, which are republics in all but name. It is true that these commonwealths, though, we may hope, less directly threatened with the wrath of heaven than the report assumes them to be, are yet not free from peril; but their peril apparently lies in the passions, the giddiness, the anarchical tendencies of the multitude, and would hardly be averted by opening another floodgate and letting in all at once the full tide of feminine emotion.

Woman, if she becomes a man, will be a weaker man. Yet she must be prepared to resign her privileges as a woman. She cannot expect to have both privilege and equality. To don the other sex she must doff her own, a process in which she will run some risk of ceasing to be, or at least to be deemed, the "angelic portion of humanity." For the time, perhaps, the ancient sentiment might linger; but the total change of relations would in the end bring a change of feeling. Chivalry depends on the acknowledged need of protection, and what is accorded to a gentle helpmate would not be accorded to a rival. Man would not be bound nor inclined to treat with tenderness and forbearing the being who was jostling with him in all the walks of life, wrangling with him in the law courts, wrestling with him on the stump, manœuvering against him in elections, haggling with him on 'Change or in Wall Street, encountering him on the race course and in the betting ring. Aphrodite, in her heart, perhaps flatters herself that her Cestus will preserve her privilege, while she gains the advantage of equality. So much poetry has been addressed to her that she may well be excused for not forming a prosaic estimate of the probable results. But the outspoken Schopenhauer has told her that beauty is rarer in her sex than in the other. It takes more to make a beautiful woman than a handsome man. Of this we may be sure, that the attractions of women generally depend upon their being women. Mrs. Mill, be it observed, remained a woman. If she had put on her wig and gown to go into court and cross-examine witnesses, or had stood against her husband for Westminster, we should have seen the great experiment really tried. That she has had social advantages while she has lain under political disabilities, woman, especially in America, can hardly deny; her sex has been an object of respect, sometimes of a worship almost fatuous, irrespective of her personal qualities. This is partly traceable to historical accident. Jonathan Oldbuck is a cynic, but he is not far wrong in saying that it was by the fantastic imagination of chivalry that Dulcineas were exalted into despotic goddesses. He might have added that Mariolatry had played its part.

Wyoming and New Zealand have made the experiment of Woman's Suffrage. Let them fairly try it, and if the result is good, let the rest of the world follow. In every field of action, except that of politics, use is made of experiment. A new engine is tested before it is put on all the railways or into all the steamships. A new remedy, however promising, is tried in one or two cases before it is applied universally. If an airship were invented, aeronauts would have to prove its safety before all the world ascended. This precaution would be taken, and not to take it would be deemed madness, however conclusive in the judgment of science the theoretical arguments in favour of the invention might be. But in politics sweeping changes are irrevocably made upon the strength of what even an advocate of the change, if he had any fairness of mind, would allow to be a mere balance of argument in its favour. Had extensions of the suffrage, or changes in the form of local government been tried in one or two districts or cities first, a pause of salutary reflection might have ensued. But political changes, for the most part, are the result of conflict, not of reasoning ; of the desire of a class for power, not of broad conviction as to the public good. Woman's Suffrage is a change fraught with the most momentous results, not only to the commonwealth, but to the household. Let Wyoming and New Zealand try it, say for ten years. The success of the Wyoming experiment is publicly proclaimed, and the universe is exhorted to do likewise, by Wyoming, whose voice is now that of the female voters. Private accounts are not so favourable, nor have the neighbouring States, which must have the clearest view of the results, been induced to follow the example. To Wyoming, for the present, Woman's Suffrage in the United States remains confined. The New Zealand experiment will be more satisfactory, though New Zealand, having no warlike neighbours, does not run the same risk in emasculating her government which is run by a European State. If at the end of ten years it appears from the two experiments that legislation and government have become wiser, more far-sighted, and more just, without any detriment to the peace and order of the home, let the world follow the example, and be grateful to those by whom the first experiment was made.

At the present juncture in Europe such an innovation would be especially perilous. The tendency to the personal ascendancy of great demagogues which has shown itself as a result of the enfranchisement of masses ignorant of political principles and questions could not fail to be aggravated by the enfranchisement of all the women, the inclination of the sex being to personal rather than constitutional government. In France, with Woman Suffrage, the Republic could hardly live.

Mr. Blair's Report ends by saying that men can have no motive for refusing the suffrage to women but the selfish one of unwillingness to part with half of the sovereign power. Selfishness in this matter would undoubtedly be not only wickedness but folly. What is good for woman is good in the same measure for man, and ought not for a moment to be withheld. One lady in her evidence warns Congress, if it will not give way, that the wild enthusiasm of woman can be used for evil as well as good, and threatens in America a repetition of the scenes of the French Commune. More terrible even than this menace is the fear of doing an injury to man's partner, and thereby a deeper injury to man himself. But the change ought to be proved good. Before man hands over the government to woman, he ought to be satisfied that he cannot do what is right himself. In an age of "flabby" sentiment and servile worship of change, we have had enough of weak and precipitate abdications. To one of them we owe the catastrophe of the French Revolution and the deluge of calamity which has followed. To man, as he alone could enforce the law, the sovereign power came naturally and righteously. Let him see whether he cannot make a just use of it, in the interest of his wife and children as well as in his own, before he sends in his resignation.

THE JEWISH QUESTION.

THE JEWISH QUESTION.

JEWISH ascendancy and the anti-Semitic movement provoked by it form an important feature of the European situation, and are beginning to excite attention in America. Mr. Arnold White, Baron Hirsch's commissioner, says, in a plea for the Russian Jews,[1] that "almost without exception the press throughout Europe is in Jewish hands, and is largely produced by Jewish brains;" that "international finance is captive to Jewish energy and skill"; that in England the fall of the Barings has left the house of Rothschild alone in its supremacy; and that in every line the Jews are fast becoming our masters. Wind and tide, in a money-loving age, are in favour of the financial race. At the same time the anti-Semitic movement gains ground. From Russia, Germany, Austria, and the Danubian Principalities it spreads to the Ionian Islands; it has broken out in France; symptoms of it have appeared even in the United States. Yet there is a persistent misapprehension of the real nature of the agitation. It is assumed that the quarrel is religious. The anti-Semites are supposed to be a party of fanatics renewing the persecutions to which the Jews were exposed on account of their faith in the dark ages, and every one who, handling the question critically, fails to show undivided sympathy with the Israelites is set down as a religious persecutor. The Jews naturally foster this impression, and, as Mr. Arnold White tells us, the press of Europe is in their hands.

In 1880, anti-Semitic disturbances broke out in Russia. A narrative of them entitled "The Persecution of the Jews in

---

[1] "The Truth about the Russian Jew," in the *Contemporary Review*, May, 1892.

Russia," [1] was put forth by the Jewish community in England as an appeal to the British heart.   In that narrative the Russian Christians were charged with having committed the most fiendish atrocities on the most enormous scale.   A tract of country equal in area to the British Islands and France combined had, it was averred, been the scene of horrors theretofore perpetrated only in times of war.   Men had been ruthlessly murdered, tender infants had been dashed to death or roasted alive in their own homes, married women had been made the prey of a brutal lust which had in many cases caused their death, and young girls had been violated in sight of their relatives by soldiers who should have been guardians of their honour.   Whole streets inhabited by Jews had been razed, and the Jewish quarters of towns had been systematically fired; in one place, Elizabethgrad, thirty Jewesses at once had been outraged, two young girls in dread of violation had thrown themselves from the windows, and an old man, who was attempting to save his daughter from a fate worse than death, had been flung from the roof, while twenty soldiers proceeded to work their will on the maiden.   This was a specimen of atrocities which had been committed over the whole area.   The most atrocious charge of all was that against the Christian women of Russia, who were accused of assisting their friends to violate the Jewesses by holding the victims down, their motive being, as the manifesto suggests, jealousy of the superiority of the Jewesses in dress.   The government was charged with criminal sympathy, the local authorities generally with criminal inaction, and some of the troops with active participation.

The British heart responded to the appeal.   Great public meetings were held, at one of which the Archbishop of Canterbury, with a Roman Cardinal, as the representative of religious liberty in general, and especially of opposition to Jew-burning, at his side, denounced the persecuting bigotry of the Russian Christians.   Indignant addresses were largely

---

[1] *Persecution of the Jews in Russia*, 1881.   Reprinted from *The Times.*

signed. Russia was accused of re-enacting the worst crimes of the Middle Ages. It was taken for granted on all sides that religious fanaticism was the cause of the riots.

Russia, as usual, was silent. But the British government directed its consuls at the different points to report upon the facts. The reports composed two Blue Books,[1] in which, as very few probably took the pains to look into them, the unpopular truth lies buried. Those who did read them learned, in the first place, that though the riots were deplorable and criminal, the Jewish account was in most cases exaggerated, and in some to an extravagant extent. The damage to Jewish property at Odessa, rated in the Jewish account at 1,137,381 roubles, or, according to their higher estimates, 3,000,000 roubles, was rated, Consul-General Stanley tells us, by a respectable Jew on the spot at 50,000 roubles, while the Consul-General himself rates it at 20,000. At Elizabethgrad, instead of whole streets being razed to the ground, only one hut had been unroofed. It appeared that few Jews, if any, had been intentionally killed, though some died of injuries received in the riots. There were conflicts between the Jews who defended their houses and the rioters. The outrages on women, by which public indignation in England had been most fiercely aroused, and of which, according to the Jewish accounts, there had been a frightful number, no less than thirty in one place and twenty-five in another, appeared, after careful inquiries by the consuls, to have been very rare. This is the more remarkable because the riots commonly began with the sacking of the gin shops, which were kept by the Jews, so that the passions of the mob must have been inflamed by drink. The horrible charge brought in the Jewish manifesto against the Russian women, of having incited men to outrage Jewesses and held the Jewesses down, is found to be utterly baseless. The charge of roasting children alive also falls to the ground. So does the charge of violating a Jew's

---

[1] *Correspondence respecting the Treatment of Jews in Russia*, Nos. 1 and 2, 1882, 1883. Presented to both Houses of Parliament by Command of Her Majesty.

wife and then setting fire to his house. The Jewish manifesto states that a Jewish innkeeper was cooped in one of his own barrels and cast into the Dnieper. This turns out to be a fable, the village which was the alleged scene of it being ten miles from the Dnieper and near no other river of consequence. The Russian peasant, Christian though he may be, is entitled to justice. As a rule, while ignorant and often intemperate, he is good-natured. There was much brutality in his riot, but fiendish atrocity there was not, and if he struck savagely, perhaps he had suffered long. For the belief that the mob was "doing the will of the Tsar," in other words, that the government was at the bottom of the rising, there does not appear to have been a shadow of foundation. The action of the authorities was not in all cases equally prompt. In some cases it was culpably slack. At Warsaw the commandant held back, though as Lord Granville, the British ambassador, bears witness, his motive for hesitation was humanity. But many of the rioters were shot down or bayoneted by the troops, hundreds were flogged, some were imprisoned, and some were sent to Siberia. That any of the military took part in the riots seems to be a fiction. It was not likely that the Russian government, menaced as it is by revolutionary conspiracy, would encourage insurrection. People of the upper class, who fancied that in the agitation they saw the work of Socialists, though they might dislike the Jews, would hardly sympathise with the rioters. Efforts were made by the government to restore Jewish property, and handsome sums were subscribed for the relief of the sufferers. Yet those who, while they heartily condemned outrage, were willing to accept proof that the Christian men and women of Russia had not behaved like demons, were saluted as modern counterparts of Haman by an eminent Rabbi, who, if the objects of his strictures had cared to retort, might have been asked whether the crucifixion of Haman's ten sons and the slaughter of seventy-five thousand of the enemies of Israel in one day, which, after the lapse of so many centuries, the feast of Purim still joyously commemorates, were not horrors as great as any which have been shown to have actually occurred at Odessa or Elizabethgrad.

The most important part of the evidence given in the consuls' reports, however, is that which relates to the cause of the troubles. At Warsaw, where the people are Roman Catholics, there appears to have been a certain amount of passive sympathy with the insurgents on religious grounds. But everywhere else the concurrent testimony of the consuls is that the source of the agitation was economical and social, not religious. Bitterness produced by the exactions of the Jew, envy of his wealth, irritation at the display of it in such things as the fine dresses of his women, jealousy of his ascendancy, combined in the lowest of the mob with the love of plunder, were the motives of the people for attacking him, not hatred of his faith. Vice-Consul Wagstaff, who seems to have paid particular attention to the question and made the most careful inquiry, after paying a tribute to the sober, laborious, thrifty character and the superior intelligence of the Jew, and ascribing to these his increasing monopoly of commerce, proceeds:

"It is chiefly as brokers or middlemen that the Jews are so prominent. Seldom a business transaction of any kind takes place without their intervention, and from both sides they receive compensation. To enumerate some of their other occupations, constantly denounced by the public: they are the principal dealers in spirits; keepers of 'vodka' (drinking) shops and houses of ill-fame; receivers of stolen goods; illegal pawnbrokers and usurers. A branch they also succeed in is as government contractors. With their knowledge of handling money, they collude with unscrupulous officials in defrauding the State to vast amounts annually. In fact, the malpractices of some of the Jewish community have a bad influence on those whom they come in contact with. It must, however, be said that there are many well educated, highly respectable, and honourable Jews in Russia, but they form a small minority. This class is not treated upon in this paper. They thoroughly condemn the occupations of their lower brethren, and one of the results of the late disturbances is noticed in the movement at present amongst the Jews. They themselves acknowledge the abuses practised by some of their own members, and suggest remedial measures to allay the irritation existing among the working classes.

"Another thing the Jews are accused of is that there exists among them a system of boycotting; they use their religion for business purposes. This is expressed by the words 'koul,' or 'kagal,' and 'kherim.' For instance, in Bessarabia, the produce of a vineyard is drawn for by lot, and falls, say, to Jacob Levy; the other Jews of the district cannot compete with Levy, who buys the wine at his own price. In the leasing by auction of government and provincial lands, it is invariably a Jew who outbids the others and afterwards re-lets plots to the peasantry at exorbitant prices. Very crying abuses of farming out land have lately come to light and greatly shocked public opinion. Again, where estates are farmed by Jews, it is distressing to see the pitiable condition in which they are handed over on the expiration of the lease. Experience also shows they are very bad colonists.

"Their fame as usurers is well known. Given a Jewish recruit with a few roubles' capital, it can be worked out, mathematically, what time it will take him to become the money-lender of his company or regiment, from the drummer to the colonel. Take the case of a peasant: if he once gets into the hands of this class, he is irretrievably lost. The proprietor, in his turn, from a small loan gradually mortgages and eventually loses his estate. A great deal of landed property in south Russia has of late years passed into the hands of the Israelites, but principally into the hands of intelligent and sober peasants.

"From first to last, the Jew has his hand in everything. He advances the seed for sowing, which is generally returned in kind — quarters for bushels. As harvest time comes round, money is required to gather in the crops. This is sometimes advanced on hard conditions; but the peasant has no choice; there is no one to lend him money, and it is better to secure something than to lose all. Very often the Jew buys the whole crop as it stands in the field on his own terms. It is thus seen that they themselves do not raise agricultural products, but they reap the benefits of others' labour, and steadily become rich, while proprietors are gradually getting ruined. In their relation to Russia they are compared to parasites that have settled on a plant not vigorous enough to throw them off, and which is being gradually sapped of its vitality." [1]

The peasants, the vice-consul tells us, often say, when they look at the property of a Jew, "That is my blood." In confirmation of his view he cites the list of demands formulated by the peasants and laid before a mixed committee of inquiry into the causes of the disorder. These demands are all eco-

____
[1] *Correspondence respecting the Treatment of Jews in Russia*, No. 1, pp. 11, 12.

nomical or social, with the exception of the complaint that Russian girls in Jewish service forget their religion and with it lose their morals. Everything, in short, seems to bear out the statement of the Russian Minister of the Interior, in a manifesto given in the Blue Book, that "the movement had its main cause in circumstances purely economical"; provided that to "economical" we add "social," and include all that is meant by the phrase "hatred of Jewish usurpation," used in another document.

Vice-Consul Harford, at Sebastopol, is in contact with the Jews of the Crimea, who, he says, are of a superior order, while some of them are not Talmudic Jews, but belong to the mild and Scriptural sect of the Karaites. He says that in his quarter all goes well.

"The spirit of antagonism that animates the Russian against the Jew is, in my opinion, in no way to be traced to the difference of creed. In this part of Russia, where we have more denominations of religion than in any other part, I have never, during a residence of fourteen years, observed the slightest indication of sectarianism in any class. The peasant, though ignorant and superstitious, is so entirely free from bigotry that even the openly displayed contempt of the fanatical Mohammedan Crim Tartar for the rites and ceremonies of the Russian Church fails to excite in him the slightest feeling of personal animosity; his own feeling with regard to other religions is perfect indifference; he enters a mosque or synagogue just as he would enter a theatre, and regards the ceremony in much the same manner that an English peasant would, neither knowing nor caring to know whether they worshipped God or the moon. As it is evident from this that race and creed are to the minds of the peasantry of no more consequence than they would be to a Zulu, the only conclusion is that the antipathy is against the usurer, and as civilisation can only be expected to influence the rising generation of Russian peasantry, the remedy rests with the Jew, who, if he will not refrain from speculating (in lawless parts of the empire) on ignorance and drunkenness, must be prepared to defend himself and his property from the certain and natural result of such a policy."[1]

Persecution is not the tendency of the Russian or of the Church to which he belongs. The Eastern Church, while it

[1] *Correspondence respecting the Treatment of Jews in Russia*, No. 2, p. 17.

has been superstitious and somewhat torpid, has been tolerant, and, compared with other orthodox churches, free from the stain of persecution. It has not even been proselyting, nor has it ever sent forth crusaders, unless the name of crusades can be given to the wars with the Turks, the main motive for which, though the pretext may have been religious, probably has been territorial ambition, and which were certainly not crusades when waged by Catherine, the patroness of Diderot and the correspondent of Voltaire. Stanley, in his "Eastern Church," dilates upon this characteristic of the Eastern Christians. He says that "a respectful reverence for every manifestation of religious feeling has withheld them from violent attacks on the rights of conscience and led them to extend a kindly patronage to forms of faith most removed from their own"; and he notices that the great philosophers of antiquity are honoured by portraits in one of their churches as heralds of the gospel.[1] Sir Mackenzie Wallace, who is the best authority, while he admits the inferiority of the Russian priests in culture, testifies strongly to their innocence of persecution, saying that "if they have less learning, culture, and refinement than the Roman Catholic priesthood, they have at the same time infinitely less fanaticism, less spiritual pride, and less intolerance towards the adherents of other faiths."[2] The educated classes he represents as generally indifferent to theological questions. The peasantry are superstitious and blindly attached to their own faith, which they identify with their nationality; but they think it natural and right that a man of a different nationality should have a different religion. In Nijni-Novgorod, the city of the great fair, the Mahomedan mosque and the Armenian church stand side by side with the Orthodox cathedral.[3] At one end of a village is the church, at the other the mosque, and the Mahomedan spreads

---

[1] *Lectures on the History of the Eastern Church*, 3d edition, p. 35. By Arthur Penrhyn Stanley, D.D.

[2] *Russia*, pp. 58, 59. By Sir D. Mackenzie Wallace, M.A.

[3] See Hare's *Studies in Russia*, p. 360.

his prayer-carpet on the deck of a steamer full of Orthodox Russians.

The ecclesiastical constitution of Russia is incompatible with religious equality. The Tsar is practically, though not theoretically, head of the Church, as well as of the State; the commander of Holy Russia as a Caliph is the Commander of the Faithful. In the interest rather of national unity than of religious orthodoxy he restrains dissent. But it is against innovation and schism within the pale of the State Church rather than against unbelief that his power has been exerted. Some Tsars, such as Peter the Great and the Tsarina Catherine II., have been Liberals, and have patronised merit without regard to creed. Nicholas was full of orthodox sentiment and in all things a martinet, yet Mackenzie Wallace has a pleasant anecdote of his commending the Jewish sentinel at his door who conscientiously refused to respond to the Tsar's customary salutation on Easter Day. No Tsar, however bigoted, has been guilty of such persecution as Philip II. of Spain, Ferdinand of Austria, or Louis XIV. Russia has had no Inquisition. That the Jews have had liberty of worship and education, the existence of 6319 synagogues and of 77 Jewish schools supported by the State, besides 1165 private and communal schools, seems clearly to prove.[1] It does not seem to be alleged that any attempt has been made by the government at forcible conversion. Whatever may have been the harshness or even cruelty of the measures which it has taken to confine the Jews to their original districts and prevent their spreading over its dominions, its object appears to have been to protect the people against economical oppression and preserve the national character from being sapped by an alien influence, not to suppress the Jewish religion.

That Christian fanaticism at all events was not the sole source of the unpopularity of the Jews might have been inferred from the fact that the relation was no better between the Jew and the heathen races during the period of declining

---

[1] *Statesman's Year-Book*, 1891, pp. 854-856.

polytheism, when religious indifference prevailed and beneath the vast dome of the Roman Empire the religions of many slept and mouldered side by side. Gibbon, who is well qualified to speak, for he was himself a citizen of the Roman Empire in sentiment, after narrating the massacres committed by the Jews on the Gentiles in Africa and Cyprus, has expressed in flamboyant phrases the hatred of the Roman world for the Jews, whom he designates as the "implacable enemies, not only of the Roman government but of human kind."[1] Tacitus speaks of the Jews as enemies of all races but their own (*adversus omnes alios hostile odium*),[2] and Juvenal, in a well-known passage, speaks of them as people who would not show a wayfarer his road or guide the thirsty to a spring if he were not of their own faith. Those who maintain that there is nothing in the character, habits, or disposition of the Jew to provoke antipathy have to bring the charge of fanatical prejudice not only against the Russians or against Christendom, but against mankind.

In Germany, in Austria, in Roumania, in all the countries of Europe where this deplorable contest of races is going on, the cause of quarrel appears to be fundamentally the same. It appears to be economical and social, not religious, or religious only in a secondary degree. Mr. Baring-Gould tells us that in Germany "there is scarce a village without some Jews in it, who do not cultivate land themselves, but lie in wait like spiders for the failing Bauer."[3] A German who knew the peasantry well said to Mr. Gould that "he doubted whether there were a happier set of people under the sun." But he added, after a pause, "so long as they are out of the clutch of the Jew."[4] Of the German, as well as of the Russian, it may

---

[1] *Decline and Fall of the Roman Empire*, Chap. xvi. "In Cyrene," Gibbon says, "they massacred 220,000 Greeks; in Cyprus, 240,000," citing Dion Cassius (I., lxviii., p. 1145), whose account, as regards numbers at all events, must be greatly exaggerated.

[2] *Hist.*, V., v.

[3] *Germany Present and Past*, Vol. I., p. 114. By S. Baring-Gould, M.A.

[4] *Ib.*, p. 127.

be said that he is not a religious persecutor. If persecution of a sanguinary or atrocious kind has sullied his annals, the arm of it was the house of Austria, with its Spanish connection, and the head was the world-roving Jesuit. In the case of Hungary, Mr. Paget, who is a Liberal and advocates a liberal policy towards the Jews, says: "The Jew is no less active in profiting by the vices and necessities of the peasant than by those of the noble. As sure as he gains a settlement in a village the peasantry become poor."[1] "In Austrian Poland," says a *Times* reviewer, "the worst of the peasant's sluggish content is that it has given him over to the exactions of the Jews." "The Jews," he adds, "are in fact the lords of the country." They are lords not less alien to the people than the Norman was to the Saxon, and perhaps not always more merciful, though in their hands is the writ of ejection instead of the conqueror's sword.

If we cross the Mediterranean the same thing meets us. In Thomson's "Morocco," we read :

"As money-lenders the Jews are as maggots and parasites, aggravating and feeding on the diseases of the land. I do not know, for my part, which exercises the greatest tyranny and oppression, the Sultan or the Jew, — the one the embodiment of the foulest misgovernment, the other the essence of a dozen Shylocks, demanding, ay, and getting, not only his pound of flesh, but also the blood and nerves. By his outrageous exactions the Sultan drives the Moor into the hands of the Jew, who affords him a temporary relief by lending him the necessary money on incredibly exorbitant terms. Once in the money-lender's clutches, he rarely escapes till he is squeezed dry, when he is either thrown aside, crushed and ruined, or cast into a dungeon, where, fettered and starved, he is probably left to die a slow and horrible death.

"To the position of the Jews in Morocco it would be difficult to find a parallel. Here we have a people alien, despised, and hated, actually living in the country under immeasurably better conditions than the dominant race, while they suck, and are assisted to suck, the very lifeblood of their hosts. The aim of every Jew is to toil not, neither to spin, save the coils which as money-lenders he may weave for the entanglement of his necessitous victims."[2]

[1] *Hungary and Transylvania*, Vol. I., p. 136. By John Paget.
[2] *Travels in the Atlas and Southern Morocco : A Narrative of Exploration*, pp. 418, 419. By Joseph Thomson, F.R.G.S.

Even if we cross the Atlantic we find the same phenomenon. Mr. Olmsted, in his "Cotton Kingdom," says:

"A swarm of Jews has within the last ten years settled in nearly every Southern town, many of them men of no character, opening cheap clothing and trinket shops, ruining or driving out of business many of the old retailers, and engaging in an unlawful trade with the simple negroes, which is found very profitable." [1]

And again:

"If his [the planter's] first crop proves a bad one he must borrow money of the Jews at New Orleans to pay his first note. They will sell him this on the best terms they can, often at not less than twenty-five per cent per annum." [2]

Mr. Stevenson says of the Jews in San Francisco:

"Jew storekeepers have already learned the advantage to be gained from this [unlimited credit]; they lead on the farmer into irretrievable indebtedness, and keep him ever after as their bond-slave hopelessly grinding in the mill. So the whirligig of time brings in its revenges, and except that the Jew knows better than to foreclose, you may see Americans bound in the same chains with which they themselves had formerly bound the Mexicans." [3]

These passages were not intended by the writers, nor are they here cited, as general pictures of the Jews, or as pictures of Jews exclusively. In the last, American sharp practice is included. The passages are cited as indications of the real source of the antagonism, tending to show that it is economical, not religious.

Light dawned on the writer's mind on this question when he had just been listening with sympathy to speeches in the British House of Commons on the anti-Semitic movement in Roumania, where, as in Russia, the number of Jews is partic-

----

[1] *Journeys and Explorations in the Cotton Kingdom*, 2d edition, pp. 252, 253. By Frederick Law Olmsted.

[2] *Ib.*, pp. 321, 322.

[3] *Across the Plains*, p. 100. By Robert Louis Stevenson.

ularly large and the feeling against them is proportionately intense. The Jewish member who appealed to the government on the subject, and the Minister who rose in response to the appeal, had both of them assumed that it was a case of religious persecution, and the Minister especially had dwelt on the mischievous influence of ecclesiastics; with how little justice, so far as the priests of the Eastern Church are concerned, we have already seen. The debate over, the writer was accosted by his friend, the late Dr. Humphry Sandwith, distinguished for his share in the defence of Kars against the Russians, who knew the Danubian Principalities well. Dr. Sandwith said that the speakers had been entirely mistaken; that religion was not the motive of the agitation; that neither the people nor their priests were given to persecution; that the government had granted aid to a synagogue; but that Jewish usurers got the simple-minded peasants into their toils and sold them out of their homesteads till the peasants would bear it no longer, and an outbreak ensued. Dr. Sandwith, being a thorough-going Liberal, would have been the last man to palliate religious persecution.

It is doubtful whether, even in the Middle Ages, the quarrel was not less religious and more economical or social than is supposed. That was the age of religious intolerance; Christian heretics, such as the Albigenses, were persecuted with fully as much cruelty as the Jews. Jews who had ventured to settle in the Catholic communities for the sake of gain, braved the same sort of peril which would have been braved by an enterprising trader who had thrust himself into Japan during its close period. But as a rule, though they were hated, they were not persecuted; they were tolerated and allowed to build their synagogues and worship God in their own way. They were regarded, not like heretics, as religious traitors, but as religious aliens. Their religious blindness, as well as their penal homelessness, was viewed as the act of God. They were privileged in misbelief. Aquinas expressly lays it down that they are to be tolerated as a useful testimony borne, though by adversaries, to the truth of

Christianity.[1] It is not true that the great Doctor of the Middle Ages sanctions the forcible conversion of the children of Jews. He raises the question and decides it in the negative.[2] An argument stated by him only to be set aside has been taken for his conclusion. In the "Corpus Juris Canonici" it is laid down that "the Jews are not to be baptised against their will or forced to it, nor to be condemned without judgment, nor to be spoiled of their goods, nor disturbed at their festivals, nor are their cemeteries to be molested or their bodies to be exhumed."[3]

By the kings, and notably by the Angevin kings of England, the Jews were protected as the agents of royal extortion, sucking by usury the money from the people which was afterwards squeezed out of the usurer by the king. Of the common people it is not, so far as we can see, the tendency to persecute on account of religion, however superstitious they may be. It is rather by the possessors of ecclesiastical power and wealth, by Archbishops of Toledo and Prince Bishops of Germany, whom dissent threatens with dispossession, or by kings like Philip II. and Louis XIV., under priestly influence, that the engines of persecution are set at work. At the time of the Crusades, Christian fanaticism being excited to frenzy, there were dreadful massacres of Jews, and forced conversions, though no reliance can be placed on the figures of mediæval chroniclers, who set down at random twenty thousand victims slain, or two hundred thousand forced conversions. The Jew at that time was odious not only as a misbeliever in the midst of the Christian camp, whose presence would turn from it the countenance of God, but as a suspected friend and ally at heart, of the Oriental power. The Jews must have foreseen the storm, and might have escaped by flight, but they were perhaps tempted by the vast harvest afforded them in the general sale of possessions by the Cru-

[1] *Summa Theologica, Secunda Secundæ,* Quæst. X., Art. xi.

[2] *Ib.,* Art. xii.

[3] Quoted by Joseph Jacobs in his *The Jews of Angevin England,* p. 185.

saders to buy equipments, while by that traffic their unpopularity was increased. But in ordinary times the main causes of the hatred of the Jews among the common people appear to have been usury and a social arrogance, which was particularly galling on the part of the alien and the enemy of Christ. In the riots the people made for the place in which the Jewish bonds were kept. At York, the scene of the worst anti-Jewish riot in England, the chronicler tells us there were two Jews, Benedict and Joce, who had built in the middle of the city houses like palaces, where they dwelt like princes of their own people and tyrants of the Christians, keeping almost royal state, and exercising harsh tyranny against those whom they oppressed with their usuries.[1] The usury was grinding and ruthless. In the Chronicle of Jocelin de Brakelond we see how rapidly a debt of twenty-seven pounds, owed to a Jew, grew to eight hundred and eighty. Jews at Oxford were forbidden by edict to take more than forty-three per cent. So it was generally. Political economy will say that this was justifiable, in the circumstances perhaps useful, and the penalty due to the Christian superstition which made the lending of money at interest an unholy and therefore a perilous trade. Nevertheless, it was hateful, at least sure to engender hate. The Lombards and Cahorsins, who, when the Jews were for a time driven from the field, took up the business, incurred the same hatred, though in their case there was no religious or social feeling to aggravate the unpopularity of the trade. A Spanish Chancellor describes the Jews as the bloodsuckers of the afflicted people, as men who exact fifty per cent, eighty, a hundred, and through whom the land is desolate, their hard hearts being callous to tears and groans, and their ears deaf to petitions for delay.[2] Savonarola, the Christian socialist of his day, revived the Monte di Pietà to rescue his people from the fangs of the Jews.

The law of the Jews themselves, be it observed, proscribes

---

[1] *William of Newbury*, quoted by Joseph Jacobs, pp. 117, 118.

[2] See *The History of the Jews from the War with Rome to the Present Time*, p. 245. By Rev. H. C. Adams, M.A.

usury in the case of a tribal brother, permitting it in the case of a stranger. "Thou shalt not lend upon usury to thy brother; usury of money, usury of victuals, usury of anything that is lent upon usury: unto a stranger thou mayest lend upon usury; but unto thy brother thou shalt not lend upon usury: that the Lord thy God may bless thee in all that thou settest thine hand to in the land whither thou goest to possess it" (Deut. xxiii. 19, 20). Hence it appears, first, that Christendom was not more superstitious on the subject of usury than were the Jews themselves; and, secondly, that the Jew regarded and treated the Christians among whom he was dwelling as strangers.

The Jews after all were not so maltreated as to prevent them from amassing what was for that time enormous wealth. And of this they appear in those days, as they sometimes do in these, to have made ostentatious and, in the eyes of natives and Christians, especially if they had been victims of extortion, offensive use. A Cortes in Portugal, in 1481, complained of Jewish luxury and display, of Jews who rode splendidly caparisoned horses, wore silk doublets, carried jewel-hilted swords, and entered churches where they mocked the worship. Jewish haughtiness seems sometimes even to have indulged in insults to the popular religion. At Oxford it mocks the miracles of St. Frydeswide before her votaries, assaults a religious procession, and tramples on the cross. At Lynn the Jews attack a church to drag out a convert from Judaism to Christianity, for whose blood they thirsted, and the people of the place are half afraid to resist them, knowing that they are protected by the king. Besides their usury, the Jews were suspected of clipping the coin. Their function as the middlemen of royal rapacity must have been most odious, not least when they handled for the king Church estates which he had wrongfully taken into his hands. In expelling them from England, Edward I., the best of kings, no doubt thought that he was doing a good deed, while his people were unquestionably grateful. The worthy Abbot Samson, of St. Edmondbury, in the same way earned the gratitude of the people of that place by ridding it of the Jews. The clearest, as well as the most terrible, case of persecution of the Jews for religion was in Spain, and there, it must be remembered, when the Jew was burned, the Christian suspected of heresy was burned at his side. Even in Spain it is not easy to say how much was hatred of religion, how much was hatred of race. For centuries the Spanish Christians had struggled for the land with Islam, and the history of Spain had been one long Crusade. The Jew was identified with Islam. A Jewish writer, Lady Magnus, in her history of her race, says:

"Both in the East and in the West the rise of Mohammedanism was, in truth, as the dawn of a new day to the despised and dispersed Jews. If we except that one bitter quarrel between the earliest followers of the Prophet and the Jews of Arabia, — and that, we must note, was no organised or systematic persecution, but rather an ebullition of anger from an ardent enthusiast at his first unexpected rebuff,— we shall find that Judaism had much reason to rejoice at the rapid spread of Mohammedanism. Monotheists, like the Jews, abhorring like them all forms of image worship, worshipping in simple fashion their one God Allah, observing dietary laws like to those of Moses, the Mohammedans both in their faith and in their practice naturally found more grounds for agreement with Jewish doctrine than with the Christian dogma of a complex Godhead, or with the undeveloped aspirations of the heathen. And besides some identity of principle and of race between the Mohammedan and the Jew there soon discovered itself a certain hardly definable kinship of habit and custom, — a sort of sympathy, in fact, which is often more effectual than even more important causes in promoting friendly relations either nationally or individually. Then, also, there was the similarity of language; for Arabic, like Hebrew, belongs to what is called the Semitic group. . . . Nearly a century of experience of the political and social results of the Mohammedan conquests must, inevitably, have made the year 710 stand out to the Jews of that time as the beginning of a grand new era in their history. Centuries of cruelty had made the wise loyal counsel of Jeremiah to 'pray for the peace of the land whither ye are led captive; its peace shall be your peace also,' a hard task for the most loyal of consciences; and in that early year of the eighth century, when Spain was added to the list of the Mohammedan victories, and the triumphant flag of the Crescent was hoisted on tower and citadel, the liberty of conscience which it practically proclaimed must have been in the widest sense a cause for national rejoicing to the Jews."[1]

[1] *About the Jews since Bible Times*, pp. 195–197. By Lady Magnus.

The kindness of the Mahomedan to the Jew may here be overrated, but the sympathy between Judaism and Islam cannot be questioned, and it meant common antipathy to Christendom, which Christendom could not fail to reciprocate, especially in its crusading mood. We sit at ease and sneer at the fanaticism of the Crusaders. But some strong motive was needed to make men leave their homes and their wives and go to die as the vanguard of Christendom on Syrian battlefields. Let us not forget that the question whether Christianity and Christian civilisation or Islam, with its despotism and its harem, should reign in Europe came to be decided, not without long and perilous debate, so near the heart of Christendom as the plain of Tours. The Jews of Southern France, like those of Spain, were suspected of inviting the invaders. If they did they were not without excuse. But their excuse could hardly be expected to pass muster with Charles Martel.

From religious intolerance in the Dark Ages, or long after the end of the Dark Ages, nobody was free. The Jew was not. He had striven as long as he had a chance, by all means in his power, unscrupulously using the Roman or the Persian as his instruments, to crush Christianity. His own law punished blasphemy with death and bade the worshipper of Jehovah slaughter everything that breathed in a captured city of the heathen. It was hence, in fact, that the Inquisitor partly drew his inspiration. Mediæval darkness had passed away when Judaism sought the life of Spinoza and scourged Uriel Acosta in the synagogue.

Although the lot of a Jew in the Middle Ages was hard in itself, it was perhaps not so hard compared with that of other classes, notably with that of the serf, as the perpetual addition of piteous epithets to his name by common writers might lead us to suppose. "Ivanhoe" is not history; Freeman's works are. Freeman says:

"In the wake of the conqueror the Jews of Rouen found their way to London, and before long we find settlements of the Hebrew race in the chief cities and boroughs of England: at York, Winchester, Lincoln, Bristol, Oxford, and even at the gate of the Abbot of St. Edmonds and

St. Albans. They came as the king's special men, or more truly as his special chattels, strangers alike to the Church and the commonwealth, but strong in the protection of a master who commonly found it his interest to protect them against all others. Hated, feared, and loathed, but far too deeply feared to be scorned or oppressed, they stalked defiantly among the people of the land, on whose wants they throve, safe from harm or insult, save now and then, when popular wrath burst all bounds, when their proud mansions and fortified quarters could shelter them no longer from raging crowds who were eager to wash out their debts in the blood of their creditors. The romantic picture of the despised, trembling Jew, cringing before every Christian whom he meets, is, in any age of English history, simply a romantic picture." [1]

The Jews found it worth their while to buy their way back again and again into lands from which they had been banished, and their existence in which is pictured by historians as a hell. If they were heavily taxed and sometimes pillaged, they were exempted from the most grievous of all taxes, service in war. Their badge, though a stigma, was also a protection, since it marked them as serfs of the king. Even the Ghetto, where there was one, would be comparatively a small grievance when nationalities, crafts, and family clans had their special quarters in cities. Any immigrant would have been less at home in the closely organised communities of feudalism and Catholicism than in the loose society of the Roman Empire. But the Jew was there by his own choice. The tenure of land in a feudal realm, being military, land could hardly be held by a Jew. But Jews were not forbidden by law to hold land in England till late in the reign of Henry III., when it was found they were getting estates into their hands by mortgage, which would have been ruinous to the feudal system. A community has a right to defend its territory and its national integrity against an invader whether his weapon be the sword or foreclosure. In the territories of the Italian Republics the Jews might, so far as we see, have bought land and taken to farming had they pleased. But before this they had thoroughly taken to trade. Under the

---

[1] *The Reign of William Rufus and the Accession of Henry the First*, Vol. I., p. 160. By Edward A. Freeman.

falling Empire they were the great slave-traders, buying captives from barbarian invaders and probably acting as general brokers of spoils at the same time. There was, no doubt, a perpetual struggle between their craft and the brute force of the feudal populations. But what moral prerogative has craft over force? Mr. Arnold White tells the Russians that if they would let Jewish intelligence have free course, Jews would soon fill all high employments and places of power to the exclusion of the natives, who now hold them. Russians are bidden to acquiesce and rather to rejoice in this by philosophers, who would perhaps not relish the cup if it were commended to their own lips. The law of evolution, it is said, prescribes the survival of the fittest. To which the Russian boor may reply, that if his force beats the fine intelligence of the Jew the fittest will survive and the law of evolution will be fulfilled. It was force rather than fine intelligence which decided on the field of Zama that the Latin, not the Semite, should rule the ancient and mould the modern world.

Religious antipathy, no doubt, has always added and continues to add bitterness to the social quarrel. Among ignorant peasants it still takes grotesque, sometimes hideous, shapes, such as the cruel fancy that the Jews sacrifice Christian children and spread pestilence. The Jew has always been felt to be a power of evil, and the peasant imagination lends to the power of evil horns and hoofs. But even the peasant imagination does not lend horns and hoofs to any power which is felt to be harmless, much less to one which has always been beneficent, as we are asked to believe that the Jews have been. The people are not everywhere fools or fiends. Let it be remembered, too, that the Jewish religion is not merely a religion of peculiar opinion. It is a religion of social exclusiveness, of arrogated superiority to Gentiles, and treatment of them as unclean, of the Pentateuch with its Chosen People, and of the feast of Purim. Milman thinks it possible that in the offensive celebration of the feast of Purim some of the calumnies about the Jews may have had their source.

People of a higher class, whom Jewish usury does not touch, object to Judaism on higher grounds. They object to it because it is at variance with the unity of the nation and threatens to eat out the core of nationality. Admitting the keenness of Jewish intelligence, they say that intelligence is not always beneficent, nor is submission to it always a matter of duty, especially when its ascendancy is gained by such means as the dexterous appropriation of the circulating medium, and when it is, as they believe, the result not of individual effort in a fair field, but of the collective effort of a united, though scattered race, aided by a press in Jewish hands. They demur to having the high places of their community monopolised, as Mr. Arnold White says they might be in Russia, by unsympathetic aliens turning the rest of the nation into hewers of wood and drawers of water. This feeling, if it is selfish, is natural, and should be charitably viewed by those who are free from the danger. Some of the opposition to Jewish ascendancy arises from dread of materialism, the triumph of which over the spiritual character and aspirations of Christian communities would, it is apprehended, follow the victory of the Jew, an impersonation of the power of wealth. Among the anti-Semites are Christian Socialists seeking the liberation of the labouring class from the grasp of usury and the money power. Herr Stoecker belongs, it seems, to this sect, and far from being an enemy of the Jewish people, is a devout believer in the Old Testament. To be opposed on social or patriotic grounds to Judaism as a system is not to be a hater of the Jews, any more than to be opposed to Islam or Buddhism as a system is to be a hater of the Mahomedan or the Buddhist.

The impression prevails that Judaism during the Middle Ages was a civilising power, in fact the great civilising power, while its beneficent action was repressed by a barbarous Christendom. The leading shoot of civilisation, both material and intellectual, was republican Italy, where the Jews, though they were not persecuted, never played a leading part. You may read through Sismondi's History almost without being made aware of their existence. Intellectually superior in a certain sense no doubt they were; their wealth exempted them from manual labour, and gave them an advantage, as it does now, in the race of intelligence. They were also practically exempted from military service. They preserved Hebrew and Oriental learning, and to them Europe owed the transmission of the works of Aristotle through Arabic translations. But in their mediæval roll of celebrated names the great majority are those of Talmudists or Cabbalists. The most illustrious is that of Maimonides, whose influence on the progress of humanity surely was not very great, albeit he was let and hindered only by the narrow and jealous orthodoxy of his own people. Jews were in request as physicians, though they seem to have drawn their knowledge from the Arabians. They had much to do with the foundation of the medical school of Montpellier; the origin of that at Salerno was Benedictine. But if they founded a medical science, what became of the medical science which they founded? At the close of the Middle Ages there was none. A Jewish physician, no doubt the most eminent of his class, is called in by Innocent VIII. His treatment is transfusion of blood. He kills three boys in the process and then runs away. Of the money trade the Jews were generally the masters, though in Italy that, too, was in the hands of native houses, such as the Medici, Bardi, and Peruzzi, while at a later period the Fuggers of Augsburg were the Rothschilds of Germany. But the Jews never were the masters of the grand commerce or of that maritime enterprise in which the Middle Ages gloriously closed. Rosseeuw Saint-Hilaire has observed in his history of Spain that their addiction was to petty trade. Showing abundant sympathy for Jewish wrongs, he finds himself compelled to contrast the "narrowness and rapacity" of their commerce with the boldness and grandeur of Arab enterprise.[1] The slave trade, which in the early Middle Ages was in Jewish hands, was not then the reproach that it is now, yet it never was a noble or a beneficent trade. Spain is supposed to have owed

[1] *Histoire d' Espagne*, Vol. III., p. 147.

her fall to the expulsion of the Jews, but the acme of her greatness came after their expulsion; and her fall was due to despotism, civil and religious, to her false commercial system, to the diversion of her energy from industry to gold-seeking and conquest, and not least to the overgrown and heterogeneous empire which was the supposed foundation of her power. England, in the period between the expulsion of the Jews under Edward I. and their readmission under Cromwell, became a commercial nation and a famous naval power; and the greatness thus achieved was English, not Gibeonite, as it would have been under Jewish ascendancy; it was part of the fulness of national life, and was prolific not only of Whittingtons and Drakes, but of Shakespeares and Bacons. As financiers it is likely that the Jews were useful in advancing money for great works; they also furnished money for enterprises such as Strongbow's expedition to Ireland. But the assertion, often repeated, that they provided the means for building the churches, abbeys, and colleges of England must be qualified in face of the fact that the greater part of those edifices was of dates subsequent to the expulsion of the Jews. Salisbury Cathedral was built before the expulsion. But we happen to know that the forty thousand marks which it cost were supplied by contributions from the Prebendaries, collections from different dioceses, and grants from Alicia de Bruere and other benefactors.[1] Judaism is now the great financial power of Europe, that is, it is the greatest power of all. It is no longer necessary, out of pity for it, to falsify history and traduce Christendom.

Of the two works on which, during the Middle Ages, Jewish intellect was chiefly employed, the Cabbala is on all hands allowed to be mystical nonsense. Of the Talmud, Dr. Farrar, assuredly no Jew-baiter, in his Preface to a volume of selections from it, says:

"Wisdom there is in the Talmud, and eloquence and high morality; of this the reader may learn something even in the small compass of the

---

[1] See Murray's *Handbook to the Cathedrals of England.* Southern Division, Part I., p. 94.

following pages. How could it be otherwise when we bear in mind that the Talmud fills twelve large folio volumes, and represents the main literature of a nation during several hundred years? But yet I venture to say that it would be impossible to find less wisdom, less eloquence, and less high morality, imbedded in a vaster bulk of what is utterly valueless to mankind, — to say nothing of those parts of it which are indelicate and even obscene, — in any other national literature of the same extent. And even of the valuable residuum of true and holy thoughts, I doubt whether there is even one which had not long been anticipated, and which is not found more nobly set forth in the Scriptures of the Old and New Testament." [1]

This judgment is fully borne out by the selections which follow, and which are made by Mr. Hershon, a known Hebrew scholar, on an impartial principle. It is supported by other independent critics, such as Thirlwall, who spoke of the Talmud as an ocean of nonsense. The writer will not presume to speak, though he looks back upon the perusal of a Latin translation of the Mishna as one of the least pleasant labours of a student's life. Dr. Deutsch's counterfeit presentment, to which Dr. Farrar refers, is a standing caution. In every page of the volume of selections we have such things as this:

"There were two things which God first thought of creating on the eve of the Sabbath, which, however, were not created till after the Sabbath had closed. The first was fire, which Adam by divine suggestion drew forth by striking together two stones; and the second was the mule, produced by the crossing of two different animals." — *P'sachim*, fol. 54, col. 1.

"The Rabbis have taught that there are three reasons why a person should not enter a ruin: 1. Because he may be suspected of evil intent; 2. Because the walls might tumble upon him; 3. And because of evil spirits that frequent such places." — *Berachoth*, fol. 3, col. 1.

"The stone which Og, King of Bashan, meant to throw upon Israel is the subject of a tradition delivered on Sinai. 'The camp of Israel I see,' he said, 'extends three miles; I shall therefore go and root up a mountain three miles in extent and throw it upon them.' So off he went, and finding such a mountain, raised it on his head, but the Holy One — blessed be He!—sent an army of ants against him, which so bored the mountain over his head that it slipped down upon his shoulders, 'from which he

---

[1] *A Talmudic Miscellany.* Compiled and translated by Paul Isaac Hershon, with introductory preface by Rev. F. W. Farrar, D.D., F.R.S.

could not lift it, because his teeth, protruding, had riveted it upon him."
— *Berachoth*, fol. 54, col. 2.

"Three things are said respecting the finger-nails: He who trims his nails and buries the parings is a pious man; he who burns these is a righteous man; but he who throws them away is a wicked man, for mischance might follow, should a female step over them." — *Moed Katan*, fol. 18, col. 1.[1]

Abraham's height, according to the Talmudists, was that of seventy-four men put together. His food, his dress, and his strength were those of seventy-four men. He built for the abode of his seventeen children by Keturah, an iron city, the walls whereof were so lofty that the sun never penetrated them. He gave them a bowl full of precious stones, the brilliancy of which supplied them with light in the absence of the sun. He had a precious stone suspended from his neck, upon which every sick person who gazed was healed of his disease, and when he died God hung up the stone on the sphere of the sun. Before his time there was no such thing as a beard; but as many mistook Abraham and Isaac for each other, Abraham prayed to God for a beard to distinguish him, and it was granted him. Every one has a thousand malignant spirits at his left side, and ten thousand at his right. The crowding at the schools is caused by their pushing in. If one would discover traces of their presence, he has only to sift some ashes on the floor at his bedside, and next morning he will see the footmarks as of fowls. If he would see the demons themselves, he must burn to ashes the afterbirth of a first-born black kitten, the offspring of a first-born black cat, put some of the ashes into his eyes, and he will not fail to see the demons. The medical and physical apophthegms of the Talmud do not give much evidence of science: "dropsy is a sign of sin, jaundice of hatred without a cause, and quinsy of slander"; "six things possess medicinal virtue: cabbage, lung-wort, beet-root, water, certain parts of the offal of animals, and, in the opinion of some, little fishes." Mr. Hershon's collection abounds with nonsense on this subject as absurd as

—————

[1] Quoted in Hershon's *Miscellany*.

anything in mediæval quackery. Other features of the work are an Oriental indelicacy and a pride of Rabbinical learning which treats illiteracy as almost criminal, looking down upon the illiterate as an American would look down upon the negro. The most superstitious of Christian writings in the Dark Ages could not be more tainted with demonology and witchcraft, nor in any monkish chronicle do we find fables so gross. Few would set the Talmud, as presented by Mr. Hershon, or the Cabbala above the works of such writers as Anselm, Aquinas, the author of "Imitatio Christi," or the authors of hymns and liturgical compositions of the Christian Middle Ages.

We have been speaking, be it observed, of the Talmud as the work and monument of Jewish intelligence and morality in the Dark Ages; we have not been speaking of the intelligence or morality of the Jews of the present day. The charge is constantly brought against Christendom of having by its barbarous bigotry repressed the beneficent action of Jewish intellect, which would otherwise have enlightened and civilised the world. The answer is apparently found in the Cabbala and the Talmud. From a perusal of the Jewish historian Graetz, it would seem that Rabbinical orthodoxy was not less opposed than Papal orthodoxy to science, philosophy, and culture. We are led to believe that, at last, Talmudic bigotry and obscurantism had prevailed, when Judaism was rescued by Moses Mendelssohn, who himself owed his emancipation to Lessing. Nathan the Wise is a philosopher and philanthropist of the eighteenth century, not a Talmudic Jew.

Still more notable, however, than the absurdities are the passages indicative of a tribal morality which prescribes one mode of dealing with those who are, and another mode of dealing with those who are not, of the tribe.

"If the ox of an Israelite bruise the ox of a Gentile, the Israelite is exempt from paying damages ; but should the ox of a Gentile bruise the ox of an Israelite, the Gentile is bound to recompense him in full."— *Bava Kama*, fol. 38, col. 1.

"When an Israelite and a Gentile have a lawsuit before thee, if thou canst, acquit the former according to the laws of Israel, and tell the latter such is *our* law ; if thou canst get him off in accordance with Gentile law, do so, and say to the plaintiff such is *your* law ; but if he cannot be acquitted according to either law, then bring forward adroit pretexts and secure his acquittal. These are the words of the Rabbi Ishmael. Rabbi Akiva says, 'No false pretext should be brought forward, because, if found out, the name of God would be blasphemed ; but if there be no fear of that, then it may be adduced.' " — *Ib.*, fol. 113, col. 1.

" If one finds lost property in a locality where a majority are Israelites, he is bound to proclaim it ; but he is not bound to do so if the majority be Gentiles." — *Bava Metzia*, fol. 24, col. 1.

" Rabbi Shemuel says advantage may be taken of the mistakes of a Gentile. He once bought a gold plate as a copper of a Gentile for four zouzim, and then cheated him out of one zouz into the bargain. Rav Cahana purchased a hundred and twenty vessels of wine from a Gentile for a hundred zouzim, and swindled him in the payment out of one of the hundred, and that while the Gentile assured him that he confidently trusted to his honesty. Rava once went parts with a Gentile and bought a tree which was cut up into logs. This done, he bade his servant go and pick him out the largest logs, but to be sure to take no more than the proper number, because the Gentile knew how many there were. As Rav Aghi was walking abroad one day he saw some grapes growing in a roadside vineyard, and sent his servant to see whom they belonged to. ' If they belong to a Gentile,' he said, ' bring some here to me ; but if they belong to an Israelite, do not meddle with them.' The owner, who happened to be in the vineyard, overheard the Rabbi's order and called out, ' What ! is it lawful to rob a Gentile ? ' ' Oh, no,' said the Rabbi evasively ; ' a Gentile might sell, but an Israelite would not.' " — *Bava Kama*, fol. 113, col. 2.[1]

The principle which animates these passages appears in a milder form in the Hebrew Scriptures, which license perpetual bondage and the taking of interest in the case of a Gentile, not in that of a Hebrew. But such a principle, however mildly expressed, was too likely to be extended in practice. Dr. Edersheim, the author of "The Life and Times of Jesus the Messiah," is favourable enough on religious grounds to the Jews; but in describing their relations to the Gentiles, as regulated by the Talmud, he says:

[1] Hershon's *Miscellany*.

"To begin with, every Gentile child, so soon as born, was to be regarded as unclean. Those who actually worshipped mountains, hills, bushes, etc.—in short, gross idolaters—should be cut down with the sword. But as it was impossible to exterminate heathenism, Rabbinical legislation kept certain definite objects in view, which may be thus summarised: To prevent Jews from being inadvertently led into idolatry; to avoid all participation in idolatry; not to do anything which might aid the heathen in their worship; and, beyond all this, not to give pleasure, or even help, to heathens. The latter involved a most dangerous principle, capable of almost indefinite application by fanaticism. Even the Mishna goes so far as to forbid aid to a mother in the hour of her need, or nourishment to her babe, in order not to bring up a child for idolatry! But this is not all. Heathens were, indeed, not to be precipitated into danger, but yet not to be delivered from it. Indeed, an isolated teacher ventures even upon this statement: 'The best among the Gentiles, kill; the best among serpents, crush its head.' Even more terrible was the fanaticism which directed that heretics, traitors, and those who had left the Jewish faith should be thrown into actual danger, and, if they were in such, all means for their escape removed. No intercourse of any kind was to be had with such,—not even to invoke their medical aid in case of danger to life, since it was deemed that he who had to do with heretics was in imminent peril of becoming one himself, and that, if a heretic returned to the true faith, he should die at once,—partly, probably, to expiate his guilt, and partly from fear of relapse."[1]

Not less significant are the Talmudic expressions of tribal pride and contempt of common humanity. "All Israelites are princes." "All Israelites are holy." "Happy are ye, O Israel, for every one of you, from the least even to the greatest, is a great philosopher." "As it is impossible for the world to be without air, so also is it impossible for the world to be without Israel." "One empire cometh and another passeth away, but Israel abideth for ever." "The world was created only for Israel: none are called the children of God but Israel; none are beloved before God but Israel." "Ten measures of wisdom came down to the world. The land of Israel received nine, the rest of the world but one only."

Critics of Judaism are accused of bigotry of race, as well as of bigotry of religion. The accusation comes strangely from

---

[1] Vol. I., pp. 90, 91.

those who style themselves the Chosen People, make race a religion, and treat all races except their own as Gentiles and unclean.

The notion that the Jews are to be maltreated because their ancestors by the hand of Pilate crucified Christ, has long been discarded and derided by all enlightened Christians. But equally baseless is the notion that Christianity owes homage to Judaism, has any particular interest in it, or any particular duty concerning it. To Talmudic Judaism, at all events, it owes nothing. Whether in its origin it owed anything to the liberal school of Hillel, we cannot tell. The Talmud is a vast repertory of legalism, formalism, ceremonialism, and casuistry. Nothing can be more opposed to the spontaneity of conscience, trust in principle, and preference of the spirit to the letter characteristic of the Gospel, in which even the Ten Commandments are superseded by the Two. The pervading intention of the Talmud is, by multiplying ceremonial barriers, to keep the Chosen People separate from the Gentiles among whom they lived, in other words, to perpetuate the tribe. Christianity is a religion of humanity. Baptism is a rite of initiation into a universal brotherhood. Circumcision, the Jewish circumcision at all events, is the mark of enrolment in an exclusive tribe. The fundamental antagonism of Judaism to Christianity was shown, not only in the murder of Christ, but in the bitter persecution of his followers. Christianity had its antecedents, but it begins with Christ: it has no relation to Talmudic Judaism but those of reaction and secession.

We have given up the fancy that the Jew is accursed. We must cease to believe that he is sacred. Israel was the favourite people of Jehovah, as every tribe was the favourite of its own god. The belief that the Father of all and the God of justice had a favourite race, made with it a covenant sealed with the barbarous rite of circumcision, pledged himself to promote its interest against those of other races, destroyed all the innocent first-born of Egypt to force Pharaoh to let it go, licensed its aggrandisement by conquest, stopped the sun in heaven to give it time to slaughter people whose lands it had invaded without a cause, and gratified its malignity by enjoining it when it took one of the cities which were given it for its inheritance to save alive nothing that breathed, ought now to be laid aside, with all its corollaries and consequences, including the passionate, and, to the Hebrew, somewhat offensive effort to convert this particular race to Christianity. We have been told from the pulpit that at the last day the world will be judged by a Jew, and a religious lady once suggested to a Jew who had been converted to Christianity that he should go on circumcising his sons. We shall have little right to complain of the tribal arrogance of the Jew so long as the Old Testament continues to be indiscriminately read in our churches and while we persist, by talking of a chosen people, in ascribing favouritism to the Almighty. The belief that "God has made of one blood all nations of men to dwell on the face of the earth," is the foundation of a religion of humanity, and Judaism is its practical denial.

Jesus called himself the Son of Man. He was a Galilean, that is, in high Jewish estimation, an inferior Jew, setting aside the "endless" or "profitless" genealogies which the writer of the First Epistle to Timothy classes with fables and bids us not to heed. Born into Judaism, he accepted it and "fulfilled" all its "righteousness," while he must have known, as his antagonists did, that his principles would subvert it. Because he did this, we have taken upon our understandings and hearts a belief in the divine authority of the Old Testament, that is, of the whole mass of Hebrew literature; we have bound ourselves to see inspiration, not only in its more elevated, spiritual, and moral parts, but in those which are not elevated, spiritual, or even moral. We torture our consciences into approval of the spoiling of the Egyptians by a fraud, the slaughter of the Canaanites, the slaying of Sisera, the hewing of Agag in pieces before the Lord, and David's legacy of vengeance; our intellects into the acceptance of the Book of Chronicles as authentic history, and of such miracles as the stopping of the sun, the conversion of Lot's wife into a pillar of salt, the speaking ass of Balaam, the destruction of the children who mocked Elisha by a bear, and the sojourn of Jonah in the belly of a whale. In church we read, with psalms of universal beauty, psalms of Oriental vindictiveness. We constrain ourselves to see divine meaning, not only in the sublime passages of Isaiah, but in the obscurest and most incoherent utterances of his brother prophets. We read theological mysteries into a love-song because it is a part of the sacred volume. Till this superstition is cast out we shall ill appreciate what is really divine in the Old Testament. Not in the darker side of the Puritan character alone are the evil effects of this idolatry to be traced.

There was much that was infinitely memorable, but recent criticism forbids us to believe that there was anything miraculous, in the history of Israel. Whatever may have been the local origin of the Jews, the race, we may be sure, was cast in the same primeval mould as the kindred races. The story of the Patriarchs and the Exodus being in all its parts —the primitive theophanies in the tents of Patriarchs, the supernatural birth of Isaac, the destruction of Sodom and Gomorrah, the transformation of Lot's wife, the wrestling of Jacob with Jehovah, the marvellous story of Joseph, the miraculous multiplication of the Israelites, the competition between the envoys of Jehovah and the Egyptian magicians, the plagues of Egypt, the drying up of the Red Sea, the forty years' wandering in the barren Sinaitic desert, the prodigies which there took place, the giants of Canaan, and the stopping of the sun—manifestly poetical, it would seem that the narrative as a whole must, in accordance with a well-known canon of criticism, be dismissed from history and relegated to another domain.[1] Of the exact process by which the finer

---

[1] It seems not unlikely from analogy that the story of the Exodus may be in part an explanation of the institution of the Passover and other Jewish rites and customs of which the origin was lost. The figures of Jewish captives on Egyptian monuments may be accounted for by Egyptian conquest. Nothing can be less satisfactory than Renan's attempt to rationalise the story of the Patriarchs and the Exodus.

spirits of Israel attained a tribal monotheism, which at last
verged on monotheism pure and simple, and carried with it
a high morality, while the grosser spirits were always hanker-
ing after the groves and images of their idolatry, no exact
account has been given us, though the prophets, as moral reformers, clearly played a great part in it.   But it involved no
miracle, since without miracle Socrates and Plato, Marcus
Aurelius and Epictetus could rise to the same level.   The
doctrine of the immortality of the soul was extraneous to
Judaism, and was rejected by one of its sects.   The tribal
idea of immortality is the perpetuation of the family in the
tribe.

   Nor is there anything miraculous, penal, or even mysterious, about Jewish dispersion or its commercial character.
The case of Israel is only one, though incomparably the most
sharply defined, as well as the most memorable, of a number
of cases of parasitism, to borrow that phrase from botany.
Other cases are those of the Armenians, the Parsees, the Greeks
of the dispersion, ancient and modern, and humblest of all,
the Gipsies, by the disappearance of whose wandering camp
with its swarthy brood from the country wayside, a feature
more dear than respectable has been taken from the landscape
of rural life in England.   The Italians, when their country
was in the hands of foreign powers, showed a tendency of the
same kind.   The dispersion of the Jews was anterior to the
destruction of Jerusalem, for Paul found Jewish settlements,
mercantile, no doubt, wherever he went.   It may have begun with the transplantation to Babylon, and have been extended by the transplantation to Egypt under the Ptolemies.
But its principal cause probably was the narrowness of the
Jewish territory, combined with the love of gain in the Jew.
The Hebrew was the near kinsman of the Phœnician, who by
the narrowness of his territory and his love of gain was likewise impelled to adventure; and Jewish parasitism is the counterpart, under another form, of that Phœnician colonisation
which, unlike the colonisation of the Greek, was strictly
mercantile in its aim.   The land of the Jew was not so mari-

time as that of the Phœnician, it had not such harbours, such store of timber for ship-building close to the water, or such sites for seaboard cities like Tyre and Sidon. Moreover when the Jewish character was being formed, the Philistine held the coast. Apparently, there was a religious party in Judea which wished to make the people simple and pious tillers of the soil, and from which emanated the ideal of that polity of husband-men with hereditary lots and a year of jubilee, ascribed by its framers to the great lawgiver of the race. But the trading instinct was too strong. In the stories of the patriarch who bought the birthright of his hungry brother, of the Jewish vizier who taught Pharaoh how to obtain the surrender of all the freeholds of his people by taking advantage of the famine, and of the Hebrews who spoiled the Egyptians by pretending to borrow jewels which they meant never to return, we see the gleamings of a character which was not likely to be content with the moderate gains of a small farming community.

Jewish parasitism, still to use the botanic metaphor, could not fail to be confirmed by the fall of Jerusalem, which deprived the dispersed nationality of its centre, though the holy city even in its desolation remained the Mecca of Judaism. Renan thinks that in the period which followed, Israel took up extraneous elements by conversion, so that the supposed purity of race is imaginary, and the identity of feature is only the imprint of a common dwelling-place and mode of life; in which case the rhapsodies of "Daniel Deronda" have little meaning. There is a passage in the Talmud which suggests that the putative descent of a Gentile from the ten lost tribes might legalise intermarriage with him.[1] But nationality was preserved by the Mosaic law, the Talmud, and circumcision, the last being probably the strongest bond of all. "That the Jews," says Spinoza, "have maintained themselves so long in spite of their disorganised or dispersed condition, is not at all to be wondered at when it is considered how they separated themselves from all other nationalities in such a way as to

---

[1] See *Yevamoth*, fol. 16, col. 2, quoted in Hershon's *Talmudic Miscellany*, p. 134.

bring upon themselves the hatred of all, and that, not only by external rites contrary to those of other nations, but also by the sign of circumcision, which they retain most religiously."

Any other race of strong vitality with the same bonds and barriers might have retained their nationality equally well. The Parsees, though a much weaker community in their origin, have retained their separate existence for eleven centuries. The Gipsies appear to have retained their separate existence for five centuries. There is therefore nothing miraculous about the wandering Jew, nor need we suppose that he is the special object either of the wrath or the favour of heaven.

Circumcision, deemed by Spinoza the bond of Judaism, is a practice which, if Jews are to be citizens, and citizens are to be patriots, owing the community not bare obedience but the allegiance of the heart, governments would seem entitled to restrain. It has nothing to do with religious opinion, nor, in repressing it, would religious liberty be infringed. It is a barbarous tribal rite, the object of which is to cut off the members of the tribe from the rest of mankind, and which performed on an infant dedicates him for life, without his own consent, to a social antagonism not less contrary to his proper relations with his fellow citizens than it is obsolete and senseless. That Jewish circumcision was really tribal, the account of its origin[1] seems to prove. That it has served the purpose of tribal isolation since the dispersion of the Jews is certain. Nor could a more effective badge or barrier have been devised.

Israel thenceforth definitely became what it has always remained, a tribe scattered yet united, sojourning in all communities, blending with none, and forming a nation within each nation. The natural tendency of a race without a country was not to agriculture but to such trades as the Jew has plied, especially the money trade. The insecurity and uncertainty of his residence would deter him from owning property which could not easily be removed. Habit became

---

[1] Exod. iv. 12.

ingrained and the attempts to form agricultural colonies of the Jews at the present day appear to be uniformly unsuccessful. Laurence Oliphant was interested in these experiments, feeling that "the great fault and weakness of the Jews was their inability for handiwork; and to train even a few into that and into a co-operative manner of life would be a great gain." [1] But the trading instinct seems to have been too inveterate even when Jews have been carried back to their own land. The Jew has thus worn everywhere the unpopular aspect of an intruder, who by his financial skill was absorbing the wealth of the community without adding to it. Not to produce but to make a market of everything has been his general tendency and forte. Among other things he has made a market of war. He bought Christian captives and spoils of the barbarian invaders of the Roman Empire. He bought up at forced sales the property of those who were departing for the Crusades. He has constantly followed in the wake of armies, making his profit out of the havoc and out of the recklessness of the soldier. General Grant found it necessary to banish Jews from his camp. On the field of Austerlitz Marshal Lannes bids one who accosts him to wait till he has stopped the depredations of the Jews.

That the Jew clings not only to his religion but to his nationality, and that the two are blended together, or rather are identical, can hardly be doubted when we find in a Jewish Catechism such a passage as this:

" *Q.* What other ordinances has God made to prevent our falling into sin ?

" *A.* Those which forbid our associating with bad men or intermarry-. ing with wicked and idolatrous nations.

    " ' Thou shalt not follow a multitude to do evil.' — Exod. xxiii. 2.

    " ' Neither shalt thou make marriage with them (the nations), thy daughter thou shalt not give to his son, nor his daughter shalt thou take unto thy son.' — Deut. vii. 3.

" *Q.* Is this latter command important ?

---

[1] *Memoirs of the Life of Laurence Oliphant*, Vol. II., p. 231. By Margaret Oliphant W. Oliphant.

"*A.* Yes, it is of the greatest moment, and the experience of the past has shown its importance.

"*Q.* In what manner?

"*A.* Whenever our people have intermarried with other nations, they have fallen into their idolatries.

> "'But they were mingled among the heathen and learned their works; and they served their idols which were a snare unto them.' — Ps. cvi. 34, 35.

"*Q.* Does the law lay much stress upon this precept?

"*A.* Yes, we are repeatedly enjoined to keep from admixture of race, and many of the laws relating to the soil are referable to this subject."

Again,—

"*Q.* Are we commanded still to keep ourselves distinct from other nations?

"*A.* Assuredly; we may love them as ourselves, help them in their need, and labour with them for the good of our fellow-creatures, but we must not intermarry with them, lest we should be led away from the Law." [1]

The Roman Catholic Church, it is true, discourages mixed marriages on religious grounds. But she does not teach her children that "assuredly they are a nation," and she does try to bring all mankind within her fold. If the Jews, as one of their chief Rabbis seems to intimate, are not a nation but a church, why do they not proselytise? How came it to be said of them, by one of their own race, that they no more desire to make converts than does the House of Lords? However, supposing religion to be the bond, it is the religion of Moses. Does not the religion of Moses separate the people of Jehovah from mankind? The Eastern Jew, the Russian or Polish Jew, and the orthodox Jew everywhere, it appears, still hold by the Talmud; Mr. Hershon, at least, says that "to the orthodox Jew the Talmud is like the encircling ocean, — inserts into and makes itself felt in every nook and corner of his existence, like an atmosphere encompasses the whole round of his being, penetrates into all centres of vitality, presses with incumbent weight upon every class irrespective of age or sex

---

[1] Jewish School Books — No. 1. *The Law of Moses, a Catechism of the Jewish Religion*, new edition, pp. 68, 69. By the Rev. A. P. Mendes.

or rank, is all-inspiring, all-including, and all-controlling, covers in the regard of the illuminated the whole field of life, and with its principles affects, or ought to affect, every thought and every action of every member of the Jewish state." The wealthy and enlightened Jew of London, Paris, or New York, perhaps, is no longer Talmudic; yet even he keeps himself much apart from the Gentiles, and if he remains a Jew at all he must observe the law of Moses, that is, a separatist law. Those who have studied the subject carefully say in fact that alike by the rich Jew of Bayswater and the Middle Class Jew of Highbury the safeguards of tribalism are kept as far as possible without actual offence to Gentile society. The "Polish" Jew, alike in Poland and in Whitechapel, is still strongly Talmudic. If the Jew keeps Christian servants in his house it is to do for him what he is not permitted to do for himself on the Sabbath.

That the Jews have, as a rule, observed the laws and performed their civic duties in the countries of their sojourn, no one will deny, and it was natural that they should not take more upon them than they could help of public imposts which to them were unsweetened by patriotism. In countries where military service is part of the duties of a citizen, as it is in Germany, they have not sought to evade it, and it is understood that they behaved well as soldiers in the German army, though they do not voluntarily enlist. Wealth has inclined them to conservatism, and the stories about their sinister activities in the French Revolution are fables, though Karl Marx and Lassalle were the founders of Socialism, and Judaism is believed to have contributed its quota to Nihilism in Russia. When a Jew plays revolutionist, we may generally expect to see him top the part. To top the part is natural when it is played in a spirit of exploitation. Some Jews have been noted as citizens for beneficence not confined to their own tribe. It is likely, too, that in lands where the Jew has been long established, the sentiment of home has grown strong enough to countervail that of tribal nationality in his breast, and to make removal very cruel. Still, he is a Jew dwelling among Gentiles. He is one of the Chosen People. He has a nationality apart, with Messianic hopes, more or less definite, of its own, and vague anticipations of future ascendancy. It seems impossible that any man should belong in heart to two nationalities and be a patriot of each. He may be a conforming and dutiful citizen of the community among which he dwells so long as there is no conflict of national interests. But when there is a conflict of national interests his attachment to his own nationality will prevail.

Mr. Oliphant, in his "Land of Gilead," dwells more than once on the great advantages which any European government might gain over its rivals by an alliance with the Jews.

"It is evident," he says, "that the policy which I proposed to the Turkish government [*i.e.* the restoration of Palestine] might be adopted with equal advantage by England or any other European Power. The nation that espoused the cause of the Jews and their restoration to Palestine, would be able to rely on their support in financial operations on the largest scale, upon the powerful influence which they wield in the press of many countries, and upon their political co-operation in those countries, which would of necessity tend to paralyse the diplomatic and even hostile action of Powers antagonistic to the one with which they were allied. Owing to the financial, political, and commercial importance to which the Jews have now attained, there is probably no one Power in Europe that would prove so valuable an ally to a nation likely to be engaged in a European war, as this wealthy, powerful, and cosmopolitan race."[1]

Perhaps the writer of these words hardly realised the state of things which they present to our minds. We see the governments of Europe bidding against each other for the favour and support of an anti-national money power, which would itself be morally unfettered by any allegiance, would be ever ready to betray and secretly paralyse for its own objects the governments under the protection of which its members were living, and of course would be always gaining strength and predominance at the expense of a divided and subservient world. The allusion to the influence wielded by the Jews

---

[1] *The Land of Gilead*, p. 503. By Laurence Oliphant.

in the European press has a particularly sinister sound. In the social as in the physical sphere new diseases are continually making their appearance. One of the new social diseases of the present day, and certainly not the least deadly, is the perversion of public opinion in the interest of private or sectional objects, by the clandestine manipulation of the press.

Such a relation as that in which Judaism has placed itself to the peoples of each country, forming everywhere a nation within the nation, cherishing the pride of a Chosen People, regarding those among whom it dwelt as Gentiles and unclean, shrinking from social intercourse with them, engrossing their wealth by financial skill, but not adding to it by labour, plying at the same time a trade which, however legitimate, is always unpopular and makes many victims, could not possibly fail to lead, as it has led, to mutual hatred and the troubles which ensue. Certain as may be the gradual prevalence of good over evil, it is a futile optimism which denies that there have been calamities in history. One of them has been the dispersion of the Jews. As was said before, it is incredible that all the nations should have mistaken a power of good for a power of evil, or have been unanimous in ingratitude to a power of good. None of them want to hurt the Jew or to interfere with his religious belief; what they all want is that if possible he should go to his own land. As it is, western Europe and the western hemisphere are threatened with a fresh invasion on the largest scale by the departure of Jews from Russia. American politics are already beginning to feel the influence. A party, to catch the Jewish vote, puts into its platform a denunciation of Russia, the best friend of the American Republic in its day of trial.

That the Jew should be de-rabbinised and de-nationalised, in other words that he should renounce the Talmud, the tribal parts of the Mosaic law, and circumcision, is the remedy proposed by M. Leroy-Beaulieu, a writer by no means unfavourable to Israel. There seems to be no other way of putting an end to a conflict which is gradually enveloping all nations.

This being done, whatever gifts and graces may belong to the race of Moses, David, and Isaiah, of the writers of the Book of Job and of the Psalms, of Judas Maccabæus and Hillel, will have free course and be glorified. If Israel has any message for humanity, as he seems to think, it will be heard. Jewish merit will no longer be viewed with jealousy and distrust as having a sinister confederation at its back; and no man need fear in the present age that in any highly civilised community he will suffer persecution or disparagement of any sort on account of his religion. But the present relation is untenable. The Jew will have either to return to Jerusalem or to forget it, give his heart to the land of his birth and mingle with humanity.

THE IRISH QUESTION.

THE IRISH QUESTION.

It is proposed that Celtic and Catholic Ireland shall be made a separate nation with a Parliament of its own, and that into this nation Saxon and Protestant Ulster shall, against its will and in spite of its passionate appeals to the honour of the British people, be forced.

Why are the Celtic and Catholic districts of Ireland, any more than the Celtic and Methodist districts of Wales, to be severed from the United Kingdom and invested with a separate nationality? One reason, or rather one motive, operating in a certain quarter presents itself to view as often as from the gallery of the House of Commons we look down upon the group of Irish members, and mark what its demeanour indicates, or read the account of the disputes between its two sections over the control of the party fund. If the Home Rule Bill were passed, these men would, besides commanding a legislature and a government, enter into the control of a great revenue and into the possession of a patronage which, as at the outset everything would have to be given away at once, would be dazzling. A fanatical hatred which breaks forth whenever it is not restrained by policy, would be gratified at the same time.

But another separatist interest besides that of the squadron of Irish politicians is at work for the dismemberment of the United Kingdom. On the other side of St. George's Channel stands the Catholic Priesthood, ready as soon as Ireland is cast adrift by Great Britain to renew its reign. It stands with the Encyclical and Syllabus in its hand, to be executed wherever and whenever it has the power.

These two interests command by organisations, political or

sacerdotal, before which the peasant cowers, the people of the Celtic and Catholic districts. The voice which we hear, though it is called that of Ireland, is theirs.

There has never been an Irish nation. The savage tribes, perpetually waging intertribal war, in whose occupation Strongbow found the island, were not a nation. The Celtic tribes and the Anglo-Saxon Pale, waging perpetual war with each other, while the wars between the tribes themselves never ceased, were not a nation. The English or Scotch and Protestant colonies in Leinster and Ulster, encircled by the Celtic and Catholic tribes, with which internecine war was still carried on, were not a nation. The dominant race of Grattan's Parliament, and the subject race which was excluded from that Parliament and treated by it as a race of political and social serfs, were not a nation. Tyrconnel's Celtic and Catholic Parliament, with its sweeping proscription of all the Saxon and Protestants, was not even so much as Grattan's Parliament the Parliament of a nation. Nor would the Parnellite Parliament be the Parliament of a nation when it proceeded, as assuredly and almost avowedly it would, to legislate in the same spirit.

There are not within the range of the United Kingdom any other two districts between which so strong an antagonism prevails as prevails between Celtic Ireland and Ulster, of which it is proposed by Liberals and philosophers to compound with the bayonet this Irish nation.

The populations of the two islands are now intermixed. There is a large Saxon element in Ireland; there are masses of Celtic Irish in Great Britain, as the British artisan knows to his cost. The language of both islands is the same; Erse, at least, is on the verge of extinction, and Ireland has no literature but the English. She has no political institutions but those which she has derived from England. She has no history of her own except one of savage wars of race and religion. The Celts have no native dynasty or centre of political unity of any kind, unless it be their religious subjection to a foreign priest.

The Channel has been a great obstacle to union, but it is now bridged by steam. If an arm of the sea were always to be fatal to union, Corsica could not be united to France, Sardinia and Sicily to Italy, Majorca and Minorca to Spain, the Ionian Islands to Greece, Prince Edward Island to Canada. The central desert of America is a good deal broader than the Irish Channel, yet it does not prevent the union of Pacific with Atlantic States. Politicians like Lord Rosebery, who propose to unite the ends of the earth under an Imperial Federation, can hardly say that nature forbids the union of the two British islands under one government. The population of the two islands is not so large as that of France, nothing like so large as that of Germany, Russia, or the United States. Not Kent itself is more thoroughly incorporated with the United Kingdom than the North of Ireland. Not Kent itself in being torn from the United Kingdom would feel a greater pang.

The map shows at once that the destinies of the two islands are linked together. The two will, in all probability, either be united or be enemies, and if they are enemies, woe to the weaker. The smaller island is cut off from the continent by the larger and thus placed under its power. Economically, the two are complements of each other, Great Britain having the wheat land and the coal, while Ireland has the grass. When people wail over the decrease of population in Ireland, they forget the numbers of Irish who find bread in the manufacturing cities of Great Britain, and who, while Ireland remains in the United Kingdom, are as much in their own country as if they were at Cork.

Territorial rapacity is folly as well as wickedness. Let every nation be content with that which by nature it has. But a nation has a right to maintain its natural boundaries against secession as well as against invasion. This Americans, at all events, cannot deny. The doctrine of rebellion as a universal right and an object of unlimited sympathy could not survive the first shot of the Civil War. By the loss of the sister island, Great Britain would be reduced to a second-rate power; amidst a circle of military nations she would live in peril. Her citizens, at least, may be pardoned for thinking that her fall would be a misfortune not to herself alone, that her influence would be missed by the nations of her hemisphere, and that European progress would lose its moderating power. Italian Liberals are among the best of Liberals. How much sympathy have they shown with Irish secession?

Irish history is a piteous tale. But there is no sailing up the stream of time. We must deal with things as they are now, not immolate present policy to the evil memories of the past. Detestable is the art of the demagogue who rakes up those memories to obtain for his schemes from passion the support which reason and patriotism would not give. No living man is now responsible for anything done seven centuries or a single century ago. He who persists in accusing England of cruelty to Ireland, when the last three or four generations of Englishmen have been as much as possible the reverse of cruel, only gives way to his temper and darkens counsel.

Race character may not be congenital or indelible. But there is no disputing that its influence has been strong and in the case of the Celt is marked. Mommsen, in a well-known passage, ends a review of Celtic character, with its graces and weaknesses, by pronouncing the race politically worthless. He holds, and declares his judgment in language too frank to be graciously repeated, that the Celt politically is only material to be worked up by stronger races.[1] Mommsen has Bismarckian iron in his blood as he has the tramp of the German armies in his style. But Bishop Lightfoot has no Bismarckian iron in his blood. He says:

"The main features of the Gaulish character are traced with great distinctness by the Roman writers. Quickness of apprehension, promptitude in action, great impressibility, an eager craving after knowledge, — this is the brighter aspect of the Celtic character. Inconstant and quar-

[1] See his *History of Rome*, Bk. V., ch. vii.

relsome, treacherous in their dealings, incapable of sustained effort, easily disheartened by failure, — such they appear when viewed on their darker side. It is curious to note the same eager, inquisitive temper revealing itself under widely different circumstances, at opposite limits both of time and space, in their early barbarism in the West and their worn-out civilisation in the East. The great Roman captain relates how the Gauls would gather about any merchant or traveller who came in their way, detaining him even against his will, and eagerly pressing him for news. A late Greek rhetorician commends the Galatians as more keen and quicker of apprehension than the genuine Greeks, adding that the moment they catch sight of a philosopher they cling to the skirts of his cloak as the steel does to the magnet. It is chiefly, however, on the more forbidding features of their character that contemporary writers dwell. Fickleness is the term used to express their temperament. This instability of character was the great difficulty against which Cæsar had to contend in his dealings with the Gaul. He complains that they all, with scarcely an exception, are impelled by the desire of change. Nor did they show more constancy in the discharge of their religious than of their social obligations. The hearty zeal with which they embraced the Apostle's teaching, followed by their rapid apostasy, is only an instance out of many of the reckless facility with which they adopted and discarded one religious system after another. To St. Paul, who had had much bitter experience of hollow profession and fickle purposes, this extraordinary levity was yet a matter of unfeigned surprise. 'I marvel,' he says, 'that ye are changing so quickly.' He looked upon it as some strange fascination. 'Ye senseless Gauls, who did bewitch you?' The language in which Roman writers speak of the martial courage of the Gauls, impetuous at the first onset, but rapidly melting in the heat of the fray, well describes the short-lived prowess of these converts in the warfare of the Christian Church.

" Equally important in its relation to St. Paul's epistle is the type of religious worship which seems to have pervaded the Celtic nations. The Gauls are described as a superstitious people, given over to ritual observances. Nor is it, perhaps, a mere accident that the only Asiatic Gaul of whom history affords more than a passing glimpse, Deiotarus, the client of Cicero, in his extravagant devotion to augury, bears out the character ascribed to the parent race." [1]

In France the Celt underwent Roman and afterwards Frankish training. What he would have been without that training Brittany, amiable but thriftless, slatternly, priest-ridden, saint-

<hr>

[1] *The Epistles of St. Paul: Epistle to the Galatians*, Introduction I. 1, 2.

worshipping, legendary, is left to tell. We know how even the Celt who had undergone Roman and Frankish training behaved in the French Revolution. Nor is it likely that the strongest and most gifted part of the race would be that which in the primeval struggle for existence was thrust away to the remotest island of the West.

The mountains, bogs, rivers, and forests, for forests there then were, of Ireland, like the isolated glens of the Scotch Highlands, helped to perpetuate the tribal divisions with their clannish ways and sentiments, the mould in which the political character of the Irish was formed; for the Celtic Irishman is still not a constitutionalist but a clansman, with clannish attachments, clannish feuds, and clannish love of political spoils. Between the general influence of race and that of the local circumstances of the Irish Celt a character was formed which is as distinct as that of any individual man, and which it would be as absurd to overlook or to pretend not to see in dealing with the race as it would be to overlook or to pretend not to see personal character in dealing with a man. That the Irish Celt has gifts and graces, or that under a good master or commander he makes a good worker or soldier, nobody who knows anything of him denies. Nobody who knows how Irish emigrants have been assisted by their kinsmen in America will deny that the Irishman has strong domestic affections and a generous heart. But nobody who is not angling for his vote will affirm that in Cork, in Liverpool or Glasgow, in New York, or in the Australian colonies, or anywhere, he has as yet become a good citizen under free institutions. Nobody who is not angling for his vote will affirm that he is by nature law-abiding, or that when his passions are excited, whether his victims be his agrarian enemies in Ireland or the hapless negroes in New York, he is not capable of dreadful crimes. The Anglo-Saxon, when he takes to rioting, may be brutal; in the Lord George Gordon riots he was brutal enough; but he does not card or hough, nor does he cut off the udders of kine. The Phœnix Park murders were a Celtic, not an Anglo-Saxon, deed.

Lists are given of Irish statesmen and commanders, such as Canning, Castlereagh, Clare, Wellington, Wellesley, Grattan, Plunket, the two Lawrences, Napier, Roberts, and Wolseley. These are Saxon, not Celtic Irish. Even Parnell and Butt before him were of that intrusive race which it was the object of their movement to expel. Of Parnell, Mr. T. P. O'Connor tells us that his manner was Saxon in its reserve and his speech was still more Saxon in its rigidity. Parnell probably owed largely to the cool tenacity of his Saxon character his despotic ascendancy over his train. There has been no Celtic leader of eminence except O'Connell, who was an agitator, not a statesman. Burke had in him a Celtic strain which showed itself in his more declamatory and passionate moods. That the Celt is politically weak, ten centuries of wail without achievement are surely proof enough.

In the North of Ireland are prosperous industry and commerce with Protestant liberty of conscience. In the South are unthrift and poverty under the dominion of the priest. The political institutions and the relation to Great Britain are exactly the same in both cases; it seems to follow that the character of the people is not.

When, beckoned by tribal revenge, the Norman Strongbow landed in Ireland, he found there no germ of national unity beyond the transient ascendancy of powerful chiefs, nor, except in the little Danish settlements of the sea-board, any elements of civilisation, unless we so designate a taste for ornament, of which the monuments are in the Celtic Museum at Dublin. Everywhere were tribal divisions and intertribal wars. The brief reign of the powerful chief, or King, as he is styled, Brian Boru, had served only to show by its result the prevalence of the centrifugal force. The Brehon Law was common to the tribes, but it was a mere repertory of tribal customs, real or imaginary; the jurisdiction of its courts went not beyond the assessment of damages or the imposition of fines; nor was there any authority to enforce it, saving habit and a precarious opinion. There was hardly any agriculture; cattle were the only wealth. There were no cities ; the Irish indeed have not founded cities either in their own land or in America, though as labourers they have helped to build many. The Church, a surviving remnant, like that in Wales, of the Church of the British Celts before Augustine, ruder than that of Rome, but not more Protestant, had for a moment marvellously shone in missionary enterprise, and, if Irish traditions are true, in pursuit of learning. But without cities it could not be opulent or imposing. It seems to have suffered severely at the hands of the Danes. It was presently crushed under the hoofs of tribal barbarism and rapacity, and stretched out its hands to Canterbury for aid. Its chief monuments are those romantic Round Towers, its refuges probably in time of raids. The chief, whose revenge had called in Strongbow, plucked after the battle from a heap of heads that of his enemy, and mangled it with his teeth.

Alarmed at the progress of his vassal, Henry II. produced and proceeded to execute a Papal Decree, awarding him the lordship of Ireland under the Pope if he would reform the manners of the people, bring their Church under the dominion of Rome, and make the island pay Peter's pence. This warrant, a laughing-stock now, was deemed valid in those days. The Anglo-Norman conquest of Ireland, falsely called the English conquest, was thus a supplement to the conquest of England by a Norman who bore the signet ring of Rome and came to subdue the national Church of England for the Papacy as well as the Kingdom for himself. The Synod of Cashel at which the Irish Church became the vassal of Rome was the counterpart of the Synod of Winchester at which the English Church bowed her neck to the same yoke. Henry received the submission of the chiefs, and though at his departure they returned to their wilds, they had become his liegemen, and he and his successors might thenceforth deem themselves lawful lords of Ireland.

Unhappily, neither Henry II. nor his successors for three centuries made good their lordship. The Norman conquest of England by a great army, with the King at its head, was complete. It gave birth over the whole country to a new order of things and to an aristocracy which presently became national, and at length the champion and trustee of national liberty. But in Ireland once only after Henry II., in the person of Richard II., did the king with the power of the kingdom for a moment appear on the scene. The centre of the English power was distant, the natural route lay through Welsh mountains, with a wild population long unsubdued or half subdued, while the arm of the sea was broad in the days before steam. A chimerical ambition diverted the power of the monarchy from its proper work of consolidating the island realm to what seemed brighter and richer fields of enterprise in France. Ireland was left to private adventure, which, from its weakness, its want of unity, the difficulties of a country ill suited for the action of men-at-arms or archers, and the mobility of the pastoral tribes, totally failed. There resulted an Anglo-Norman Pale, with Dublin and the grave of Strongbow for its centre, carrying on incessant war with the tribes, which continued to war with each other and to lift each others' cattle at the same time. Some of the Anglo-Norman Barons, finding tribal even more lawless than feudal anarchy, doffed the hauberk, donned the saffron mantle of Irish tribalism, and became chiefs of bastard Septs. The Crown, by enactments which sound like an inhuman perpetuation of the estrangement between the races, strove to prevent this lapse of the Englishry into barbarism, but strove in vain.

Without a king, the feudal system, introduced into Ireland, lacked its regulative and controlling power. The grantees of great fiefs were counts palatine without a suzerain. When, by the degeneration of the Anglo-Norman lords, the chief was blended with the feudal baron, the result seems to have been a mixture of the evils of both systems. The earl-chieftain became the leader of a band of lawless and insolent mercenaries or gallowglass, who were quartered, under the name of Coyne and Livery and other titles of extortion, on the hapless people. The historic thread, if slight, is not invisible which connects these Bosses with the Bosses of New York.

The very presence of royalty, as a power superior to all

these anarchies, did good. The sojourn of Lionel, Duke of Clarence, son of Edward III., produced a momentary reformation. "Because," says Sir John Davis, "the people of this land, both English and Irish, out of a natural pride, did ever love and desire to be governed by great persons." If British monarchs could only have seen this and done their duty!

Bad was only made worse when Ireland was invaded by Edward Bruce, brother of the Norman adventurer, who had won for himself the throne of Scotland. The campaign was like those of the Bruces and Wallace in their own lands, one of merciless destruction. The death blow was dealt to the ambition of Edward Bruce by the generalship of John de Bermingham, which turned the wavering scale in favour of British connection. But Bruce, though he was called in by the Irish chiefs, seems to have experienced the fickleness of Irish alliances. The Irish Annals of Clonmacnoise declare that he was slain "to the great joy and comfort of the whole Kingdom in general, for there was not a better deed, that redounded more to the good of the Kingdom since the creation of the world, and since the banishment of the Finè Fomores out of this land, done in Ireland, than the killing of Edward Bruce; for there reigned scarcity of victuals, breach of promises, ill performance of covenants, and the loss of men and women, throughout the whole Kingdom, for the space of three years and a half that he bore sway; insomuch that men did commonly eat one another, for want of sustenance, during his time." [1]

Nothing is more cruel or more hideous than a protracted struggle of semi-civilisation with savagery. A native was to the Englishman as a wolf, and the native skene spared no Englishman. Nothing could prosper. In the little English sea-board towns, petty commonwealths in themselves, there was order and some commerce. Galway preserves in her architecture and her legends the picturesque and romantic

[1] Quoted by A. G. Richey, LL.D., in his *Short History of the Irish People*, pp. 196, 197. Edited by R. R. Kane, LL.D.

traces of her trade with Spain. Elsewhere was nothing but turbulence and havoc. A Parliament there was in the Pale, but it was a scarecrow. Judges there were in the Pale, after the English model, but they had little power to uphold law. The Church was feeble, coarse, and almost worthless as an instrument of civilisation. What there was of it was rather monastic than parochial, the monastery being a fortalice, and, in a general reign of crime, probably drawing endowment from remorse. Only the Friars were zealous in preaching. The Church seems not to have acted as a united body, to have held no synods, and to have been intersected, like the people, by the race line. Ecclesiastics fought like laymen, and appear to have been as little revered. - A chieftain pleaded as an excuse for burning down a cathedral that he had thought the Archbishop was in it. In the Celtic districts the calendar of ecclesiastical crimes, or crimes against ecclesiastics, given by the Four Masters between 1500 and 1535, comprises Barry More, killed by his cousin, the Archdeacon of Cloyne, who was himself hanged by Thomas Barry ; Donald Kane, Abbot of Macosquin, hanged by Donald O'Kane, who was himself hanged ; John Burke, killed in the monastery of Jubberpatrick ; Donaghmoyne Church, set on fire by M'Mahon during mass ; Nicholas, parson of Devenish, wrongfully driven away by the laity ; Hugh Maguinness, Abbot of Newry, killed by the sons of Donald Maguinness ; the Prior of Gallen, murdered by Turlough Oge Macloughlin ; O'Quillan, murdered, and the Church of Dunboe burned, by O'Kane.[1]

While England was torn and her government paralysed by the War of the Roses, the Pale was reduced to a district comprising parts of four counties, and defended by a ditch. Had there been among the Celts any national unity or power of organisation, here was their chance of winning back their lands. But they were fighting among themselves just as fiercely as they fought with the Pale. As Richey says, patriotism did not exist ; there was no sentiment broader than

---

[1] Richey, p. 284.

that of the clan, nor was the rival clan less an object of enmity than the Englishry.

Soon the chance of the Celts was lost. Out of the wreck of the aristocracy in the civil war rose the powerful monarchy of the Tudors. In Ireland conquest resumed its march. Henry VII. brought the Irish Parliament under the control of the Privy Council by Poyning's Law. Henry VIII. crowned himself King of Ireland, instead of being only Lord under the Pope. The policy first tried was that of ruling Ireland through great native chiefs. This failing, dominion was advanced by arms. Could the full force of the monarchy have been thrown on Ireland, there would have been a merciful end of the struggle. But the greater part of that force was engaged upon the continent, first by the vanity of Henry VIII., or the schemes of his minister, and afterwards by the dire exigencies of the conflict with the Catholic powers. Here, as elsewhere, the unwise parsimony of Elizabeth starved the service. Instead of systematic subjugation, there were hostings or military raids, and the soldiers, being unpaid, lived by rapine. The conquest was very slow, and forms an exceptionally cruel page even in the cruel history of the conflict between the half-civilised and the savage. As the Red Indian is to the American frontiersman, so was the Irishman under the Tudors to the Englishman in Ireland. The gentle Spenser, in speaking of him, forgets the language of humanity. Spenser, like Raleigh, was one of a body of adventurers who took part in the conquest and were paid by sweeping confiscations of native land. Nothing can be more horrible or heartrending than the pictures of the state of the island and its people, drawn by the conquerors themselves.

That the Irish at this time were uncivilised is clear. Cuellar, a Spaniard, who had been thrown among them, says:

"The habit of those savages is to live like brutes in the mountains, which are very rugged in the part of Ireland where we were lost. They dwell in thatched cabins. The men are well made, with good features, and as active as deer. They eat but one meal and that late at night, oatcake and butter being their usual food. They drink sour milk because they have nothing else, for they use no water, though they have the best in the world. At feasts it is their custom to eat half-cooked meat without bread or salt. Their dress matches themselves — tight breeches and short, loose jackets of very coarse texture ; over all they wear blankets, and their hair comes over their eyes. They are great walkers, and stand much work, and by continually fighting they keep the Queen's English soldiers out of their country, which is nothing but bogs forty miles either way. Their great delight is robbing one another, so that no day passes without fighting ; for whenever the people of one hamlet know that those of another possess cattle or other goods, they immediately make a night attack and kill each other. When the English garrisons find out who has lifted the most cattle, they come down on them, and they have but to retire to the mountains with their wives and herds, having no houses or furniture to lose. They sleep on the ground upon rushes full of water and ice. Most of the women are very pretty but badly got up, for they wear but a shift and a mantle, and a great linen cloth on the head rolled over the brow. They are great workers and housewives in their way. These people call themselves Christians and say mass. They follow the rule of the Roman Church, but most of their churches, monasteries, and hermitages are dismantled by the English soldiers and by their local partisans, who are as bad as themselves. In short, there is no order nor justice in the country, and every one does that which is right in his own eyes. The savages are well affected to us Spaniards, because they realise that we are attacking the heretics and are their great enemies. If it was not for those natives who kept us as if belonging to themselves, not one of our people would have escaped. We owe them a good turn for that, though they were the first to rob and strip us when we were cast on shore, from whom and from the three ships which contained so many men of importance those savages reaped a rich harvest of money and jewels." [1]

The Lord Deputy Sidney wrote in 1567 of the people of Munster and Connaught:

" Surely, there was never people that lived in more misery than they do, nor as it should seem of worse minds, for matrimony among them is no more regarded in effect than conjunction between unreasonable beasts. Finally, I cannot find that they make any conscience of sin, and I doubt whether they christen their children or no ; for neither find I place where it should be done, nor any person able to instruct them in the rules of a

[1] Duro's *Armada Invencible*, Vol. II., pp. 358–360. Quoted by Mr. Richard Bagwell in his *Ireland under the Tudors*, Vol. III., pp. 185, 186.

Christian; or if they were taught, I see no grace in them to follow it; and when they die, I cannot see they make any account of the world to come."[1]

Sidney may have been an adverse witness, but he was a man of high character, and in describing that which was before his eyes we may believe that he spoke the truth.

The wars of the Irish chiefs among themselves did not cease and were hardly less cruel than that waged upon the natives by the invaders. "It is but fair," says the learned and impartial Richey, "to judge the Celtic tribes by their own historians, not by the reports of English statesmen concerning them. The Annals of the Four Masters are thoroughly imbued with the Irish spirit of this period. Although detailed as to the annals of the Ulster and Connaught clans, they pass by without notice many of the transactions of Leinster and Munster, and the events they record do not comprise the entire history of the period; yet the analysis of the annals from 1500 to 1534 gives the following results: Battles, plundering, etc., exclusive of those in which the English government was engaged, 116; Irish gentlemen of family killed in battle, 102; murdered, 168,—many of them with circumstances of great atrocity; and during this period, on the other hand, there is no allusion to the enactment of any law, the judicial decision of any controversy, the founding of any town monastery, or church; and all this is recorded by the annalist without the slightest expression of regret or astonishment, and as if such were the ordinary course of life in a Christian nation."[2]

Another and a terrible element of evil had now come in. To the enmity of race that of religion had been added. The history of Ireland must henceforth be read not by itself but in connection with the great European struggle between Catholicism and Protestantism, in which to its ruin the island was involved. England and the Pale had become Protestant, at least, had revolted from the Pope. This was enough to make

----

[1] Quoted by Mr. Bagwell, II., 113.
[2] Pp. 247, 248.

the native Irishman more Papal than before. Moreover, the form in which the new faith was presented to the Irish was most unhappy. Anglicanism, sober, decorous, and genteel, has never suited the hot and enthusiastic Celt. The dissolution of the monasteries bore hard on Ireland, where the Church was eminently monastic; so did iconoclasm, the images and relics being dear to the Irish heart. Disaffected Ireland presented itself to the Catholic powers as the point for a diversion against England. Spanish and Italian troops landed, and the tragedy of Smerwick, where a body of Italian troops was put to the sword after surrender by the Lord Deputy Grey, might be compared to the atrocities perpetrated by the Roman Catholic soldiery of Alva and Parma, or afterwards by that of Tilly. The alliance did not prevent the savage Irish from stripping and murdering the crews of the Armada cast upon their coast. But Catholic Ireland had become the feeble satellite of the Catholic powers, of whose acts she was deemed the accomplice, and another vial of wrath was thus poured out.

By the beginning of the reign of James I. the conquest had been completed after a fashion; the last great chief had been dispossessed; the last tribe had been broken up; Ireland had been carved into English shires; English institutions and English law, the land-law of England among the rest, ostensibly prevailed. James I. was weak, but he was cultured and he had Bacon at his ear. He tried to endow Ireland with English civilisation. He called a Parliament for all Ireland. When it met there was a division on the Speakership. While the majority was out, the minority seated its man in the chair. The majority, when it returned, seated its man in the other man's lap. Under James, however, was founded the Scotch colony in the north of Ireland, the beginning of Ulster, the hope of industry, commerce, and civilisation.

It seems pretty clear that for the people the change from the tribal to the manorial system in itself would have been a blessing. Whatever the fancy about clan brotherhood might be, the fact, according to the best authority, appears to have been that the humble clansman was more degraded, more trampled on, more plundered by the coshering chief, with his brigand tail of gallowglass, than ever was tenant or peasant under the lord of a manor. The owners and lenders of cattle, which constituted wealth and was the indispensable means of livelihood in a grass country, appear to have been not less tyrannical than are owners of land. The law might not be rational or suitable; but the people, at all events, were brought under the domain of law, with the hope that the code would become rational and be administered with justice. Unhappily, the lord of the manor was a stranger by race and by religion, while to the chief there had been an hereditary tie which had partly reconciled his clansmen to his oppression. The land, confiscated by James I. as the property of the rebel chiefs, was, in theory at least, the property not of the chief but of the tribe, though the chief being a local despot, this may have been a distinction rather than a difference. How deep the sense of the wrong thus done sank into the heart of the people, and how far the recollection has lived and helped to sustain agrarian war, are questions about which authorities are not agreed. The sequel proves clearly enough that the Celts bitterly resented the transfer of the land to the stranger.

Nothing can keep the peace between hostile races on the same soil but an authority superior to them both and wielded by an impartial hand. Strafford was born to rule, and his despotism in Ireland would have been beneficent had he not been under the necessity of providing a force to support absolutist and High Church reaction in England. This drove him into sweeping confiscations of land under form of law. At the same time, by the policy which made Ireland a lever of Stuart conspiracy against English liberty and religion, yet another vial of wrath was poured out.

By the quarrel between Charles and the Parliament an opportunity was once more given to the Celts. They embraced it by either murdering outright, or casting out to perish of destitution and nakedness all the Protestants on whom they could lay hands. Dublin narrowly escaped. To doubt that there was a massacre seems absurd, whether the massacre was premeditated or not, and however great the exaggerations may have been. Could Clarendon, with the best possible means of information and no tendency to magnify Puritan wrongs, have said that forty or fifty thousand Protestants had been killed if there had been no killing at all? There followed a general insurrection headed by ecclesiastics, with the Jesuit in the background, and a revolutionary government was formed at Kilkenny under the presidency of a Papal Envoy. The English force was not only small, but divided against itself, and might have been easily overcome. But the Celts showed their usual lack of the powers of organisation and self-government. The party whose chief aim was the recovery of the land quarrelled with the party whose chief aim was the restoration of the Church. No one worthy to command appeared. There ensued a murderous, aimless, and bootless civil war, in which fearful atrocities were committed on both sides, and quarter was given on neither. The Irish population of Island Magee, though not involved in the rebellion, was massacred, man, woman, and child, by the Scotch garrison of Carrickfergus. According to the Protestant historian, Borlase, Sir W. Cole's regiment performed the exploit of starving, of the vulgar sort whose goods were seized on by it, seven thousand. One redeeming incident alone there was. The evangelical virtues of the Protestant Bishop Bedell protected him and those who took refuge with him from the rage of the Catholics. He was made a prisoner, but was treated with kindness by his captors, and when he died the Irish army buried him with military honours, and joined over his grave in the prayer that the last of the English might rest in peace.

At last on the wings of victory came Cromwell, and with one terrible stroke made peace. The great man himself deplored the necessity, in which some of his worshippers now exult. Quarter in those ages was not given to a garrison which after summons had stood a storm. The Catholic and

Imperial armies put to the sword not only the garrison but the inhabitants of captured cities. The Irish Catholics had given no quarter. Rinuccini, the Papal Envoy, reports with exultation that after a victory no prisoners were taken; "every one," says the holy man, "slaughtered his adversary, and Sir Phelim O'Neill, who bore himself most bravely, when asked by the colonels for a list of his prisoners, swore that his regiment had not one, as he had ordered his men to kill them all without distinction."[1]

With the ruthlessness common to all parties in those days, Cromwell deported or sent into exile a good deal of the loose savagery which the civil war had left behind. That he meant to extirpate the Irish people is a fiction, but he did mean to extirpate Irish barbarism, and to plant law, order, and industry in its room. Confiscation of land there was on a terrible scale to satisfy the claims of the soldiers, who had been paid in land-scrip. But this struck the Catholic proprietors, who had played their game and lost, not the peasantry, who, if they chose to work, would probably be under better, certainly under thriftier, masters. Cromwell proclaimed to the Catholics liberty of private conscience. The Mass in those days he could not have tolerated if he would, and when we consider what the Mass is, what it has done, and how soon the common people would have been weaned from it, we may be rather disposed to wink at this departure from religious liberty. The Protector treated Ireland as "a clean paper," to use his own expression, for the introduction of legal reforms for which the professional "sons of Zeruiah" were too strong in England. But the greatest of all the benefits conferred by him alike on Ireland and Great Britain was the Union, which he was able to accomplish without buying anybody, by simple exercise of a might which in this case assuredly was right. It is almost heartrending to think that the Irish Question was settled in the right way nearly two centuries and a half ago.

Of the acts of the Restoration the worst was the dissolution

---

[1] *The Embassy in Ireland*, p. 175, Annie Hutton's translation.

of the Union. Protestant proprietary in Ireland had interest enough partly to hold its ground. But the strong arm of beneficent and civilising power was gone, and the hapless country and its people were left to their own courses again. Another consequence of the Restoration, big with evil, was the re-establishment of the Anglican State Church in Ireland.

James II. renewed the attempt of his father against English liberty and religion, and in a form more dangerous and hateful than that in which it had been made by his father, a form which threatened with extinction the political and spiritual life of the nation. Once more Ireland had the misfortune to be used as the lever of the Stuart policy. England saw with disgust and dismay regiments of Irish Papists moving along her highways. Ireland was put into the hands of Tyrconnel, who, though a reckless ruffian, was accepted as the leader of the Catholic Celts at that time. Under this man's auspices a Celtic and Catholic Parliament passed an Act of Attainder proscribing at one swoop, without regard to age or sex, the whole Protestant proprietary of Ireland. It is Tyrconnel's Parliament, a Celtic and Catholic Parliament, not Grattan's Parliament, a Parliament of Protestant gentry, which it is now proposed to revive.

Overwhelmingly outnumbered and driven to bay behind the mouldering walls of Derry, the stronger race showed in extremity a force which in extremity it may show again. The result, as all know, was the victory of that race and the miserable subjection of the Celt. The most warlike of the Celtic youth went, and for a century afterwards continued to go, as food for powder and at the same time as the soldiery of reactionary despotism, into the service of the Catholic kings. In that service Irish soldiers of fortune won distinction, though Brown and Wall are not Celtic names.

Then followed the era of the penal code, cruel and hateful. Mark, however, that the penal code was not intended, like the religious codes of Roman Catholic countries and the Inquisition, to rack conscience and compel apostasy, but to keep the Celts disarmed, socially and politically as well as physically, and prevent them from repeating, as, if the power had reverted to their hands, they would have repeated, the acts of Tyrconnel's Parliament. Remember too what was being done in countries where Roman Catholicism reigned. Remember how in every Roman Catholic kingdom Protestantism was treated as treason; how Louis XIV. was banishing the Huguenots, butchering them, sending their ministers to the galleys; how the *autos da fé* were going on in Spain; how the Jesuit was still busy everywhere with his conspiracy for the extirpation of Protestantism by the Catholic sword. Forty years after this the Roman Catholic Prince Bishop of Salzburg expelled the whole Protestant population from his dominions. Irish history in these times, to be fairly read, must be read, not by itself, but in connection with that of the great conflict between Protestantism and Roman Catholicism over all Europe. Not a few of the exiled Huguenots settled in Ireland, ocular warnings of the fate which the Protestants might expect if their enemy were unchained. When danger passed away and cruel fear subsided, the penal code was practically relaxed, the growing spirit of religious indifference and free-thinking embodied in Chesterfield's Lord-Lieutenancy helping the process, and before the *autos da fé* had come to an end the Roman Catholics in Ireland, though politically unenfranchised, as a Church had become practically free; free, at least, so far as a Church could be while another Church, and that of the minority, was established by the State.

To the High Church bishops of the Anglican establishment, the Roman Catholics were less the objects of persecuting antipathy than the Presbyterians in the north of Ireland, in whom lay the hope of industry, commerce, and civilisation for the rest of the island. Of these, the bishops succeeded in harrying many out of the country, and sending them to fight, with hearts full of the bitterness of wrong, against Great. Britain in the American Colonies. The Anglican Church itself did nothing, and could do nothing, either for religion or for civilisation. Its system was fatally unsuited to the people. It never made converts, where thorough-going and fervent Protestantism, if it had only had a free course, might have made many. In Francis Newman's "Phases of Faith," there is a remarkable account of the impression which a Protestant preacher of that type did make. The Anglican Church showed all the worst marks of an establishment. Not only did it not advance or propagate; it sank into miserable lethargy, its churches were left unrepaired, sinecurism and pluralism abounded in it, half a dozen parishes were clubbed together to make an income for one man, to collect tithes was its chief care, and Irish parsons lived in English cities on pretence that there was no parsonage in their parishes, spending the money which the tithe-proctor wrung for them from a starving peasantry. In addition to the usual evils of establishment, the State Church of Ireland had those of a Church alien to the people; it had also those of a political garrison. Its heads were political intriguers, some of them, such as Stone, of the worst class. Swift could say that the British government appointed pious and learned men to the Irish bishoprics, but they were all waylaid on Hounslow Heath by highwaymen, who robbed them of their letters patent and stole into their sees.

In the early part of the eighteenth century Ireland desired union. Union was withheld. The refusal was, saving the dissolution of Cromwell's united Commonwealth, the most calamitous blunder that British statesmanship ever made. If the sons could ever deserve to suffer for the sins of the fathers, the England of our generation would deserve to suffer for this misdeed. Commercial jealousy was, in all probability, the main cause. Commerce has served civilisation well; but there is also a heavy account against her for inhuman cupidity, monopoly, and commercial war. But in Ireland's expression of desire for union the voice of her true interest had been heard.

Instead of union, to Poyning's Law, subjecting the legislation of the Irish Parliament to the control of the Privy Council, was added the Act of George I., declaring that the British

Parliament had power to legislate for Ireland. Thus Ireland was placed in the position of a dependency with a vassal Parliament; that arrangement manifestly pregnant with jealousy, discord, and revolt, to which, after decisive experience of its results, the sagacity of British statesmen now desires to return. The fetters imposed on Irish trade, particularly on the trade in wool, the Irish staple, for the supposed benefit of the English trader, bespoke the evil spirit which was universal in those days, and were counterparts of those which were laid on the trade of the American Colonies, and, fully as much as any stamp or tea tax, were the cause of the American revolt. Their iniquitous pressure, together with the friction inevitably caused by the political arrangement, the abuses of the Irish pension list, and the aspirations excited by the possession of a Parliament, gave birth, among the dominant race at least, to a sort of bastard nationality, which began to assume the form of a struggle for independence. A bastard nationality only it was, since the mass of the people remained political and social serfs. Molyneux sounded the first note in a treatise on the power of the British Parliament to bind Ireland. Swift, though he hated and despised the country to which his character had banished him, out of mere revenge and mischief, played, and of course played venomously, a patriot's part.

The manorial system has not a little to say for itself, both economically and socially, so long as the landlord pays for improvements, does his duty, resides on the estate, and maintains kindly relations with his people. But of the Irish landlords many were absentees, rack-renting their tenants through merciless middlemen. Those who were resident were commonly aliens in religion, and as a class improvident and worthless, though some of them, especially those of old families, were popular with the peasantry, not the less on account of the reckless profusion which often brought them to ruin. More oppressive and insolent than the great landlord was the squireen. The landlord rack-rented and yet did not provide improvements. Hence agrarian conspiracy under the name of Whiteboyism, and outrage which assumed forms, only too familiar to the cruelly excitable Celt, such as carding, houghing, and mutilation not only of men but of cattle. It was, in fact, a desperate social war for the land, in which on both sides ferocity reached an almost heroic pitch. A party of Whiteboys entered a house in which were a man, his wife, and their daughter, a little girl. The three were all together in the same room. The ruffians rushed into the room, dragged the man out of the house, and there proceeded to murder him. In the room where the woman and the girl remained, there was a closet with a hole in its door, through which a person placed inside could see into the room. The woman concealed the little girl in this closet, and said to her, "Now, child, they are murdering your father downstairs, and when they have murdered him, they will come up here and murder me. Take care that while they are doing it you look well at them, and mind you swear to them when you see them in the court. I will throw turf on the fire the last thing to give you light, and struggle hard that you may have time to take a good view." The little girl looked on through the hole in the closet door while her mother was being murdered. She marked the murderers well. She swore to them when she saw them in a court of justice; and they were convicted on her evidence.

The people multiplied heedlessly, their Church practically encouraging them, as it everywhere does, in improvidence. As the land generally would not well bear grain, even if the holdings had been large enough, the only food by which the swarms could be maintained was the potato, precarious from its liability to disease, as well as barbarous, to force which the soil was recklessly exhausted by burning. The results were peasants living on potato mixed with seaweed and a reign of misery which Swift grimly characterised by proposing in a horrible tract that babies should be used as food.

Praise and thanks are due to the Catholic priesthood for having been the comfort and the guide of the Irish peasant in his darkest hour. On the other hand, the influence of an anti-economical and obscurantist Church must be the same every-where, the same in Ireland as in Spain, Portugal, Southern Italy, Brittany, and the Valais. Had Ireland been left wholly in the hands of a Spanish or Calabrian priesthood, what would have been its state now? The history of Roman Catholic society affords us no reason for believing that the priest would have bearded the landlord in the interest of the peasant. It affords all possible reason for believing that he would have complacently shared the fruits of rack rent. This, at least, is what he did in Spain, in Italy, and in France down to the time of the Revolution. The history of Ireland as it has been is dark enough. What it might have been without British connection we cannot tell. That it would have been bright and happy, there is nothing either in the Irish horoscope at the time of the Norman conquest or in any subsequent manifestations to lead us to assume.

When Great Britain was worsted in the struggle with the American Colonies, and had France, Spain, and Holland, as well as the Colonists, at her throat, the Irish Protestant gen-try, who after all depended for their ascendancy and almost for their existence as an order on their connection with her, took advantage, without any false chivalry, of her distress to extort from her Parliamentary independence. This she was fain to concede; though, had she not been unnerved by faction as well as depressed by defeat, a few regiments of regular troops would probably have sufficed to quell the Vol-unteers. Grattan, in rhetorical ecstasy, on his knees adored the newly-risen nation in presence of a Parliament which traced its pedigree to the Parliament of the Pale, and was holding in social and political bondage three-fourths of the Irish people.

Left to themselves, the two Parliaments would have speedily flown asunder. They did, in fact, fly asunder on the question of the Regency, and a rupture of the Kingdom was averted only by the recovery of George III. Generally they were held together in uneasy wedlock by Castle patronage, including all the rich bishoprics and deaneries, and sheer corruption, together with a large number of nomination boroughs in the gift of the Crown. But there was a still stronger though latent bond. Grattan's Parliament of Protestant proprietors knew, amidst all its patriotic declamation against British tyranny, that with British connection its own life was bound up. Had it broken with England, Tyrconnel's Parliament would have taken its place. It never dared to grant Catholic Emancipation or Parliamentary reform. About its last measure was an Act of Indemnity for the illegal infliction of torture by the lash on suspected Catholics. It must always have remained what it was, a scion of the Parliament of the Pale. Eloquent speakers it had. Its corruption, its orgies, its duelling, are facts not less certain. The evidence of Sir Jonah Barrington is enough.

Pitt, strong in his great majority, and lifted above commercial prejudices by the teaching of Adam Smith, projected a liberal measure of commercial union for Ireland. He was baffled as much by Irish jealousy of anything that came from England as by British prejudice or faction. He designed for Ireland political reform, the abolition of corruption and abuses, and a measure of justice to the Catholics. As a harbinger of that policy, Fitzwilliam was sent to Ireland. But Fitzwilliam was headlong where he ought to have been most cautious, prematurely proclaimed his mission, and began to dismiss powerful friends of government. Pitt was at the head of a coalition ministry, of which one wing was strongly Tory. The consequence was a break-down of Pitt's liberal policy, and at a moment which unhappily proved to have been critical.

Then came the French Revolution, and called into activity the free-thinking republicanism which the intolerant bishops of the State Church had helped by their vexations to foster at Belfast. Disturbance, once set on foot among the dominant race, spread, as it had done in the time of Charles I., to the subject race, taking the usual form of agrarian conspiracy and outrage. The Catholics having risen, the Protestants turned on them as their immemorial enemies, and there ensued over certain districts a reign of terror carried on by the Protestant yeomanry, whose practices were flogging, pitch-capping, picketing, and half-hanging, as those of the Catholics were shooting, carding, and houghing. Of the Catholic priesthood a few favoured the insurrection, and one afterwards became the rebel general; but most of them shrank from anything connected with the French Revolution, and not on their order rests any of the responsibility of this civil war. At this time they were generally educated abroad, and identified with the Continental Church which the Revolution was threatening to destroy. Meantime Wolfe Tone, the only real leader whom the Celtic insurrection produced, a brave, gay, clever, and sincere, though light and rather tipsy, man of action, had won the ear of the French Revolutionary government and obtained from it a promise of assistance. In fulfilment of that promise came an armament commanded by Hoche, which was only prevented from landing by weather, and which had it landed must for a time have overrun Ireland, though it would presently have been cut off by the British fleet. Winds and waves saved the Kingdom. Napoleon, left supreme by Hoche's death, liked not the aspect of Irish insurrection and refused to repeat Hoche's attempt. "Ireland," he said to the Directory, "has made a diversion for you; what more do you want of it?" To the furies of civil war, however, those of invasion had been added. It is useless to recount the infernal history of 1798, the passions of which only the vilest demagogism would wish, for political purposes, to revive. Amidst that murderous chaos the one power of mercy, let the traducers of England take it as they will, was the regular army of Great Britain.[1]

[1] "The respect and veneration with which I heard the names of Hunter, Skeret, and Stewart . . . pronounced, and the high encomiums passed on the Scotch and English regiments, under whose protection the misguided partisans of rebellion were enabled to return in safety to their homes, convinces me that the salvation of the country was as much owing to the forbearance, humanity, and prudence of the regular troops as to their discipline and bravery. The moment the militia, yeomanry, and Orangemen were separated from the army, confidence was restored." — Wakefield's *Ireland*, II. 372. The answer made to this by those who begrudge

Grattan's Parliament and the system upon which it stood had sunk, with social order, in blood and flame. That Pitt had contemplated union before is most likely. Union now was evidently the only course. To take both races and religions under the broad ægis of the Imperial Parliament was the sole chance of ending a civil war of devils between them, and of saving the weaker race from the vengeance which would have been hailed upon it by the stronger. Best of all would it have been to follow the example of Cromwell: declare Ireland united to Great Britain, and call her representatives to the Imperial Parliament. On this Pitt did not venture. The alternative was to compound with a powerful oligarchy for the loss of its field of ambition and patronage. This was done, and it was dirty work, as Cornwallis bitterly complains. But it would not have been done by a man so upright and sensible as Cornwallis, had he not been profoundly convinced of the necessity and righteousness of the measure. That the Union was carried by bribery has been conclusively disproved by Dr. Dunbar Ingram,[1] whose treatises they only refuse to read who do not desire to know the truth. The money which has been mistaken for bribes was compensation for the loss of nomination boroughs given under the authority of Parliament in accordance with the notions of that day, and given without distinction to supporters and opponents of the Union. That the measure was not carried by British force is proved by Cornwallis's confidential statement that in July, 1799, when the political struggle was at its height, the force remaining in Ireland was sufficient to preserve peace, but totally incompetent to resist foreign invasion. In September,

honour to the British army is that Wakefield was not an official writer, and that he wrote fourteen years after the event; as though most historians were official, and a writer could not remember an important and impressive circumstance for fourteen years. The troops, of which Abercrombie spoke of as " only formidable to their friends," were not the regulars, but the militia. (See Cornwallis's Despatch, Sept. 25, 1798.)

[1] *Two Chapters of Irish History*, and *A History of the Legislative Union of Great Britain and Ireland.*

1798, he reckoned his effective force of British regulars at
four regiments, comprising in all eighteen hundred men, and
his total force of all kinds did not exceed forty-five thousand.
There was no rising of any importance against the Union even
in Dublin, which, as the capital, had most to lose.   The leaders
of the Catholics are alleged to have been decoyed by a
promise of Emancipation.   No pledge was given by Pitt; to
what extent expectations were held out it is difficult to decide.
But there was a motive for acquiescing in the measure, which
amidst recondite speculations and conjectures is too much
left out of sight.   All who had property to be plundered or
throats to be cut were likely to embrace the only visible mode
of escape from a sanguinary chaos.   That there was a concerted destruction by British statesmen of their papers relating to this period, to conceal their infamy, is an imagination
worthy of those who seem to think that there was no honour
or beneficence in British statesmen before their own day.[1]

Some of the leading opponents of the Union, such as Foster,
Ponsonby, and Parnell, ratified the act when it was done by
the acceptance of large sums as compensation.   Grattan sat
in the Imperial Parliament for an English nomination bor-
ough and there voted for a Coercion Bill.   Plunket likewise
sat in the Imperial Parliament.   He had said that he would
resist Union to the last gasp of his breath and the last drop of
his blood, that he would swear his children at the altar to
eternal resistance to it.   Afterwards as a member of the United
Parliament and the great advocate of Catholic Emancipation
there, he said: "As an Irishman I opposed that union; as an
Irishman I avow that I did so openly and boldly, nor am I now

[1] The sole basis for the statement appears to be a passage, misread by
the eyes of prejudice, in Ross's Preface to the Cornwallis Correspondence;
the existence of which correspondence is itself a confutation of the statement.   Ross uses "purposely," in contrast to the neglect by which he
says some of the papers have perished.   He does not hint at concert, and,
of the papers purposely destroyed, some were destroyed at a late date
and by persons not implicated in the transactions.   He says that all
facilities were given to his investigations both at the State Paper Office
and in Dublin Castle.

ashamed of what I then did. But though in my resistance to it I had been prepared to go the length of any man, I am now equally prepared to do all in my power to render it close and indissoluble. One of the apprehensions on which my opposition was founded, I am happy to say, has been disappointed by the event. I had been afraid that the interest of Ireland, on the abolition of her separate legislature, would come to be discussed in a hostile Parliament. But I can now state — and I wish when I speak that I could be heard by the whole of Ireland — that during the time that I have sat in the United Parliament, I have found every question that related to the interests or security of that country entertained with indulgence, and treated with the most deliberate regard." [1]

That the Union was politically unfair to Ireland cannot be pretended. She has always had her fair share of the representation. She has now twenty-two members more than she is entitled to have, and thus swells to thirty-four Mr. Gladstone's majority, which would rightly be only twelve. For some years under the reign of the Whigs, her members held the balance between the parties, and, as we have good reason to know, hold it now.

To all the offices, honours, and employments of the Empire, the native of Ireland has been admitted on a perfect equality with the other citizens of the United Kingdom. India has had two Irish Viceroys; natives of Ireland now command the British armies; the Indian Civil Service and the Indian offices at home are full of Irishmen.

If the Irish representation in the House of Commons has been weak in character and has been disgraced by a series of adventurers of the Sadleir type, this has not been due to any unfairness in the terms of union, nor is it now good reason for giving Ireland over to such hands. If Ireland may fairly complain that Parliament has sometimes neglected her needs to spend its time in faction fights, England, Wales, and Scot-

---

[1] *Plunket's Life*, II. 104. Quoted by T. Dunbar Ingram in his *History of the Legislative Union of Great Britain and Ireland*, pp. 93, 94.

land may do the same, and the remedy is the abolition of party government, not the erection of another House of party. If Parliament is overburdened with local matters, the remedy is, at all events, to throw off a part of the burden on local assemblies or authorities generally, not to repeal the union with Ireland. Ignorance of Ireland has been pleaded by Mr. Gladstone as an account of his change of mind, and he may extend the plea, it is believed, to Mr. Morley, his reputed partner in the authorship of his Bill. But Parliament, as a body, has not been uninformed; it has had a hundred Irish members to inform it. To say that British statesmen have not cared for Irish questions, that the Irish problem has not received their anxious, their painfully anxious, attention, is most unjust, as every one who has lived among them knows.

Pledged or unpledged, Pitt desired, and did his best to carry, Catholic Emancipation. That he was insincere and secretly counted on the King's resistance is a vile calumny, for which no shadow of proof has been produced. He was baffled by the intrigue of Wedderburn and the bishops. If he took time, it was only because he wished to get his Cabinet perfectly united on the question before he approached the King. He paid the debt of honour by resignation. He afterwards returned to power without insisting on Catholic Emancipation. But was he to leave the nation leaderless in extremity, or was he to depose the King? Pitt, acting in tremendous times, sometimes erred. The contrast between the brightness of the first half of his career and the cloud which overhung the second half is one of the saddest things in our history. But he was an upright English gentleman; he was a sincere lover of his country; he never left the path of honour, practised deceit, or uttered untruth. We could as easily imagine him traducing his country in a foreign press as giving a pledge to the Catholics and secretly relying on the King's bigotry for a release.

Catholic Emancipation, like all domestic reform and improvement, whether for Ireland or Great Britain, was delayed till the end of the mortal conflict with revolutionary France, and afterwards with the brigand empire to which she had given birth. Then it came with other liberal measures, though not in the best way, and when by postponement it had lost much of its grace. There followed another pause, after which came the disestablishment of the State Church. In respect of religious equality, Ireland is now in advance of the other two Kingdoms, verifying in this case Cromwell's saying that she offered a clean paper for the trial of reformers. Disestablishment might have come earlier if some of the Irish members in the House of Commons would have devoted their attention to justice for Ireland instead of devoting it to the Galway Packet Contract, as for more than one session they did. Whatever pledge had been given, whatever expectation had been held out to the Catholics at the time of the Union, was now virtually fulfilled. The compact, if compact the deed could be called which was written with the finger of necessity, was now perfectly made good, and the last stain of moral invalidity was removed.

Ireland also received from the Imperial Parliament a system of national education which the priests, saving a few Liberals, such as Moriarty, opposed, and which, if Home Rule were granted, the priests would to-morrow overturn. Nor can it be truly alleged that the Irish since the Union have been subject to social disparagement in the slightest degree, whatever discredit may have been brought upon them in former days by Irish heiress-hunters and adventurers. To say that they have been treated with more studied contumely than the negro in the United States is the very delirium of calumny. If men behave as Irish members behave in the House of Commons, they will draw odium on themselves and those who sent them there. Otherwise, the peculiarities of Irish character, like those of English or Scotch character, may have been objects of harmless jest, objects of hatred they have never been. There are no better mirrors of public sentiment than the public schools and the universities; let any one who has been at them say whether he ever knew an Irish youth insulted or ill-treated on account of his place of birth.

About thirty years ago the writer, during a summer spent in Ireland, enjoyed the intimate converse of some of the best Irish patriots and Liberals. These men were staunch Unionists, and would never hear of any paltering with that question. They saw the necessity of social and economical reforms, but the only political grievances, so far as the writer remembers, of which they complained in connection with the Union, were the expense and trouble of going to Westminster for private bill legislation and for appeals to the House of Lords. The first grievance might be removed by allowing Irish committees of the two Houses of Parliament for private bills to sit in the vacation at Dublin, and to report to Westminster. The second might be mitigated by the institution of a delegate court, though the unity of the Supreme Court could not be broken without breaking the unity of law. A capital grievance is now made of the Vice-Royalty, or Castle government, as it is styled, which is dubbed an Austrian Satrapy. The Vice-Royalty is, no doubt, a relic of dependence. In 1850, a bill for its abolition passed the House of Commons by an overwhelming majority, and was dropped in deference to protests from Ireland.

Whatever may have been the shortcomings of Parliament in legislating for Ireland between the Union and this outbreak, it may safely be said that the spirit of legislation has been just. The measures, so far as their intention has been fulfilled, have always made for justice. To treat Ireland with kindness and indemnify her for sufferings past, has been the general desire of the English people. Foreign statesmen, as impartial observers, have seen this. Guizot, though an admirer and student of English institutions, was not an Anglo-maniac, and as Prime Minister of France he had quarrelled more than once with British governments. It was about 1865, before the disestablishment of the Irish Church, that he was heard to say that the conduct of England towards Ireland for the last thirty years had been admirable. He was reminded that to do Ireland complete justice, disestablishment was still required. He assented, but at the same time emphatically repeated his encomium. This may be contrasted with the language of American-Irish conventions, which charge the British Parliament with organising famine in Ireland to destroy the people whom it has not been able to extirpate with the sword.

Coercion Bills, alas! there have been many, but they have been generally agrarian, not political. It cannot be said that for agrarian outrage they have not been needful. Government cannot abdicate its primary functions, nor can a country be left to savage and murderous lawlessness, though the law may require change. When for giving unpopular evidence a man and his family of seven were burned alive in their house, and outrages of this kind were protected by conspiracy; when a farmer for defending his house against nightly ruffians was shot at the chapel door in the presence of hundreds, who connived at the murder; strong measures could hardly be avoided if civilisation was to be saved. Most European governments would have declared martial law. That of Italy, which is liberal enough, represses agrarian conspiracy by armed force. The number of the Coercion Bills, though it sounds appalling, is really a proof of the constant effort to do without coercion and go back to the ordinary course of law.

Since the Union, not only has there been no civil war or serious conflict between the races and religions in Ireland, but there has been no political rebellion or revolutionary movement of the slightest force. O'Connell's repeal agitation took no hold, and at last degenerated into a protracted farce or an excuse for levying O'Connell's "rent" from the people. Smith O'Brien's insurrection, in 1848, though the air of Europe was charged with revolution, ended in ridicule and a cabbage garden. Other political conspiracies have flashed in the pan. This last, it seems, had its origin, not among Irish patriots, but among Irishmen of the Anglican Church, who resented disestablishment, so that it may be regarded as the last service rendered by a State Church to the State.

The commercial grievances which existed before the Union

have been wholly swept away. Great Britain has opened for Irish produce the best market in the world. She has given employment in her manufacturing cities to hundreds of thousands of Irish who would have starved on their own soil. Her capital would open up Irish resources if it were allowed, and were sure of receiving dividends in money, not in bullets.

Whatever appearance of strength political disaffection has shown has been derived from agrarian discontent. This is emphatically true of the present rebellion. It cannot be doubted that the agrarian question in Ireland called for legislative interposition. From causes already mentioned, the manorial system had there failed. Absenteeism was only part of the evil, and some of the estates of absentees were very well and liberally managed, though to the Irishman, of all men, nothing can make up for the absence of his social chief. The root of the mischief lay not so much in the system of tenure as in the swarming of the people, under a Church which practically discourages economy, over a soil unfit for grain, and on which they could be maintained only by the treacherous potato. Rents were raised to an excessive amount by the desperate bidding of the people against each other for the land which was their only means of subsistence. There would be distress from over-population in the Roman Catholic Province of Quebec as there is in Roman Catholic Ireland, were there not a ready outlet into the United States. Unless thrift could be given to the Irish peasant with security of tenure, he would soon be in the hands of the money-lender, who neither resides nor remits, and the more money-lenders were shot the higher interest would be. The Church, too, would probably lay her hands on a large part of that which the landlord had resigned. Those who write most sympathetically on Irish sorrow, if they write at all fairly, do not omit to mention the indisposition of the Irish peasant to steady labour; and the defect, whether inborn or produced by long discouragement, is now too probably ingrained and cannot fail to tell. Still, Irish tenure called for reform. Possibly, it may have been necessary to provide for the general abolition of the dual ownership. But this should have been done by the hand of deliberate caution and impartial justice, not by lawless violence, class passion, and the unscrupulous malignity of faction. As it is, faith in contracts, the foundation of commerce and almost of civilisation, has been seriously shaken in the process, and property has been made generally insecure. Purchasers under recent Acts of Parliament, such as the Encumbered Estates Act, purchasers from the State under the Disestablishment Act have been despoiled or marked for spoliation without compunction, or rather with insolent delight. The present Ministers saw what morality and the national honour required. They showed this by their first proposals on the subject, which recognised the claim of the landlords of Ireland to protection and indemnification. They appear to think that they can draw the line of "rapine" at Ireland; and the factory lords who vote with them seem to think that they can draw the line at property in land.

In 1847 the potato brought its periodical dearth on the most frightful scale. Great Britain, charged with organising famine to extirpate the Irish, did everything in her power for their relief. To let in food for Ireland, the fiscal system was suspended and the ports were thrown open, which O'Connell had said only an Irish Parliament would do. The present leader of the Irish party in the House of Commons has borne witness as a historian to the good-will and generosity shown on that occasion by the English people.

There was, nevertheless, a vast exodus to America and a proportionate increase of Irish influence, both on the domestic politics of the United States and on the relations between the United States and Great Britain. What Irish influence on American politics and on the affairs of American cities is, it is needless to say. The Irish immigrants, for two generations at least, do not become American citizens, but remain Irish, prosecuting their clan feud. They keep their national or rebel flag, and annually unfurl it in face of American nationality over the City Hall at New York. The name it probably was that drew them into the Democratic party.

Into that party, at all events, they went. They almost to a man supported slavery, notwithstanding the generous protests of O'Connell. At the time of the Civil War, rising at New York, they abused and butchered negroes, till the Americans brought up troops, and instead of passing Coercion Bills proceeded to quell murderous lawlessness by summary execution. It may safely be said that on that day twenty times as many Irish fell as have suffered for political offences since the Union. To proclaim indemnity for crime committed on political pretexts would be to put society at the mercy of any brigand who chose to say that his object in filling the country with blood and havoc was not plunder, but anarchy or usurpation. Irish influence upon the relation between the United States and Great Britain has given rise to acts of political subserviency and breaches of international comity on the part of American legislatures, presidents, and statesmen, of which patriotic Americans in private own themselves ashamed. British opponents of Irish domination are, in fact, labouring to redeem the politics of both nations from a noxious and humiliating yoke. American Fenianism has reinforced Irish Fenianism with rhetorical vitriol, and, what is of more consequence, with money, the large contributions of which, being at all events for a sentimental object, would be creditable to the race were it not pretty certain that they are to a great extent enforced. But here the danger from American Fenianism ends. To enlist the American people in their own clan feud and drive the Republic into war with Great Britain is the constant object of Irish efforts. But the Americans, whatever their politicians may deem it necessary to say, have no intention of being enlisted in any one's clan feud, and will never go to war in an Irish quarrel. Nor will they put up with Irish conspiracy beyond a certain point. A strong reaction was caused by the murder of Dr. Cronin.

To the sister island, also, there was increased exodus, and the dreadful Irish quarters of Liverpool and Glasgow became more crowded than before. Irish colonisation of Great Britain, while it practically helps to answer the charge of

British cruelty to Ireland, is a serious matter for England and Scotland in a political, a social, and an industrial point of view. "There are no Irishmen," says Mr. T. P. O'Connor, "more fierce or resolute in the national faith than the Irishmen who settle in England or Scotland." "They are far more extreme in their views," he adds, "than the majority of the Irish in America." He depicts them as a caste with a feeling of estrangement from those around them. In confirmation of his description, it may be said that not all of those who, at the time of the Phœnix Park murders, were going about in Irish quarters of British cities, saw reason to believe that, as Mr. O'Connor says, the blow struck in the Irish cause was regarded by the whole Irish race with unmixed sorrow. It is by the Irish vote in not a few cases that British constituencies have been turned in favour of Home Rule.

Such, in general outline, is the story. From what part of it would any reasonable and patriotic man draw the inference that it would be good for Great Britain and Ireland, or for either of them, to erect Celtic and Catholic Ireland into a separate nation? Whatever unity Ireland has, whatever she has of constitutional government, of free institutions, of civilisation, has come to her from her partner in the Union, though, owing to unhappy circumstances either of nature or of history, it has come to her in a cruel way. The past may be deplored; undone it cannot be; by an unwise policy its evils may be renewed. We see into what hands Ireland would pass. There in the House of Commons, turning the debate into a brawl, sits the Home Rule Parliament of Ireland. In Mr. T. P. O'Connor's lively sketch of the recent history of Irish parties, it is instructive to note the pervading assumption that the Irish politician who comes within reach of corruption will infallibly be corrupted. Mr. O'Connor describes to us the way in which, under O'Connell the "Liberator," the system was worked. "A profligate landlord, or an aspiring but briefless barrister, was elected for an Irish constituency as a follower of the popular leader of the day and as the mouthpiece of his principles. When he entered the House of Commons he soon gave it to be understood by the distributors of State patronage that he was open to a bargain. The time came when in the party divisions his vote was of consequence, and the bargain was then struck, the vote from him and the office from them." Under the auspices of the Repeal Association there was returned, Mr. T. P. O'Connor says, "instead of seventy independent and honest Irish representatives, a motley gang of as disreputable and needy adventurers as ever trafficked in the blood and tears of a nation." As it was in O'Connell's time so, according to the same authority, it continued to be afterwards. "Since the break-up of the Butt party, a number of his most prominent followers have accepted office, and the few that still retain places in the House of Commons have, with scarcely an exception, gone over to the Liberal party, and are notoriously as open to employment as the cabbies in Palace yard." Let him who accuses us of treating Irish politicians with disrespect see what estimate is formed of them by their own kin. The O'Shea case gave us a measure of the independence of Irish constituencies. What sort of security would there be against the appearance of a series of Sadleirs and Keoughs in a Parliament at Dublin? These battles of Parnellites and Anti-Parnellites over the money-bag of the agitation, do they not show us what is to be expected in the way of disinterestedness as well as of concord?

At first the priest will probably share the power and the spoil with the patriot. There is no use in saying that the Roman Catholic Church would not do what it is a necessity of its nature to do, what it tells you plainly in the Syllabus and Encyclical that it claims a right to do, and what it has everywhere done to the full extent of its power. It would begin by putting an end to the popular system of education which the United Parliament has established, or turning the common schools into organs of ecclesiasticism and their teaching into a preparation for the first communion, as it has done in Quebec. It would proceed formally or informally to establish itself, and in so doing it need fear no opposition from

Gladstonian Liberals like Mr. Morley, who are fain to palliate its tyrannical action in the elections and to uphold the sinister rule which enables the priest to oversee and dictate the illiterate vote. Mr. Morley's case is instructive because he bitterly denounced Mr. W. E. Forster for apostasy from sound Liberal principles in recognising religious schools. Small, to judge from all experience and from such an analogy as that of priestly rule in Quebec, would be the modicum of political freedom which the peasant would be allowed by his Church to enjoy when the last legal safeguard was withdrawn. In time, perhaps pretty soon, a rupture would come between the priest party and the revolutionary party, to which the more thorough-going Fenians both in Ireland and America belong, and which is affiliated to the revolutionary party in Europe. The torch of intestine discord would then be kindled once more. Between the two islands the relations could not fail to be hostile, when Ireland was a separate nation, owing her existence to successful rebellion, and setting out with bitter hatred in her soul. Let people who talk sentimentally about a union of hearts, instead of listening to the voice in Ireland, subdued to the tones of a sucking dove while the work of disunion is being done, listen to the genuine accents of Chicago, or let them look into the graphic pages of Mr. T. P. O'Connor, scan the portraits of the Parnellite leaders painted there, and draw their inference as to the direction which such men would give Irish sentiment and policy towards Great Britain when they had an Irish Parliament in their hands.

To a moral certainty, Ireland would become a thorn in the side of Great Britain. To sustain herself against her powerful neighbour, she would attach herself to some foreign enemy of England, as the tribes attached themselves to Spain in the sixteenth century, and as Scotland attached herself to France before the Union. This Great Britain could not and would not endure. Ireland would be reconquered and the circle of woe would revolve again.

The effect on Irish prosperity of a patriot and priestly

government is not hard to foretell. Capital would fly the island; employment would fall off. There would be another exodus, and the British artisan who votes and shouts for dismemberment would pay the penalty in an increased measure of the most depressing of all competition, unless he should insist on immigration laws, in which case misery would abound in Ireland. When this rebellion broke out Ireland was doing well, commerce was improving, the deposits in the savings banks had increased, and pauperism had been greatly diminished.

There is no reason for believing that the mass of the Irish people want a separate Parliament. Nobody who knew them well ever said that their aspirations were political. It is the land that they want, and they are Home Rulers only because they are told that a Home Rule Parliament would give them the land. It is probable that at this moment most of them would be glad to be under a strong and just government, enjoying their improved holdings in peace. They are wanting in political independence, and through the whole course of these events have been completely under the control of the terrorist organisations or the priests. If it could be said with regard to the Union that the compact was morally invalid because it had been carried by force, fully as much may it be said with regard to Home Rule that the compact would be morally invalid as having been passed under lawless coercion.

With respect to the case of Ulster, all that need be said more is that we shall only get what we deserve if the noble province, thrust by us in spite of her passionate appeals to our good faith out of the nationality to which she belongs, and forced to accept the yoke of all that she most abhors, instead of our best and firmest friend should become our bitterest enemy. Nor is this unlikely to be the result.

It is needless again to discuss Mr. Gladstone's Bill. It was torn to pieces by Lord Selborne in the Lords' debate, while the ministers in charge of it could reply only by vague assertions that in spite of probabilities all would turn out well, or with an insolent levity, which shows in what spirit, sure of their mechanical majority, they are dealing with the fundamental institutions of the country. The measure is a hopeless jumble of the National, Imperial, Federal, and Colonial systems. Nobody imagines that it could work or that it is in truth anything but a complicated mask for the surrender of Ireland to the rebellion. Mr. Redmond feels sure enough of the subserviency of the government, the life of which is practically in his hands, to proclaim openly that the measure is not final; in other words, that the end is to be complete independence, or, as Mr. Parnell said, "the severance of the last link which binds Ireland to Great Britain." Mr. Parnell said this when he chose to speak the truth, and if he afterwards disclaimed the statement, we know from his own lips what his disclaimer was worth.[1] On the morrow of Home Rule the Union Jack will be hauled down over Ireland, the rebel Green will take its place, and the last Lord-Lieutenant, if he is a Gladstonian, will humbly lend a hand on the occasion. "If any man attempts to haul down the American flag, shoot him on the spot;" so said the Unionist General Dix at the time of Secession. Americans remember the day.

Under the Parliamentary system, if there are two Parliaments, there are two nations. The Crown is called, ironically as it may be supposed, the golden link. A golden link with a vengeance it was in the days before the Union. But it has now no mass of patronage, no bribery fund, no nomination boroughs in Ireland. Had the government meant to preserve the Union, it would have welcomed, instead of repelling, as it did, amendments distinctly asserting the supremacy of the Imperial over the Irish Parliament. In order to make sure that the ostensible safeguards shall not be real, and at the same time to keep the British party of surrender in power, Ireland is, besides a Parliament of her own, to have a garrison of eighty Irish members in the Parliament of Great Britain. The affected indifference of the government about this part of

[1] See the evidence of Mr. Parnell before the Special Commission, May 3, 1889: *Report of the Proceedings before the Commissioners.* Reprinted from *The Times*, Vol. II., pp. 798, 799.

their measure only betrays the depth of the design. Was such a cup of shame ever put to the lips of a great nation? If England needs to be disciplined for her rejection of a political Messiah, this bill does it with a vengeance. Neither in America or elsewhere has she an enemy who does not watch its progress with delight. To have voted for it, if the nation ever recovers its sense and spirit, will be a brand. Notoriously of those who voted for it many spoke in private against it. They trusted to the Lords to throw it out. These same men will now court popularity by swelling the cry against the Lords. Then perhaps they will read homilies on the knavery of American politicians.

It is needless to discuss again the false, and for the most part absurd, analogies which have been adduced to lull the British people into dismemberment: that of Iceland, a petty community a thousand miles from Denmark; that of Canada, a colony three thousand miles off, and virtually independent; that of the Scandinavian Kingdoms, whose union is not home rule but federation, and is, moreover, going to pieces before our eyes; that of Germany, which again is a confederation tending probably towards a closer national unity; or the uneasy but co-equal wedlock of Austria and Hungary, which presents no point of real resemblance, historical, ethnological, or structural, to the measure proposed for Ireland. These analogies have not much figured in recent debates. Nor can anybody imagine that the position of States in a federation such as the States of the American Union or the Provinces of Canada, each with its own local government on the same footing and all sharing alike in the federal government, bears any resemblance to that of a vassal State such as Ireland would be made by the Home Rule Bill. The only real analogies are those of vassal Parliaments, and these all point distinctly the same way. Alike in Ireland before the Union, in the American Colonies, and in Canada, the institution of a vassal Parliament, by the aspirations which it excited and the friction which it induced, gave birth to a struggle for complete independence, which in the case of the

American Colonies ended with the Revolution, and in the case of Canada with a twofold rebellion. The Irish politicians who will be the leaders of the Parliament at Dublin, have all, according to an admiring chronicler, been distinguished by their burning hatred of British rule, as well as by what he would style the fervour, and others might style the venomous violence, of their patriotism. Is it likely that their hatred of British rule would become love or even toleration of British supremacy?

If there is any other analogy really in point, it is that of the Protestant minority under the rule of a Roman Catholic majority in the Province of Quebec, from which, controlled as the domination by the priesthood there is by the influence of a Protestant confederation, Ulster may learn what her doom under Home Rule would be, and how the Exchequer of a Catholic Parliament would be likely to deal with the strongbox of Belfast.

It is not Ulster or Protestantism alone that desires the preservation of the Union, but almost the entire wealth and intelligence of Ireland, whether Protestant or Catholic. American enemies of Great Britain, while they abet Mr. Gladstone's policy, admit that he has hardly a supporter among the classes in which, if education and responsibility are essential to political wisdom, the political wisdom of Ireland must reside.

To turn the United Kingdom into a confederation is possible if you will begin by restoring the divisions of the Heptarchy together with the contemporary divisions of Scotland, Wales, and Ireland. You will then have the material for a confederation, which is a large group of tolerably equal States. A federation of England, Scotland, Wales, and Ireland would be an everlasting cabal of the three lesser States against the greater. To the reconstruction of the United Kingdom on the federal system the only objection is that the nation, and still more certainly the Empire, would go to pieces in the process.

The Home Rule Bill was carried through the House of

Commons by the help of twenty-two Irish votes, to which, by the admission of the author of the Bill itself, Ireland had no title. It is now to be palmed upon the country, which is known to be adverse to it, by uniting with it a number of incendiary proposals, and carrying the whole lump by means of appeals to class passions, local antipathies, and the lure of socialistic confiscation. Civil war is a dreadful thing; but there are things even more dreadful than civil war. Submission to the dismemberment of the nation by the sinister machinations of a morally insane ambition, would in the end work more havoc than the civil sword. "I am prepared," said the constitutional and cautious Peel, "to make the declaration which was made, and nobly made, by my predecessor, Lord Althorp, that, deprecating as I do all war, but, above all, civil war, yet there is no alternative which I do not think preferable to the dismemberment of this Empire."

To that dread arbitrament, however, the Irish Question has not yet come. The first object of all British citizens ought to be to insist that this Bill, which is not an ordinary law, or a law at all, but a fundamental change of the national constitution, shall be fairly submitted as a single issue to the constituencies of the United Kingdom.

PROHIBITION IN CANADA AND THE UNITED STATES.

PROHIBITION IN CANADA AND THE UNITED STATES.

It is evident that English politics are beginning to be disturbed, like those of the United States and Canada, by the formation of a Prohibitionist party. The party usually calls itself that of Temperance. But though we may wish to be courteous, we cannot concede a name which not only begs the question at issue, but is a standing libel on those who take their glass of wine or beer without being in any rational sense of the term intemperate. Temperance is one thing, total abstinence is another, and coercion, at which these reformers aim, is a third. As Temperance implies self-restraint, there can be no Temperance, in the proper sense of the term, where there is coercion.

The "Temperance" people are not usually inclined to listen to anything so rationalistic as the lessons of experience. They tell you that with them it is a matter not of expediency but of principle; that their cause is the cause of Heaven; yours, if you are an opponent, that of the darker power; and they intimate, with more or less of gentleness and courtesy, what, if you persist in getting in Heaven's way, will be your deserved and inevitable doom. To those, however, who in practical matters regard the dictates of experience as principles, and who wish before committing themselves to a particular kind of legislation to know whether it is likely to do good or harm, the result of Canadian or American experiment may not be uninstructive.

In 1878 the Canadian Parliament passed the Canada Temperance Act, more commonly called the Scott Act. The purport of this Act may be described as county and city option. It enables any county or city adopting it by a simple majority of the electors to prohibit the sale of any liquor within the district for local consumption under penalty of a fine of fifty dollars for the first offence, a hundred for the second, and two months' imprisonment for the third. When adopted, the Act remains in force for three years, after which, upon a petition signed by one-fourth of the electors, it may again be submitted to the vote, and if there is a majority against it, repealed.

In the Province of Ontario there are forty-two counties and eleven cities. Twenty-eight counties and two cities adopted the Act, most of them in 1884 and 1885. In 1888 ten counties, nine of them at once, repealed it; and in the following year the remaining Scott Act counties and cities also returned to license law. The majorities for repeal were overwhelming. In Ontario the Scott Act is generally regarded as impossible of resuscitation, and the advocates of prohibitive legislation are turning their minds to other measures. This is a genuine verdict of the people. The liquor-trade had exhausted its power of opposition in the early part of the contest; in fact it hardly appeared in the field without doing mischief to its own cause.

The general result where the Act was tried appeared to have been the substitution of an unlicensed and unregulated for a licensed and regulated trade. The demand for drink remained the same, but it was supplied in illicit ways. It was found by those who were engaged in the campaign against the Scott Act that the lowest class of liquor-dealers were far from zealous in their opposition to prohibitive legislation. They foresaw that the result to them would be simply sale of liquor without the license fee. Drunkenness, instead of being diminished, appears to have increased. A memorial signed by three hundred citizens of Woodstock, including nearly all the principal men of business and professional men, but nobody connected with the liquor-trade, said: "The Scott Act in this town has not diminished but has increased drunkenness; it has almost wholly prevented the use of lager beer, which was becoming an article of common consumption; it has operated to discourage the use of light beverages, substituting therefor in a large measure ardent spirits, and it has led to the opening of many drinking-places which did not exist under the license law, and to the sale of liquor being continued till hours after midnight." "From my own observation," said a leading physician of the same place, "and the most trustworthy information privately and publicly received, I am satisfied that the most extensive illicit traffic prevails in Woodstock, that the abuse of intoxicating liquors is greatly on the increase here, and that there is a lamentable increase of drinking among the younger men of the community." At Milton, in the county of Halton, the effects were found to be the same as at Woodstock. Before the adoption of the Act there were but five places in which liquor was sold; after the adoption of the Act there were no fewer than sixteen, and owing to the persecution of the hotels the traffic was thrown into the lowest and worst hands. Forty-eight men of business, including the Mayor and Chief Constable, signed a declaration that the Act had signally failed to reduce intemperance; that the trade, instead of being in respectable hands, was in those of the bottle-hawkers and keepers of low dens; that the effect of the Act had been the substitution to a great extent of spirituous liquors for malt, wine, or cider as beverages; that drunkenness, lawlessness, and perjury were much more prevalent than they had been under license; and that the Scott Act instead of removing temptation from the young had had the contrary effect, and cases of juvenile drunkenness had become shockingly frequent. Scores of petitions were sent to Parliament from county councils or other municipal bodies declaring the failure of the Act.

Wine, beer, and cider may or may not be injurious, but at all events they are not so injurious as ardent spirits; they stimulate less to criminal violence, the evil against which in dealing with this subject, society is most concerned to guard. A natural tendency of Prohibition, however, as the evidence cited seems to show, is to substitute ardent spirits, which, containing a great amount of alcohol in a small bulk, are more easily smuggled, for the lighter drinks of which the bulk is greater. It is well that the attention of philanthropy, of practical philanthropy at least, should be specially called to this point. Not only does Prohibition appear practically to encourage the use of ardent spirits; the spirits which it encourages, being sold by the lowest dealers, are apt to be of the most pernicious kind; sometimes they are literally poison.

It is true that in some places where Prohibition prevails the liquor-shop no longer invites the passer-by with open doors. But the illicit liquor-seller is probably more active than the licensed publican in thrusting his temptation upon those who are most likely to yield to it, especially on the young. A clandestine drinker is sure to be a deep drinker. He is sure to drink, not with his meals, but in the specially pernicious form of drams. He is sure to drink in bad company. He is sure also to contract sneaking habits, and to lose respect for himself as well as respect for the law.

Witness after witness testifies to the prevalence of perjury in liquor-cases, and this evidence is supported by that of judges and magistrates in the United States and England. The people were morally dragooned by a powerful organisation and strong ecclesiastical influence into voting for the Act. The pulpit of the Methodist Church, which is very powerful in Canada and has thoroughly identified itself with Prohibition, thundered in favour of the measure, and the Methodist farmers obeyed. But no pulpit-thunder will make the people in their hearts believe that to drink or sell a glass of beer is really criminal, or support the execution of the law as if they did. Archdeacon Farrar himself, in his controversy with the late Baron Bramwell, repudiates as uncharitable and absurd the doctrine that there is anything morally wrong in the use of fermented liquor. He says that he has never preached abstinence as a matter of duty, even to confirmation classes or to national schools. He admits that moderate drinking is a perfectly lawful enjoyment, and that multitudes of men indulge in it who are wiser and better than he is himself. Agreeing at heart with this, the people, though they have voted as their preacher bade them, cannot bring themselves to take part in ruining a neighbour, sending him to gaol, and perhaps leaving his wife and children destitute, for that which in their conscience they do not regard as criminal. They refuse to back the ministers of the law. When forced to give evidence they prevaricate and too often commit what is morally perjury. The *Bruce Herald* declared that the Act in that county, though nominally in force, was "dead as Julius Cæsar," adding that the idea that the law would be sustained by reverence for authority soon vanished, and that prosecutions failed from the unwillingness of witnesses to give evidence against the hotel-keepers, who had public sympathy on their side, the people feeling that the Act sought to destroy a business and to confiscate property erected under the sanction of previous law. Have we not in the history of the poaching bred by tyrannical game-laws and the smuggling bred by excessive customs-duties, abundant proof of the danger of putting the moral sense of the people at variance with the law ? To break the law is always wrong, but it is also wrong to make laws which, as they are unsupported by any moral obligation, the people are sure to break.

The testimony borne by municipal councils in all parts of Ontario to the fact that there was an increase of drunkenness under the Act was not invalidated by the decrease, in some counties, of the number of arrests for that offence. Under the prohibitive system the liquor-seller, his trade being illicit, is afraid to call, as the licensed tavern-keeper does, for the intervention of the police. He does his best to conceal the drunkard whose detection would be the betrayal of his own breach of the law.

The Prohibitionists themselves hardly show confidence in their own moral code. They do not propose to punish a man for drinking a glass of ale, though the drinking and the selling being parts of the same transaction, both must be criminal or neither. The framers of the Scott Act did not even go so far as to make the manufacture of liquor a crime. They confined themselves to harassing the retail trade, as though, so long as the drink was made, it could fail to find its way through some channel to thirsty lips.

In the Province of Quebec the Scott Act has been adopted by five counties, of which two have repealed it. In the French province this question, like all other public questions, is apt to become one of race. In the Maritime Provinces the Act has been extensively adopted, and only in the cases of two cities or rather large towns and one county has the Act been repealed. But the organised public opposition, independent of the liquor-interest, which in Ontario arrested the progress of the Act and turned back the tide, has hitherto been wanting in the Maritime Provinces. The people of those Provinces, moreover, to judge from their behaviour in the political sphere, are peculiarly submissive to pressure of the sort which the Prohibitionist party and the clergy who support it bring to bear. But the Act, though not generally repealed, is described as practically a dead letter by provincial journals, which call for its repeal on that account.

The writer was in the North-West Territories, where the law imposed by the central government, under pressure of the Temperance vote, was Prohibition qualified by a power of giving permits vested in the Lieutenant-Governor. He was assured, on what appeared to be the best possible authority, that the law was a disastrous failure, that anybody could get liquor who wanted it, and that the only fruits of the system were smuggling, perjury, secret drinking, and deterioration of the liquor. The liquor is sure to be of the worst quality, because the dealer will thus indemnify himself for the risks of a contraband trade, while his own character and that of his drinking-place will inevitably be low. Attention is once more called to this feature of the question, and to the tendency of the system which makes the trade contraband to the displacement of the lighter drinks by ardent spirits which are easily smuggled.

In the Territories so bad were the effects of the prohibitory law that the Territorial Legislature recently passed a License Law, which went into effect in May, 1892. The evidence given before the Canadian Prohibition Commission later in that year was generally favourable to it compared with the prohibitory measure.   Amongst the witnesses were the chief officers of the North-West Mounted Police, judges, lawyers, and others, and there was conclusive testimony to the large amount of smuggling and to the manufacture of deleterious liquors.   One witness testified that thousands of shipments of liquor were made into the Territory in kegs or packages concealed in other goods, often in a car of bacon or a bag of rice, sugar, or nails.   Often, too, liquor came in bottles of preserves or pickles, or canned goods or temperance drinks.   Sometimes four hundred gallons of liquor at once were conveyed by teams hundreds of miles inland, and evaded the vigilance of the officers.   The supply of liquor was irregular; a consignment was often on its arrival surrounded by friends of the consignee, and the whole of it was quickly consumed.   This led to a great amount of drunkenness, and, in the dearth of liquor which followed, to the consumption of eau de Cologne, pain-killer, Florida water, essences of various kinds, and even red ink.   A favourite punch concocted in the Territories was pain-killer, Jamaica ginger, strong tea, sugar, and molasses.   These deleterious compounds, witnesses swore, produced a number of deaths.   Their effect, as well as that of some whiskeys imported into the Territories or illicitly manufactured there, was stated to be maddening. A judge said that of the only two cases, among forty or fifty criminal cases, due to the abuse of liquor, one, a case of murder, was clearly due to a poisonous compound manufactured by an illicit distiller whose only appliances were some lead pipe and some barley.   The compound was the fruit of Prohibition. This failure of Prohibition is notable, for though the country has a long frontier, the risks encountered in carrying liquor far into the interior were very great, the Mounted Police being numerous and vigilant, while the question had not, as in other cases, become involved with politics.

Besides contempt of the law and perjury the country has been filled with ill blood.   Nothing is more odious or poisons the heart of the community more than the employment of spies and informers, to which it has been necessary and will always be necessary for Prohibitionism to resort.   Dickens holds up the mirror to nature in his description of the Claypoles and their trade.   Men who have been imprisoned and ruined for plying a trade which they can hardly feel to be criminal, as only the other day they were holding licenses for it from the State, are naturally not grateful for such treatment.   Their vindictiveness and hatred of the spies has led to several outrages, and once or twice to the use of dynamite.

To force the sentiment of the people into accordance with the law is the more difficult, since all the time their Church is holding up for their imitation a model of character which is not "temperate" in the Prohibitionist sense of that term.   In commenting on the miracle at Cana, Archdeacon Farrar contrasts the "genial innocence of Christ's system" with the "crushing asceticism of rival systems."   By way of reconciling this discrepancy desperate efforts are made to uphold the astonishing theory that the *oinos* of the Gospel was not fermented wine but syrup.   The ruler of the feast at Cana, it seems, expressed his surprise that the best syrup had not been produced till the guests had well drunk; the accusers of Christ in calling Him a winebibber meant only that he was a syrupdrinker: it was on syrup that the Corinthians got drunk at the celebration of the Lord's Supper: Paul advised his friend to take a little syrup for his stomach's sake; and the same Apostle enjoined the Church in electing deacons not to choose those who were given to excess in syrup!   To such paltering with what every one educated enough to be a clergyman must know to be the truth, we rather prefer the preacher who said boldly that if Christ were again to come on earth and persisted in celebrating the Eucharist with wine, He would have to be excluded from His own Church.   To drag the Gospel into this discussion on the Prohibitionist side is hopeless.   There is no more of fanaticism than there is of formalism in that volume. When St. Paul bids us not drink wine if thereby our brother is made to stumble, he couples eating meat with drinking wine, showing that in his opinion both in themselves are innocent.

The Gospel bids us have regard to the weakness of our brother; but it does not bid our brother be weak or us to countenance his weakness by unjust and unwise legislation.

The effect even of less violent and hazardous measures of coercion in Canada appears to have been pretty much the same. The supporters of the Scott Act did not venture to put it to the vote in Toronto, but finding themselves powerful in the City Council, they proceeded to wage a war of extermination on the taverns. At one stroke they cut off seventy-five licenses. They were warned that this arbitrary measure, while it might ruin the tavern-keepers, would not diminish the demand for drink; that while there was a demand there would be a supply, and that the tavern-keepers whose licenses were withdrawn would not starve if they could help it, but would ply an illicit trade. The result was a large increase of the number of cases of drunkenness before the magistrate and an unusually drunken Christmas. Nor could the Prohibitionists find any way of parrying the natural inference better than an insinuation that drinking had been promoted by the powers of darkness for the special purpose of discrediting their policy.

It may be argued with some force that when the Scott Act was adopted by some counties and not by others the moral perceptions of the people in the counties that did adopt it would be disturbed by the vicinage of a different code. But even if the Prohibitionist code were imposed on a whole nation the difficulty, if diminished, would not be removed. To make an Eleventh Commandment you must obtain the concurrence of the civilised world, intercourse and communication between all the parts of which are now too active for a sectional morality. Put all Canada under Prohibition, and every Canadian who visits a foreign country will be apt to come back a heretic, and to propagate his heresy on his return. Literature, moreover, from Homer to Dickens is full of the other view.

The results of coercive legislation in the United States, wherever the experiment has been tried, seem to tally with those of coercive legislation in Canada. Maine is the "banner-

State" of Prohibition. It has been trying the system for over forty years, more than time enough to kill the liquor-traffic, if the liquor-traffic was to be killed. Yet of Maine, "Gail Hamilton," who must know it well, said in the *North American Review*: "The actual result is that liquor is sold to all who wish to obtain it in nearly every town in the State. Enforcement of the law seems to have little effect. For the past six years the city of Bangor has practically enjoyed free rum. In more than one hundred places liquor is sold and no attempt has been made to enforce the law. In Bath, Lewiston, Augusta, and other cities no real difficulty is experienced in procuring liquor. In Portland, enforcement of the law has been faithfully attempted, yet the liquor-traffic flourishes for all classes from the highest to the lowest. . . . In a journey last summer for hundreds of miles through the cities and through the scattered villages and hamlets of Maine, the almost universal testimony was 'you get liquor enough for bad purposes in bad places, but you cannot get it for good purposes in good places.'" "What works against Prohibition," the writer adds, "is that in the opinion of many of the most earnest total-abstinence men, the original Maine-Law State after thirty years of Prohibition is no more a Temperance State than it was before Prohibition was introduced." It appears that upwards of 1000 people in the State paid United States retail liquor-tax, though Archdeacon Farrar was informed that the trade had been completely driven out of sight. The Maine Prison Report for 1884 said: "Intoxication is on the increase; some new legislation must be made if it is to be lessened. In many of our counties Prohibition does not seem to affect or prevent it." In the city of Portland (population 34,000) in 1874 the arrests for drunkenness were 2318. But drunkenness was not confined to the cities. Every one of the sixteen counties furnished its quota. The number of committals for drunkenness for one year was 1316 for a population of 648,000, while in Canada, an area at that time not under the Scott Act, with a population of 661,000, and a town population as large as that in Maine, showed only 593 committals, less than half the number of those in the model State of Prohibition. General Neal Dow himself, upbraiding his former party for its slackness in the cause, complained of the number of low drinking-places infesting the cities of Maine. The New York *Sun* after investigation carried on through its correspondent, said: "The actual state of affairs in Maine is perfectly well understood by every Maine man with eyes in his head, and by every observant visitor to Maine. In no part of the world is the spectacle of drunken men reeling along the streets more common than in the cities and larger towns of Maine. Nowhere in the world is the average quality of the liquor sold so bad, and consequently so dangerous to the health of the consumer and the peace of the public. The facilities for obtaining liquor vary in different parts of the State, from the cities where fancy-drinks are openly compounded and sold over rosewood bars, to the places where it is dispensed by the swig from flat bottles carried around in the breeches pockets of perambulating dealers. But liquor, good or bad, can be bought anywhere." Perjury, the *Sun* correspondent also stated, as usual, was rife. The most recent evidence is to the same effect. In the cities of Maine, though the law has been forty-six times amended to sharpen its teeth, liquor, generally of a bad kind, is freely though clandestinely sold. "Pocket peddling" is rife and presses the temptation on the young. The city of Bangor has openly taken itself out of the law, and established a liquor system of its own. In Portland the city government sells liquor nominally for medicine, but really also as a beverage, and the agency is a scene of falsehood, jobbery, and corruption. The corruption of city officers is an almost inevitable and a serious consequence of the system. Some of those who have administered the law in Maine are among the strongest advocates of repeal and of a return to the license system. They tried to give effect to the law. They fine, they imprison, they perhaps ruin one set of liquor dealers, and the only result is that a worse set succeeds.

Nor has Maine fulfilled the golden promises held out by

Prohibition of immunity from crime and enhanced prosperity. Though the population of the State has been stationary, the statistics of crime have increased. In 1873 the number of committals to gaol was 1548; in 1884 it was 3672. The pauper rate of the cities was large compared with that in other States. More recent statistics seem not much to alter the case. All statistics of this kind may require qualification on account of changes in population or trade. But Prohibition at all events cannot be said to have put an end to crime or pauperism in Maine. If that State has advanced socially, or morally, or economically, it has not advanced farther than other States similar to it in general respects but without a prohibitive law. Prohibition has been the platform of one of the political parties; otherwise it seems not unlikely that there might have been a repeal of the law and a return to the license system. Entanglement of a social and moral question with the tactics and hypocrisy of a political party is an evil attendant of Prohibition. The integrity even of churches is in some peril. "The Methodists," said General Neal Dow, "are a very great body of religionists in this country, and always at their conventions they form very grand resolutions against the liquor traffic. There is hardly any language in the English tongue that they do not use against the liquor traffic. Nice men they are and educated men too, but after that they go directly round and vote for rum. The Presbyterians all do the same thing, and the Congregationalists will do the same. When I have occasion to speak to them I say, 'I would rather you would resolve against temperance and pray against temperance, and then vote against rum, rather than you would pray and resolve against intemperance and then go and vote for rum.'"

Vermont has also been trying Prohibition for more than forty years. Here the city population is comparatively small, so that the system has the fairest chance; while the legislature, under the pressure of the "Temperance vote," has piled one repressive enactment upon another, heaped up penalties, and at last given the police power to enter any house without a warrant. The result after thirty years was reported by Mr.

Edward Johnson in the *Popular Science Monthly* for May, 1884. He states that "for all practical purposes the law is an absolute dead letter." There were at the time of his writing in the State 446 places where liquor was sold, and though the population was well-nigh stationary there was a marked increase in their number. " A large proportion of the dram-shops are on the principal streets, and there is no concealment of the illegal traffic. Spasmodic attempts to enforce the law are made in the larger places, but are utterly futile. Of enforcing the law, as the laws against burglary and larceny are enforced, nobody dreams for a moment." "Such," says Mr. Johnson, "is the unsatisfactory result of Vermont's thirty years' experience of the Prohibitory liquor-laws." "One might," he adds, "go still further and speak of the perjury and subornation of perjury for which the law is in a sense responsible, of the disregard and contempt of all law which the operation of this law tends to foster and encourage, and of cognate matters which will occur to the reflective reader; but perhaps enough has been said in showing the failure of the law to accomplish the object for which it was enacted." No attempt, so far as we know, has been made to controvert Mr. Johnson's statements, or to refute the conclusion which he draws from them, and which is that men cannot be dragooned into virtue; that is, not by State interference with practices not in themselves criminal, but only by State interference with positive crime.

Massachusetts also for a series of years tried Prohibition. The result is embodied in the Report of a joint committee of both Houses of the Legislature (1867), which ought to be in the hands of all those who wish to be guided by experience in this matter. That Report, founded on the best evidence, states that the law, if by its operation it diminishes the number of open places of drinking, does so only to multiply the secret places, that more liquor and worse liquor was drunk, that drunkenness had increased almost in direct ratio to the closing of public places of sale, and that there was more of it in Boston than there had been at any previous time in the history of the city. "The mere fact," says the Report — in words to which we would call special attention — "the mere fact that the law seeks to prevent them from drinking rouses the determination to drink in many. The fact that the place is secret takes away the restraint which, in more public and respectable places, would keep them within temperate bounds. The fact that the business is contraband and liable to interruption, and that its gains are hazardous, tends to drive honest men from it and to leave it under the control of dishonest men, who will not scruple to poison the community with vile adulteration." In conclusion, the Report submits that so long as there is a demand for liquor there will be a supply, licensed or illicit, and recommends regulated freedom as the best policy.

In Iowa again Prohibition has been on its trial. A correspondent of *Harper's Weekly*, recommended as thoroughly trustworthy by a journal itself very careful of its statements, reported that Prohibition in the cities of Iowa meant free liquor. A correspondent of the New York *Nation* testified to much the same effect, adding that the local organ of Prohibition itself admitted the failure. Dr. Dio Lewis, the Cato of dietists, said that he had touched at several of the large cities on a tour to the Rocky Mountains, and among other things had inquired into the practical benefits reaped from Prohibition. In places where he had been assured that drink could not be had for love or money he had seen drunkards reeling in the streets. In Iowa City, where Prohibition was supposed to be enforced, he saw from seventy-five to a hundred kegs of beer delivered on trucks from a brewery. His practical conclusion was that Prohibition was a wild theory; "that as a preventative it had not met the claims of its supporters, and as an aid to the cause of Temperance was a failure." Dubuque is a city of about 35,000 inhabitants. Its business Directory comprises two breweries, six bottlers, thirty-five hotels, ten wholesale liquor places, and a hundred and eighty-one saloons. The annual expense to the liquor-seller in the way of "license" is small: he pays the United

States Government tax of $25, and twice a year is formally prosecuted and fined $50 by the municipality. Druggist shops are turned into liquor shops with a few drugs in the window.

In Kansas, the State of Governor St. John, the chosen chief of Prohibitionism, where the most stringent Prohibition had been enacted, the result, according to Dr. Gardner, was that the drug-stores were little more than rum-shops, and that their number was astonishing. In one town of four thousand people, fifteen of them were counted on the main street. Leavenworth, with a population of 23,000, has a hundred and seventy-five places where liquor is sold. In Kansas City the police collected in 1882 $45,000 in fines for illegal sale of liquor. There is a general tendency to convert Prohibition, where it prevails, practically into license by taking the fees under the guise of fines. In Tongawoxie, a small town in Kansas where there was no saloon before Prohibition, there are three or four now. This is against the theory that Prohibition works well in small places though in large cities it works ill. At Topeka in Kansas there are no saloons. But there were none when Prohibition was introduced, popular feeling being against them. A proof that it is popular feeling that is strong, not prohibitive law. The Canadian Commission, however, has been making careful inquiry in Kansas and the results of its investigations will soon appear.

It seems that experience has always pointed the same way. Under James I. and Charles I. a series of Acts was passed to suppress tippling, the effect of which evidently was only to suppress the respectability of the tavern-keepers, who at last were found to be unable to pay fines, so that Parliament had to resort to flogging as a penalty. The failure is the more significant because the Executive was so strong, and was sure to be backed in this case by the Puritan Parliament. The Gin Act of George II. was found to have made bad worse, and had to be repealed. Even in Puritan Connecticut, where the pressure of ecclesiastical authority was tremendous, the historian tells us that "rules against excess in drinking and in apparel were attempted, with the usual want of success." Heaven appears in no place or time to have prospered what we are told is its own cause.

The difficulty of even enforcing vaccination in places where it is widely resisted, shows how arduous a task is coercive legislation when it is not backed by popular conviction, which, if it is in favour of the principle, will produce the effect without coercive law.

About ten years ago, a mass meeting of the friends of Temperance, connected with the Church Temperance Society, was held at Chickering Hall, at New York. The hall was full to overflowing; speeches were made by Mr. Warner Miller, Rev. Dr. Greer, the Bishop of Delaware, Mr. Seth Low, and Father Osborne. The sense of the meeting was evidently in favour of high license, as practically the best safeguard against intemperance. Dr. Greer dwelt on the failure of Prohibition in Rhode Island, declaring that "the State was not less wicked as a Prohibition State than as a low-license State; that the tactics to which reputable citizens resorted to evade the law created a spirit of lawlessness; and that, with regard to the city of Providence, numerous clubs had sprung up there, where the citizens could drink their fill and be sheltered from publicity or arrest."

By voluntary associations, such as Teetotal societies and the Bands of Hope, and still more by the general advance of morality, of intelligence, and above all of medical science, great improvement has been made in Canada as it has elsewhere. Old inhabitants tell you that forty or fifty years ago drunkenness was very common among our farmers, and that many of them regularly went home from market the worse for liquor. Now the Canadian farmers are a very sober race. There is a certain amount of drunkenness, as well as of other vices, in our cities, but a large proportion of the cases are those of recent immigrants. The writer would be inclined to say, judging from outward appearances, that Toronto, compared with other cities in which he has lived, is sober as well as orderly. It has indeed been proclaimed from the Prohibition platform that there are seven, or even ten, thousand deaths from drinking in the Dominion every year. This would be from a third to one-half of the total number of male adult deaths. About the time when this announcement was made, the Mortuary Statistics gave the total number of deaths from alcoholic causes in eight principal cities and towns in one month as two. In England likewise, the evil habit of drinking has been greatly reduced, without any restrictive laws or restraint of any kind, mainly by the increasing influence of medical science, and in connection with the general progress of hygienic reform. It should be observed that voluntary effort will be weakened by coercive legislation. Prohibition, if universally enforced, would break up Teetotal fraternities and Bands of Hope; and unless it was itself successful in extirpating the desire for drink, that desire might any day break out again on a large scale, and find no organisation on foot to resist its sway.

Before the British Parliament consents to extreme legislation, let it at all events appoint a Commission of Inquiry to report to it on the results of prohibitory legislation in Canada and the United States. The Commissioners, will probably find that impartial opinion on the continent pronounces Prohibition a failure, and inclines decidedly in favour of the plan of high licenses with stringent regulation. That stringent and exceptional legislation is required for the liquor-traffic nobody doubts. Nor do the respectable members of the trade deprecate it; for nothing can be less conducive to their interest than drunkenness and disorder on their premises. It is quite possible that a stricter code may be necessary in England than is necessary in the United States or Canada. There is nothing, thank Heaven, on the American continent like the gin-palaces of London.

A license fee as high as a thousand dollars (200*l.*) has been proposed, and the prospect of revenue is tempting to the municipalities. But if the system is overstrained its effect will practically be the same as Prohibition; it will call into existence in towns and cities an illicit trade, which of all results is the worst. To diminish the demand for liquors by moral agencies has been shown to be practicable, both in Canada and among the upper classes in England; to diminish the supply without diminishing the demand seems to be impracticable, resort to what expedients you will.

It is as needless to dilate on the evils of intemperance as it is to dilate on the evils of small-pox. The only question is whether prohibitive legislation cures or rather aggravates and propagates the disease. But the advocates of coercion have surely overstated the connection between drinking and crime. From their language it might be supposed that if we could only stamp out drinking, crimes of all kinds would cease, our gaols would stand empty, and we should be at liberty to disband the police. If it were so, no measures, provided they were effective, could be too strong. But can we believe that cruelty, lust, covetousness, vindictiveness, malice, and the other evil tendencies of human nature in which crime has its source, are all the offspring of drink, and that with drink they would depart? Do they not manifest themselves, in germ at least, in children whose lips have never touched the glass? Among the poorer classes seasons of distress are seasons of crime, though the power of buying liquor is diminished. Is there no crime in Mahomedan countries, which keep the Prophet's law? Is there none in Spain, the people of which are remarkable for their temperance? It is natural that the criminal classes should also be given to drink, as they are to gross sensuality of other kinds; but it does not follow that their addiction to drink is the sole, or even the principal, source of their crime. Prisoners, too, are apt to plead drink in extenuation of their offences, especially since they know that philanthropy will hail their plea. A remarkable article on diet appeared in 1885 from the pen of Sir Henry Thompson, in which he avowed his belief that not only the bodily but the moral evil arising from intemperance in eating was as great as that arising from intemperance in drink. Certainly, we should not look for more malevolence in a drinker of any but the worst whiskey or rum than in one who, like too many people in America, over-eats himself daily with fat and ill-boiled pork, or beefsteak cooked in the deadly frying-pan, as well as with half-baked bread and greasy pie, washing down the whole with copious draughts of the most abominable green tea. The Maine Prison Report for 1884 says: "Intemperance is not a cause of crime; it is a crime more against society and against the family than against the State." The words are a little ambiguous, but they certainly do not mean that intemperance is the sole source of crime. The warden of the Maine State prison, reviewing the declarations made of each convict between the years 1880 and 1887, found that of 375 convicts 194 declared that they used no liquor, 163 that they used some liquor, and 88 that they were intemperate.

Whether we or any of us ought entirely to renounce alcohol it is for science to determine. If science pronounces that we ought, there can be little doubt that the growing intelligence of humanity will gradually conform to the decision, as it is already conforming to the decision of science by other changes of habit. But one can hardly help thinking that even with regard to the physical effects of alcohol there has, at all events, been a good deal of exaggeration on the "Temperance" platform. The sort of spirits to which Prohibition drives people, as we have seen, is poison indeed. But surely it is only in a metaphorical sense that the name can be applied to liquors which a man has drunk through a life of eighty, ninety, even a hundred years. In Manitoba there are two bodies of Mennonites, of which one drinks spirits or fermented liquors, while the other abstains; and a person who has a great deal to do with the Mennonites, and whose evidence is to be trusted, told the writer that the section which drinks is rather superior in progressive energy to the section of abstainers. No part of our Canadian population is more industrious or worthier than the Germans of Waterloo County, Ontario, who, like all Germans, drink beer. That alcohol does not nourish, supposing it to be true, is not much to the purpose. If alcohol does not nourish, it exhilarates. Tea, which some Prohibitionists drink in floods, and on which they spend as much money as others do in beer, does not nourish, but it soothes. Possibly the exhilaration produced by wine may sometimes have been a necessary antidote to melancholy, which would otherwise prey fatally on the mind. The Psalmist, who praised wine as making glad the heart of man, though he lived before science, may have spoken with the voice of Nature. But let medical science decide; to her, not to the religious or political platform, the question belongs.

The Temperance platform has also beyond doubt grossly exaggerated the effect of moderate drinking in tempting onward to excess. To maintain that a man who is in the habit of taking daily a glass of wine or beer must inevitably contract a craving which will lead to his becoming a drunkard, is necessary, no doubt, for the justification of those who advocate indiscriminate repression; but nothing can be more flagrantly at variance with obvious facts. An ordinary English gentleman takes a glass of wine daily at dinner without feeling any more tempted to swallow the whole contents of the decanter than he is to swallow the whole contents of the mustard-pot from which he takes a spoonful with his beef. A man may play a game of cribbage with his wife without becoming a gambler. If Johnson found abstinence easier than temperance, it was because he had once been intemperate. He knew that his own case was peculiar. To most men, as they require physical enjoyment of some kind, temperance is easier than abstinence. The Spaniards regularly drink wine, yet Croker, in his " Travels in Spain," says, " The habitual temperance of these people is really astonishing; I never saw a Spaniard drink a second glass of wine." Another English tourist says, " In all our wanderings through town and country, along the highways and byways of the land from Bayonne to Gibraltar, we never saw more than four men who were the least intoxicated." Mr. Bryant, the American author, has confirmed this account. A clerical advocate of our Scott Act once said that he would no more think of putting liquor within reach of the people, than of putting a knife within reach of a baby. Supposing a glass of ale to be a knife, the reverend gentleman's fellow-citizens are not babies. Among the extreme advocates of coercion are, it is believed, men who have themselves been given to drink, and who cannot understand the existence of self-control.

From communities vexed by arbitrary legislation those who rebel against arbitrary legislation, or do not wish to have their tastes and habits regulated by a tyrannical majority, will depart. It seems that the Germans, excellent settlers, but unwilling to give up their lager beer, have been driven from Maine. Against lager beer as well as cider and other light drinks Prohibition, as has already been said, discriminates; their bulk in proportion to the alcohol making them unsuitable for contraband sale.

The taste for fermented liquors, if not congenital, seems to be immemorial and almost universal. Its traces appear in all the mythologies, Hindu, Hellenic, Roman, and Scandinavian. Probably the use of such liquors is coeval with cookery, which also has been the source of much evil as well as of much pleasure to mankind. It is very likely that a great change in human diet, as well as in human beliefs and institutions, is coming; but it is not likely that this change will come suddenly, or that diet, being complex, will undergo a revolution in one of its elements without a corresponding revolution in the rest. Vegetarianism has many advocates, and there are symptoms of gradual progress in that direction since the days in which a Homeric hero devoured a whole joint of meat and the bard sang of the work of the shambles with as much gusto as he sang of the harvest and the vintage. It is certain that most people eat too much meat and are the worse for it, though it has not yet been proposed on that account to shut up the butchers' shops and send the butchers to gaol. Fermented drinks may be discarded and cookery with them; a refined and intellectual world may be content to sustain its grosser part with bread and water from the spring; and our Christmas cheer may be remembered only as the habit of primeval savages with wonder and disgust. But in questions of diet, as has already been said, it is for medical science, not for the sentiment of the platform or for religious enthusiasm, to decide.

We have seen how in Vermont, Prohibitionism, exasperated by its inevitable failure, heaped up penal enactments, and at last invaded the most sacred liberties of the citizen and the sanctuary of his home. It is the tendency of all tyranny, whether it be that of a sultan, a crowd, a sect, or a party of zealots, when it finds itself baffled, to pile on fresh severities instead of reconsidering the wisdom of its own policy. Prohibitive legislation in Canada has not failed to betray the same arbitrary spirit. There is a clause in the Scott Act (sec. 12) setting aside the common legal safeguards of innocence. It provides "that it shall not be necessary for the informer to depose to the fact of the sale as within his own personal or certain knowledge, but the magistrate, so soon as it appears to him that the circumstances in evidence sufficiently establish the infraction of the law, shall put the defendant on his defence, and in default of his rebuttal of such evidence shall convict him accordingly," — convict him, in short, and send him to prison on hearsay, if in the opinion of the magistrate, who may be a strong partisan, he fails to prove his innocence. There is a clause (122) requiring a man when interrogated respecting previous convictions to criminate himself, which seems intended for the very purpose of breeding mendacity. There is a clause (123) compelling husband and wife to give evidence against each other. When the wife has sent the husband to prison, what will the wedlock of that pair thenceforth be? Which of the two is the greater sin, to refuse to give evidence under the Scott Act, or to break the marriage vow, which bids husband and wife to cherish and protect each other? There is no appeal on the merits from the arbitrary decision of the magistrate, and zealots have not been ashamed to demand in the plainest terms the appointment of partisans to the bench. It never occurs to them to consider whether intemperance itself is a worse vice than injustice.

The treatment of the hotel and tavern keepers has also been utterly iniquitous. These men have been earning their bread by a trade which, when they entered it, was not only licensed by the State, but deemed by everybody perfectly reputable; and therefore when their trade is suddenly suppressed they are apparently entitled to the same compensation which any other trade in the same circumstances would receive. But compensation is inconvenient and might fatally weight the measure. It is necessary, therefore, to put the tavern-keeper out of the pale of justice; and to do this pulpit and platform vie with each other in kindling popular passion against him. He is represented not only as the agent of a traffic to which it is desirable to put an end, but as a criminal and the worst of criminals, as a poisoner and a murderer, "steeped to the elbow in the blood of civilisation." Yet money made by the poison which he sells is accepted even by the most scrupulous of the Churches for its religious objects, while one Church, at least, which has synodically declared for total Prohibition, counts many dealers in liquor among its members.

We do not want a selfish and isolated liberty. Milton himself did not want a selfish and isolated liberty; at least, he deliberately sacrificed his eyesight rather than decline to serve the State. But after all this struggling against the paternal despotism of kings and popes, we do want a reasonable measure of freedom and of self-development. We do want it to be understood, as the general rule, that

> " All restraint,
> Except what wisdom lays on evil men,
> Is evil."

In case of extremity, such as war or plague, we are of course ready for strong measures, provided they are effectual. Not only war or plague, but any peril of such a kind that the State alone can deal with it, warrants the intervention of the State. Nobody would desire to set arbitrary and pedantic bounds to the common action of the community for the preservation of the whole. It might be necessary, and therefore lawful, to close the taverns of the nation, were the nation becoming the hopeless slave of drunkenness, as it might be necessary, and therefore lawful, to close the race-courses if the nation were becoming the hopeless slave of turf-gambling. But in an ordinary way we submit that, whether in the hands of kings or majorities, political power is a trust held for definite purposes, which do not include interference with your neighbour's diet, or any of his personal habits, any more than they include the limitation of his industry or the confiscation of his property. The Prohibitionist thinks that by doing a little injustice he can do a great deal of good, and so probably have thought all tyrants who were not absolutely insane.

If fanaticism in pursuit of the one cherished object tramples on justice and natural affection, how can it show any more regard for the claims of political duty? A citizen is manifestly bound in the exercise of his suffrage to consider all the qualifications of the candidate and all the interests of the State. But Temperance organisations in Canada have formally resolved to exclude, so far as they can, from all public offices, even from that of a school-trustee, any one who will not pledge himself to the support of their policy. There may be other issues before the country of the most vital importance, but they are all to be sacrificed to the one end of the sect. The man may be qualified in every respect to be a legislator: he may even be a total abstainer; but if he does not believe in prohibitory legislation, and refuses to submit his conscience to that in which he does not believe, he is to be excluded from public life, and the State is to be deprived of his services. On the other hand, the most transparently dishonest submission is accepted as a title to support. A fierce electoral contest is going on with forces evenly balanced, and everybody is in doubt about the result. Suddenly it is announced that one of the candidates has consented to take the Prohibition pledge. There is no concealment as to his motive; but he gets the Prohibitionist vote, and by its help rides in over the head of his more scrupulous rival, while eminent Christians and religious journals applaud a triumph gained over public morality by fraud and lying. It is needless to say that Prohibitionism becomes a marketable commodity among politicians, and furnishes the ladder by which knavery climbs to the mark of its ambition.   It is now, perhaps, after Irish clanship, the most noxious of the sectional organisations, the number of which is always on the increase, and which are destroying the character of the citizen, and rendering elective government impossible by treating the State as an oyster to be opened with the knife of their vote for their own particular end.

Once more then, and with increased emphasis, let us suggest that before the British Parliament commits itself to prohibitive legislation it should send a Commission of Inquiry to the United States and Canada, or at least wait for the report of the Canadian Commission which is now investigating the subject, and which embraces in the scope of its inquiry not only Canada but the United States.

APPENDIX:

COMMUNISM IN THE UNITED STATES.

THE ONEIDA COMMUNITY AND AMERICAN SOCIALISM.

This paper appeared in the *Canadian Monthly* of November, 1874. It was suggested by a visit of two days paid by the writer to the Oneida Community, then under the Presidency of Mr. Noyes. Mr. Noyes has since died, and his death proved irreparable to his Community.

In "History of American Socialisms," by J. Humphrey Noyes, founder and father of the Oneida Community, we are presented with an instructive enumeration of the various socialistic experiments made in America, chiefly within the last fifty years.[1] This enumeration furnishes the basis for an induction. That religious communities succeed, while the non-religious invariably fail, is the inference drawn by Mr. Noyes, whose own community is religious. "The one feature," he says, "which distinguishes these (the prosperous) communities from the transitory sort, is their religion; which in every case is of the earnest kind, which comes by recognised *afflatus*, and controls all external arrangements." "It seems then," he adds, "to be a fair induction from the facts before us that earnest religion does in some way modify human depravity, so as to make continuous association possible, and insure to it great material success."

To the writer the facts suggested a different conclusion; but before embracing it he wished to see the Oneida Community. The Oneida Community is, at all events, not afraid

---

[1] Mr. Noyes had embodied in his work the researches of Macdonald, an ex-socialist, who devoted himself to the preparation of materials for a history of the movement.

of being seen. The writer was one of some five hundred visitors in the month of September alone. Upon applying for the requisite permission he was received with the most courteous hospitality, and allowed freely to satisfy his curiosity, so far as the shortness of his visit would permit. He came away confirmed in his previous opinion.

Communities of steady, sober, and industrious workers, held together by a religious bond, or by the influence of a venerated chief, will make money; if they have no separate families there will be no family interests to draw them apart; if they are childless, or have few children, their money will accumulate; their wealth will become a new bond, but will at the same time put a stop to proselytism, so that the extension of the community will be limited by the number of its children, and if it has no children, it will become extinct. A practical assurance of this fact, which might have been taken for granted without any experiment, the writer believes to be the net upshot of the eighty experiments which have been made, many of them on a very costly scale. In other words, he believes that the law of success or failure is not a religious law, but an economical law, and one of the most commonplace kind. The utmost that religion or sentiment of any sort has done is to form the original bond of union, and invest the prophet-chief with the necessary power.

If religion could sustain a communistic association, success would have been assured to Hopedale, founded at Milford, Massachusetts, in 1841, by about thirty persons from different parts of that State, under Rev. Adin Ballou. This Community was, to use Mr. Noyes's own expression, intensely religious in its ideal. In the words of its founder, it was "a church of Christ, based on a simple declaration of faith in the religion of Jesus Christ, as He taught and exemplified it, according to the Scriptures of the New Testament, and of acknowledged subjection to all the moral obligations of that religion." No person could be a member of it who did not cordially assent to that declaration. It was "to afford a beginning, a specimen and a presage of a new and glorious social Christendom — a

grand confederation of similar communities — a world ultimately regenerated and Edenised." Nor was a leader wanting,
for Mr. Ballou, besides being an ardent enthusiast, was evidently in point of ability no ordinary man. He strove hard for
success. He set the example of labour by working, and working vigorously, with his own hands. We are told that he would
sometimes be found exhausted with labour, asleep on the
sunny side of a haycock, and that the only recreation he had
was occasionally to go out into the neighbourhood and preach
a funeral sermon. The result, however, was a total failure,
which Mr. Ballou ascribes to the lack or the decline of religious enthusiasm, but which, at all events, assumed a decidedly
economical form. Mr. Ballou was superseded as President by
Mr. Draper, who, being a keen business man, and in partnership with a brother outside, sacrificed the interests of the
Community to those of his firm, got three-fourths of the stock
into his own hands, and ultimately compelled Mr. Ballou to
wind up.

It was enough to ruin Hopedale that it accepted, among
other Christian principles, that of "connubiality," which must
have created separate interests and have prevented the accumulation of money, while industry was probably slackened by
want of the full stimulus of competition and by reliance on
the community. Mr. Draper would not have found it so easy
to operate on the stock of the Oneida Community or the
Rappites.

There are two great groups of experiments, all failures,
which Mr. Noyes characterises respectively as Owenite and
Fourierist, the Owenite utopias being founded on the principle of Communism, the Fourierist on that of Joint-Stock
Association, though the two principles are apt to run into each
other, and it is difficult to say exactly to which class any particular experiment belongs. The two fits of national enthusiasm, however, seem clearly marked. The first commenced
with the visit of Robert Owen to the United States, in 1824,
the second was brought on twenty years later through the
dissemination of Fourierism by Brisbane in Horace Greeley's
paper, the *New York Tribune*.

"Robert Owen is a remarkable character. In years nearly seventy-five; in knowledge and experience superabundant; in benevolence of heart transcendental ; in honesty without disguise; in philanthropy unlimited; in religion a sceptic; in theology a Pantheist; in metaphysics a necessarian circumstantialist; in morals a universal excusionist; in general conduct a philosophic non-resistant; in socialism a Communist; in hope a terrestrial elysianist; in practical business a methodist; in deportment an unequivocal gentleman." Such is the portrait, drawn by the sympathising hand of a fellow visionary, of the great Social Reformer who was to deliver the world from the monstrous trinity of man's oppressors — Private or Individual Property, Irrational Religion, and their concomitant, Marriage. Owen had tried organised philanthropy in Scotland; but for Communism he sought a more fitting cradle amidst the wild lands and crude ideas of the new world. He was received with enthusiasm; the Hall of the Representatives at Washington was assigned him as a lecture room, and the President, the President elect, all the Judges of the Supreme Court and a number of the Members of Congress were among his hearers, while the large private fortune which, while he included private property in the trinity of evil, he had not scrupled to retain, furnished him with the means of trying his experiment on the largest and most costly scale. He purchased a fine property of 30,000 acres at Harmony, in Indiana, just vacated by the Rappites, who left behind them good buildings and well cultivated fields, so that "terrestrial elysianism" here escaped the hardships which have proved fatal at once to utopias founded in the wilderness. Some 800 people were drawn together by the prospect of unbounded happiness. In the course of eighteen months New Harmony had seven successive constitutions. About a year after the foundation, "in consequence of a variety of troubles and disagreements, chiefly relating to the disposal of the property, a great meeting of the whole population was held, and it was decided to form four separate societies, each signing its own contract for such part of the property as it shall purchase, and each managing its own affairs; but to trade with each other by paper money." Mr. Owen had not shown sufficient confidence in his own theory to give up his hold either on the land or on the power. We are told that he was now beginning to make sharp bargains with the independent Communists. "He had lost money, and no doubt he tried to regain some of it, and used such means as he thought would prevent further loss." Yet he chose this time for a solemn re-promulgation of his communistic creed under the title of the *Declaration of Mental Independence.*

"Disagreements and jealousies." "Many persons leaving. The *Gazette* shows how impossible it is for a community of common property to exist, unless the members comprising it have acquired the genuine community character." "Although there was an appearance of increased order and happiness, yet matters were drawing to a close. Owen was selling property to individuals; the greater part of the town was now resolved into individual lots; a grocery was established opposite the tavern; painted sign-boards began to be stuck up on the buildings, pointing out places of manufacture and trade; a sort of wax-figure and puppet-show was opened at one end of the boarding-house; and everything was getting into the old style." It is useless, as Mr. Noyes says, to follow this wreck further. The destructive forces of roguery and whisky seem to have mingled with the fundamental impracticability of the scheme in bringing on the final catastrophe. Owen complained that he got the wrong sort of people, the dishonest, the intemperate, the idle, the apathetic, the selfish, instead of the honest, the temperate, the industrious, the active-minded and the self-sacrificing. But we should say he got the right sort of people for the purpose of a social reformer who undertakes by the application of his regimen to purge human nature of its vices and transform society. The inventor of a patent medicine might as well complain that he got the sick and not the healthy to operate on. One of the qualifications prescribed by Owen for the members of his Community was a conviction of the fact that the character of man is formed for, and not by, himself. The people of New Harmony showed practically that they were fully possessed of this qualification.

Mr. Owen afterwards became a Spiritualist and a believer in Special Providence. If he had been so before, Mr. Noyes seems to think, the result of the experiment at New Harmony would have been different. We will touch on this point hereafter. Here it is important to notice that, whatever may have been his theory, Owen did not attempt any practical innovation on the subject of marriage; at least he did not attempt to annihilate the separate family or to check the propagation of children.

Another great experiment on Mr. Owen's principles was made at Yellow Springs, in Ohio, the present site of Antioch College, the coeducational university, so that there seems to be something Radical in the soil. This Community consisted of about a hundred families, and included professional men, teachers, merchants, mechanics, farmers, and a few common labourers. "In the first few weeks all entered into the new system with a will. Service was the order of the day. Men who seldom or never before laboured with their hands, devoted themselves to agriculture and the mechanic arts with a zeal which was always commendable, though not always according to knowledge. Ministers of the Gospel guided the plough; called the swine to their corn instead of sinners to repentance; and let patience have her perfect work over an unruly yoke of oxen. Merchants exchanged the yard-stick for the rake or pitchfork. All appeared to labour cheerfully and for the common weal. Among the women there was even more apparent self-sacrifice. Ladies who had seldom seen the inside of their own kitchens went into that of the common eating-house (formerly hotel) and made themselves useful among pots and kettles; and refined young ladies, who had all their lives been waited upon, took their turn in waiting upon others at the table. And several times a week all parties who chose, mingled in the social dance in the great dining-hall." This continued for three months.   Then — "the industrious, the skilful, and the strong saw the products of their labour enjoyed by the ignorant, the unskilled, and the improvident; and self-love rose against benevolence.   A band of musicians insisted that their brassy harmony was as necessary to the common happiness as bread and meat; and declined to enter the harvest-field or the work-shop.   A lecturer upon natural science insisted upon talking only while others worked.   Mechanics, whose day's labour brought two dollars into the common stock, insisted that they should in justice work only half as long as the agriculturist, whose day's work brought but one."   It is strange that these words should have been written by one who is himself a Communist.

With New Harmony and Yellow Springs, went to "that limbo near the moon" the ghosts of a number of other abortive attempts of the Owenite epoch.   The history of the failure in some cases is traced, and it is clear that the result was due to the irresistible action of the economic laws which the projectors had undertaken to supersede; in other cases the end is shrouded in pathetic silence, but we may be sure that the course of events was essentially the same.   It is sad to think of the waste of earnest, perhaps heroic effort, and of the disappointment of generous hopes.   Owen had his qualities, but to call him a genius of the first order is preposterous.   Genius in art produces high works of imagination; but genius in action does not indulge in impracticable reveries, and cover the world with the wrecks of schemes the failure of which common sense might have foreseen.

That any one in his senses should have followed Fourier, has always seemed to us one of the most curious facts in the history of opinion.   This visionary believed that the grand mistake, and the source of all disorder and misery, was the habit of attempting to restrain our passions, and that by letting them all loose, and giving free play to every kind of propensity and idiosyncrasy, we should produce complete equilibrium and perfect harmony in society.   His plan of material felicity is hallucination verging upon lunacy.   To match this he had a philosophy of history than which wilder nonsense never was penned, even on that seductive theme. Nevertheless, he possessed some sort of electricity which called into activity the utopian tendencies of other men. About twenty years after the appearance of Owen, the conditions of soil and atmosphere in the United States being then favourable to fungoid growths, a crop of Fourierist *Phalanxes* sprung up like mushrooms, and, like mushrooms, died. The economical reasons of their death are such as common sense would at once suggest, and are disclosed with almost ludicrous distinctness. "The transition," says Mr. Noyes, always clear-sighted, except with regard to his own peculiar phase of the illusion, "from the compulsory industry of civilisation to the voluntary, but not yet attractive industry of association, is not favourable to the highest industrial effects. Men who have been accustomed to shirk labour under the feeling that they had poor pay for hard work will not be transformed suddenly into kings of industry by the atmosphere of a Phalanx. There will be more or less loafing, a good deal of exertion unwisely applied, a certain waste of strength in random and unsystematic efforts, and a want of the business-like precision and force which makes every blow tell, and tell in the right place. Under these circumstances many will grow uneasy, at length become discouraged, and, perhaps, prove false to their early love." Mr. Noyes proceeds to say that these are temporary evils and will pass away. They may be suspended by the strong hand of a chief like Mr. Noyes, but they will pass away only with human nature.

The passionate expressions of enthusiasm, the confident belief that under Fourier, "the Columbus of social discovery," the caravels of enterprise were again touching the shore of a new world, the first chilling contact with the inexorable reality, the struggle, sometimes a gallant one, against overmastering fate, the inevitable break-up, the voice of faith trying to rise triumphant over the wreck of hope, are enough to touch any heart less stern than that of an economical Rhadamanthus. But comedy is mingled with the tragedy. A scene at the opening of the Clermont Phalanx reminds us of one in "Martin Chuzzlewit." "There were about one hundred and thirty of us. The weather was beautiful, but cold, and the scenery on the river was splendid in its spring dress. The various parties brought their provisions with them, and toward noon the whole of it was collected and spread upon the table by the waiters, for all to have an equal chance. But alas for equality! On the meal being ready, a rush was made into the cabin, and in a few minutes all the seats were filled. In a few minutes more the provisions had all disappeared, and many persons who were not in the first rush had to go hungry. I lost my dinner that day, but improved the opportunity to observe and criticise the ferocity of the Fourierist appetite." At Prairie Home there was an Englishman named John Wood who was imperfectly Fourierised. John, having blacked his boots, put away the brushes and blacking. "Out came a Dutchman and looked out for the same utensils. Not seeing them, he asked the Englishman for the 'prushes.' So John brings them out and hands them to him, whereupon the Dutch-man marches to the front of the porch, and in wrathful style, with the brushes uplifted in his hand, he addresses the assem-bled crowd: 'He-ar! lookee he-ar! Do you call dis commu-nity? Is dis common property? See he-ar! I ask him for de prushes to placken mine poots, and he give me de prushes and *not give me de placking!*'" Occasionally we catch a glimpse of the form of a speculating Yankee floating like a shark among the flat fish, with no visionary intentions. The members of the communities generally appear to have been honest and loyal to the common cause, but at the end of the Sodus Bay experiment we are told that "each individual helped himself to the movable property, and some decamped in the night, leaving the remains of the Phalanx to be disposed of in any way which the last men might choose."

Fourierism finally staked its existence on the success of the North American Phalanx, which was planted not in the wilderness but near New York City. This Community, con-sisting of only a hundred members of both sexes, starting with a capital of $28,000, and supported by the dead-lift efforts of the leaders of the school, dragged on its existence for twelve years. But the inevitable did not fail to arrive. "Most of them," says an observer, "are decent sort of people, have few bad qualities and not many good ones, but they are evidently not working for an idea. They make no effort to extend their principles, and do not build, as a general thing, unless a person wanting to join builds for himself. Under such circumstances the progress of the movement must necessarily be slow, if ever it progress at all. Latterly the number of members and probationers has decreased. They find it necessary to employ hired labourers to develop the resources of the land." The powers of talking, directing others, and grumbling, were found to be possessed in a high degree by those who had little power of work. At meals the best of the food was taken by those who had stayed at home, while "the swinked hedger," coming late from the field and then having to wash, got the worst. Eighteen hundred was Fourier's pet number of members for a Phalanx. The people were asked what would have happened if the North American Phalanx had consisted of that number: they answered that it would have broken up in two years.

Brook Farm stands by itself, and Hawthorne's "Blithedale Romance" has made it sufficiently familiar to the general reader. It would be an injustice to call it "a pic-nic," or to say that "half the members worked while the other half sketched them from the windows." It was a little Boston utopia, in which a number of men, afterwards notable in the intellectual world, sowed their philosophic wild oats, and gratified the literary man's fancy for manual labour, sharpening their wits no doubt at the same time by intercourse with each other. If they seriously believed that men trained to work with the brain could, with advantage to themselves or to society, take to working with their hands, they were the victims of a strange illusion. The effective combination of manual with mental labour, as a system, is impracticable. Both draw on the same fund of nervous energy, which, when drained by one sort of labour, is unable to supply the other.

Mr. Noyes is of opinion that among the causes of failure in all these cases, was the universal propensity to invest in land and engage in the business of farming. Factories, he thinks, are more suitable for communistic experiments. But surely, if the *afflatus* is the decisive thing, the investment ought not to be of so much consequence.

With the principles of common property or associated labour, there mingled in these utopias all the other chimeras and fanaticisms of the day:—Individual Sovereignty—Labour Exchange—Paper Currency—Transcendentalism—Swedenborgianism—Vegetarianism—Blumerism—Woman's Rights—Anti-domestic-servantism—Spiritualism. Everything impracticable, in short, came to find a place for putting itself in practice outside the conditions of existence. Mr. Noyes traces the connection of Socialism with religious revivals, and shows that people who were preparing their Ascension robes were the unconscious harbingers of the Fourierist movement. The Skeneateles Community had, as one of the articles of its programme, "a disbelief in the rightful existence of all governments built upon physical force," and proclaimed "that they were organised bands of banditti, whose authority was to be disregarded"; that it would not vote under such governments, or petition to them, but "demanded that they should disband"; that it would do no military duty, pay no taxes, sit on no juries, give no testimony in "courts of so-called justice"; that "it would never appeal to the law for a redress of grievances, but use all peaceful and moral means to secure their complete destruction." The relation between the sexes was of course one of the fields for innovation. Robert Dale Owen carried not only the law separating the property of married women from that of their husbands, but the divorce law of Indiana. As a general rule, the mother of all these "notions" was New England, who will have to take care that she does not become as great a source of mischief to this continent as South Carolina, though in a different way.

The failures we have seen. Now what were the successes, and what was the reason of their success. Was it *afflatus*, or something more commonplace? The list drawn up by Mr. Noyes in 1870 is as follows:

Beizel's Community. — Has lasted one hundred and fifty-six years; was at one time very rich; has money at interest yet; some of its grand old buildings are still standing.

The Shaker Community. — Has lasted ninety-five years. Consists· of eighteen large societies, many of them very wealthy.

The Zoar Community. — Fifty-three years old and wealthy.

The Snowberger Community. — Forty-nine years old and "well off."

The Ebenezer Community. — Twenty-three years old, and said to be the largest and richest Community in the United States.

The Janson Community. — Twenty-three years old and wealthy.

The Oneida Community, which is also a commercial success, we omit for the present, undertaking hereafter to show that its case is covered by our induction.

All the communities enumerated are religious. But they are not the only religious communities. Hopedale, as we have said, was religious in the highest degree, and its religion was a better one than that of these ignorant and fanatical little sects. Even the spirit-rapping communities might claim to be placed on a level, in the spiritual scale, with the saltatory religion of Shakers. But Hopedale, as we have seen, was strongly Conservative with regard to marriage. That which is at once common to all the successful communities, and peculiar to them, is the rejection of marriage, whereby in the first place they are exempted from the disuniting influence of the separate family; and in the second place, they are enabled to accumulate wealth in a way which would be impossible if they had children to maintain.

The members of Beizel's Community are strict celibates; so are the Shakers; so are the Rappites; so are the Snowbergers. The Ebenezers permit marriage "when their guiding spirit consents to it"; but the parties have to undergo some public mortification; and the Community at its foundation, to meet the difficulties of the struggle, resolved that for a given number of years there should be no increase of their population by births, which resolution was carried into effect. Among the Zoarites, marriage is now permitted. But we are told that at their first organisation it was strictly forbidden, not from religious scruple, but as an indispensable matter of economy; that for years no child was seen within their village; and that, though the regulation has been removed, the settlement retains much of its old character in this respect. The Jansonists, though they do not forbid marriage, hold that a "life of celibacy is more adapted to develop the life of the inner man." In fact these associations are not so much communistic as monastic, and belong to a class of phenomena already familiar enough to economical history.

The Rappites, a set of enthusiasts who expected the speedy advent of the Millennium, called their first two settlements Harmony. Their third, by a significant change of name, they called Economy. They are not only wealthy, but millionnaires of the first order. We are not surprised to learn that they do not proselytise, though converts enough might undoubtedly be found to a doctrine even more extravagant than Rappism, if it were endowed with twenty millions. The Silver Islet Company would be about as likely to desire proselytes.[1] Those who have visited the Community report that all its members are advanced in years. The end of Rapp's Millennium is in fact a tontine, which will terminate in a Rappite Astor.

We are far from saying that in these cases the religion had nothing to do with the result. It collected and united a body of enthusiasts, whose very fanaticism, being of the coarsest kind, was a guarantee for their belonging to a class accustomed to manual labour and to submission; it helped to hold them together through the first struggle for subsistence; and, what was perhaps the most important point of all, it led them

---

[1] When this was written the Silver Islet on Lake Superior was yielding immense riches.

to render implicit obedience to a prophet-chief, who, whether fanatic or impostor, was pretty sure to be an able man. The ascendancy of the prophet-chief is evidently the mainspring of Mormonism, which is also a great material success. But we very much doubt whether even the strong hand of Brigham Young could hold together for a year a Utah combining the separate family and free propagation of children with community of goods.

The Oneida Community,[1] a visit to which suggested the subject of this paper, was founded in 1847, by the Rev. John Humphrey Noyes, a man whose ability is written on his brow, on the pages of his vigorously-written books, and on the work of his organising hands. He was, by his own confession, a religious enthusiast of the wildest and most erratic kind. Libertinism he has not confessed, though by loose and sensational versions of his words, it has been made to appear that he has done so.[2] The form of religious enthusiasm in which he ultimately landed was *Perfectionism*. The gist of the Perfectionists' creed, if we rightly comprehend it, is that the second coming of Christ took place in the lifetime of St. John; that the reign of Law in every sense then finally gave place to that of the Spirit; that now, the believer united with Christ, and "confessing holiness," is above all ordinances, including the ordinance of marriage, and perfectly free from sin. This sounds like Antinomianism, but we are told that it is only "anti-legality." At all events it is not the professed belief of the Perfectionists that one of their number cannot do wrong. There is a series of subordinate articles, some of them highly mystical, while others, introducing Spiritualism, have probably been grafted on the religion since its first promulgation.

---

[1] Since this was written Mr. Noyes, then at the head of the Community, has died.

[2] An incident, however, which is related by Mr. Noyes himself in the *Oneida Circular*, and which occurred in 1846, indicates plainly enough that a case of elective affinities was the immediate source of his theory about the relations between the sexes, and of his practical application of that theory in the Oneida Community.

The Bible is implicitly received, though with Perfectionist interpretations. Scepticism is denounced. Much is made of special interpositions of Providence, and of Providential "signals." Form of worship the Perfectionists have none. They only confess Christ before each other, and communicate religious thought in their family gathering. The Sabbath is not distinguished from the week except by cessation from work. This religion is proclaimed to be still the bond of union among the members of the Community. They will tell you that they are held together by Father Noyes' love of Christ, and by their love of Father Noyes.

The Community at Oneida numbers two hundred. At Willow Place, on a detached portion of the same domain, are nineteen more; and there are forty-five in a branch at Wallingford, Connecticut. All these are supposed to constitute one family, with the founder as father. The property is held in common; there are no separate interests, incomes, or allowances whatever. The several members of the family are presented with such money as they may require from time to time, just as children are furnished with pocket money by their parents, the only restriction being family duty. The other characteristic feature of the system is one which it is difficult to describe in language at once measured and adequately expressive of the feelings of repugnance with which it must be regarded by every one who acknowledges the Christian rule of morals. The marriage tie is totally discarded. The male and female members of the Community pair with each other for a time, and for a time only; not promiscuously, but under the authority of the Community, which appears to be guided in regulating these matters partly by the policy of restraining the increase of its numbers, partly by physical rules connected with what is styled the scientific propagation of children. The initiative is assigned to the woman, who makes it known to the authorities when she is willing to become a mother. She is not permanently wedded to one partner, but may have two or three in succession. So that the "permanence" predicated of Oneida unions, in the *Circular*, must have reference not to the individual parties, but to the family aggregate. The parental relation is not ignored, but it is merged in the Community, the children being brought up together as brothers and sisters in common nurseries. There are certain supplementary portions of the system which its inventor is in the habit of bringing without reserve before the public, but over which ordinary sentiment enjoins us to draw a veil.

During the early years of the Community few children were born to it, though of late, and apparently in connection with the growth of its wealth, the number of births has been allowed to increase. And thus we have again the two familiar and simple conditions of success, exemption from the disuniting influence of the separate family, and the facility for the accumulation of wealth attendant on the absence or paucity of children. Communism, in fine, can be rendered practicable only by a standing defiance of morality and nature.

In the case of the Oneida Community the measure of commercial success has been large. A strong business head has controlled its financial operations as well as its internal economy. The principle that *afflatus* eschews land and delights in factories has been carried into effect with the most gratifying result. The Community owns a farm of 650 acres, highly cultivated, round its mansion; but its chief investments, and the source of its opulence, are three factories, — one of traps, one of silk goods, and one of canned fruit. The trap factory, which seems a singular line of business to be chosen by Perfectionism, is a monument of one of the original members of the Community, who was a trapper and a maker of traps. The canned fruit of Oneida enjoys the highest reputation, and we do not doubt the truth of the assertion that the business might be greatly extended if the Community chose to borrow capital. Manual labour, though not repudiated by members of the Community, as the writer can testify, is now chiefly performed by hired hands, of whom there are about 150 in the factories, besides some negroes employed in the coarser housework. The members of the Community, as a general rule, are now, like other capitalists, the employers and directors of labour. They are apparently good employers, and, in case of any attempt to disturb them on the ground of their defiance of established morality, they feel secure in the attachment of the people around them, many of whom, we are told, are English immigrants. It is a remarkable proof of the confidence of the Community, both in its own cohesiveness and in its ability to face scrutiny, that it has ventured to send several of its young men to the Scientific Department of Yale College, in order to supply itself with the scientific element requisite for its manufacturing purposes.

The mansion is a spacious and handsome range of buildings, fitted up simply, but with every comfort. Its public rooms are a double dining-hall, a large parlour, with a stage for the gatherings and amusements of the whole family, and other parlours for the meeting of smaller circles. Round it are well-kept grounds, to which the Community admits neighbours and visitors with liberality which must somewhat interfere with the purposes of its own enjoyment. With the charms of green lawns, shady walks, and gay flower-beds, are combined views of a valley, which, in its rich cultivation and the soft outlines of the hills surrounding it, reminds the traveller of England. There are croquet grounds, which appear to be in constant use. A few miles off, by the side of a lake, the Community has a hunting-box, called Joppa, to which excursions are frequently made. Pleasure evidently has its due place among the objects of existence, and is organised with care and on a liberal scale. Teams in sufficient number appeared to be at the service of the brethren. Music is much cultivated, and, by a refinement of humanity, the practising room is a separate building, at some distance from the mansion. In winter, intellectual pursuits and self-culture are the order of the day. The writer was told that an old lady had taken up Greek and acquired the power of reading the New Testament in the original tongue.

The library is furnished with books of all kinds, and New York papers are on the table. The Community, however, is politically quietist, and its members never vote. Political divisions might disturb the family, though the writer was told that the members were all in spirit New Englanders, and would vote with the Republican party. They escaped the military draft through the error of two officials, each of whom supposed the Community to be in the jurisdiction of the other.

"This reform means trousers," said a female advocate of Woman's Rights the other day in the United States. The ladies of the Oneida Community have adopted the Blumer costume, though in a mitigated form. Mr. Hepworth Dixon has recorded his opinion that this dress is becoming. He could hardly extend his commendation to the practice of cutting the hair short in male fashion, which is also universal among the Oneida ladies; at least, if he did, we should be unable to agree with him.

Cookery is not delegated to inferior hands, but done by those of the Perfectionists themselves. The fare is simple but most excellent. There appear to be no rigorous ordinances about diet. As a matter of habit and taste, meat is sparingly eaten, but vegetarianism is not enjoined. Stimulants are banished from the board, but the use of them is not morally proscribed; at least they are offered to a guest. Tobacco is denounced by Father Noyes. One of the brethren was living entirely on brown bread and baked apples, at an expense to the Community, as he reckoned, of twelve cents a day. But this was voluntary, and the motive was dietetic. While there is no appearance of luxury, asceticism is equally unknown.

Among the members of the Community are persons of various social grades and degrees of education — ex-clergymen and ex-lawyers, as well as mechanics; though there must obviously be a limit intellectually to the class disposed to believe in Perfectionism and Father Noyes. If you ask how order and harmony are preserved in so large and so heterogeneous a family, the all-sufficing answer is, through the institution of mutual criticism. Every member of the Community, in turn, is compelled thus to submit himself to the organised influence of social opinion, in order that he may be warned of his social faults and constrained to address himself to their cure. The author of "New America" had the good fortune to witness one of these singular operations, which at that time were performed in the great parlour by the Community at large. But the duty has since been delegated to a Committee of Criticism, which summons before it the person to be criticised, together with those who are most intimate with him and best qualified to point out his defects. It is asserted that the system perfectly answers its purpose, and that at the same time it has the effect of banishing from the Community irregular backbiting and malevolent love of scandal. It may be doubted, perhaps, whether this or any other gentle instrument of government would work so well if within the velvet glove were not felt the iron hand of Father Noyes, though the members of the Community speak with confidence of the self-sustaining power of the system, and profess to look forward without fear to a demise of the paternal crown.

To preserve the unity of the family, all the members are assembled for an hour every evening in the great parlour. Matters of interest to the whole Community are then brought forward and discussed, correspondence is read, sympathy is expressed with the sick, professions of religious sentiment are exchanged. To give the assembly a domestic air, three or four tables were disposed over the room with groups of women at work around them. But it would not do. The assembly was not a family circle: it was a meeting, though a meeting of people agreed in conviction, and well acquainted with each other. In the very unanimity of opinion and sentiment there was an undomestic ring. In the same manner the repasts in the common hall lack the character of a family meal. Dinner is a table d'hôte, at which those who partake of it do not even sit down together, but separately, each when he pleases, between certain hours, just as they do in a hotel. And this was the general impression made on the writer by what he saw of Oneida. He felt that all the time he was in a great hotel, an hotel where people boarded all the year round, and were on friendly terms with each other, but still an hotel and not a home. Mention has been already made of the departure from the original institution of family criticism, and the delegation to a committee of the function, once performed by the Community at large. This is obviously a symptom of disintegration, while the necessity under which the committee finds itself of summoning special witnesses proves that within the great circle of the Community inner social circles are formed. In fact, without some miraculous enlargement of the range of human affections, it is absurd to talk of forming a family of two hundred people. They may be under the same paternal despotism, but they can be a family in no other sense of the term. To preserve the domestic unity of the three establishments, Oneida, Willow Place, and Wallingford, will be still more beyond human power.

The children, as has been already said, are regarded as children of the Community, and are brought up together on that footing. The mother is allowed to take part in nursing them as much as she pleases, but she is not required to do more. Undeniably they are a fine, healthy-looking, merry set of infants. But we need not jump from this fact to a conclusion in favour of Scientific Propagation, and all its repulsive incidents. The Oneida children are reared under conditions of exceptional advantage, which could not fail to secure health to the offspring of any but positively diseased parents, whose union no coarse intervention of anthropological science is needed to forbid. The nurseries, with everything about them, are beautiful. Large play-rooms are provided for exercise in winter. The nurses are not hirelings, but members of the Community who voluntarily undertake the office. Every precaution is taken against the danger of infection. A simple and wholesome dietary is enforced, and no mother or grandmother is permitted to ruin digestion and temper by administering first a poison from the confectioner's and then another poison from the druggist's. Lessons may perhaps be learned from the nurseries of the Oneida Community, but not the lesson for which the Community cites a long roll of the hierophants of science, that it is good in human unions to disregard, or treat as secondary, the selective instinct of affection, <u>and to breed</u> human beings as we breed horses or swine.

It is by no means surprising that the Perfectionists should not be anxious to make proselytes to the possession of the Oneida estate, and the three flourishing factories upon it, any more than the Rappites are anxious to make proselytes to their millions. We read in the *Circular*, under the head of Admissions:

"These Communities are constantly receiving applications for admission which they have to reject. It is difficult to state in any brief way all their reasons for thus limiting their numbers; but some of them are these: 1. The parent Community at Oneida is full. Its buildings are adapted to a certain number, and it wants no more. 2. The Branch-Communities, though they have not attained the normal size, have as many members as they can well accommodate, and must grow in numbers only as they grow in capital and buildings. 3. The kind of men and women who are likely to make the Communities grow, *spiritually and financially*, are scarce, and have to be sifted out slowly and cautiously. It should be distinctly understood that these Communities are not asylums for pleasure-seekers or persons who merely want a home and a living. They will receive only those who are very much in earnest in religion. They have already done their full share of labor in criticising and working over raw recruits, and intend hereafter to devote themselves to other jobs (a plenty of which they have on hand), receiving only such members as seem likely to help and not hinder their work. As candidates for Communism multiply, it is obvious that they cannot all settle at Oneida and Wallingford. Other Communities must be formed : and the best way for earnest disciples generally is to work and wait, till the Spirit of Pentecost shall come on their neighbors, and give them communities right where they are."

It appears that from a pretty early period regard was had to "financial" as well as to "spiritual" qualifications; for the amount of property brought in by members of the Community and its branches up to 1857 was, according to the *Handbook*, $107,000. This, and cheapness of living in common, must of course be taken into account in estimating the commercial success of the Community, and tracing it to its real source.

That the Oneida Community, or any one of the group to which it belongs, has solved any great problem for humanity, or even tried any experiment of general interest, the writer sees not the slightest ground for believing. Of course nothing which involves celibacy can be extended beyond a few circles of fanatics, such as the monks in former days, or the Shakers in ours; and the abolition of the family is, except within the same narrow limit, equally impracticable as well as utterly revolting. In addition to which, such a mode of living as that adopted by the Oneida Community, and essential to the application of their principles, is wholly at variance with the general conditions of industrial life. Close to the mansion of the Community runs a railroad on which they ship their goods, and which is necessary to their subsistence. Can they imagine it possible to organise the life of the people employed upon that railroad after the model of their own? They send some of their goods across the ocean. Do they think that the sailors who carry these goods can be gathered with their families into a communistic home?

There is at Brooklin, on the Southern shore of Lake Erie, another community which has attracted notice from numbering among its members an Englishman of some distinction, Mr. Laurence Oliphant. About this association little is known,[1] even among the people at Oneida, whose curiosity it naturally excites. But it appears to be not a counterpart of Oneida, but a small group of householders living under the presidency of Mr. Harris, the prophet of a religion akin to Swedenborgianism, and entrusting their property to his hands. So long as that property holds out, the Community may of course continue to exist without impugning any of the received laws of political economy, or introducing any new principle into the world.

It is true that there may be points worthy the attention of the social pathologist in connection with the tendencies which

[1] This, it will be borne in mind, was written in 1874. The mystery of the Lake Erie Community has been since revealed. The revelation confirms what is said in the text.

have called these strange structures into existence, though the subject is too extensive to be discussed at the close of this paper. Among the impelling motives have evidently been the discomfort and the waste attendant on the domestic economy of our separate households, which advancing civilisation will surely teach us in some degree to mitigate. Another motive is the desire of escaping from the gloom and dulness of excessive family isolation into more mixed and more cheerful society. The family is the centre of happiness; but at the same time a man and woman can rarely be so gifted as, after the honeymoon, to be absolutely sufficient for each other. The writer of this paper was once the guest of a friend residing in the neighbourhood of London, and in the middle of a district of suburban villas. On his noticing the number of houses bespeaking opulence which was visible on every side, his friend replied, "Yes, and you would suppose there was a great deal of good society here. There is absolutely none. It is impossible to bring these families together for any social purpose whatever. The man goes up to his place of business in London every morning; stays there till he returns home for dinner, then reads the newspaper the rest of the evening. For two months in each summer the family goes to a watering-place where it lives in a private lodging by itself. That is the whole existence of these people." A dreary and a truncated sort of existence it is. Unfortunately it is not confined to the suburbs of London. We need in Canada, as much as anywhere, to learn the art of preserving the happiness of the family by supplementing it with the enjoyments of more general society in a cheap and reasonable way.

Communism, in a certain sense, was no doubt the original condition of mankind; at least tribal not private ownership of land is the rule of primeval history: and probably this union of interest served an important purpose in the foundation of primitive States. A temporary communism has also played a memorable part in the commencement of great religious or social enterprises. The first preachers of Christianity for a time had all things in common, and so had the founders of New England. Monachism was also communistic, and partly in virtue of its detachment from the ties and cares of property, it was able to perform a mighty work in the conversion of the Barbarians, and the foundation of Christian civilisation. Besides these limited instances, extensive though vague manifestations of the communistic sentiment have generally attended the great crises of history, such as the Reformation, and the English and French Revolutions. It is difficult to believe that such yearnings of humanity, though premature and abortive, are without any significance. "Property has its duties as well as its rights," is a sentiment the distinct expression of which is comparatively of recent date. It may perhaps gain force and ascendancy till, in the course of ages, the right of property is by a spontaneous process virtually merged in social duty. The saying of the Greek dramatist, as to the Omnipotence of time, has acquired new meaning from the late revelations of science and historical philosophy. But the attempts of American Socialists and Communists at once to transmute humanity by founding utopias, have all come to nothing. For the present, the only seat of communism, and the proper sphere of the communistic sentiment, is the family, if the Woman's Right party will only have the wisdom to let it alone.

THE UNITED STATES.

An Outline of Political History, 1492-1871.

By GOLDWIN SMITH, D.C.L.

Third Edition. With Map. Crown 8vo, $2.00.

"His survey of events is luminous, his estimate of character is singularly keen and just, and his style is at once incisive, dignified, and scholarly. . . . No one who takes up Mr. Goldwin Smith's volume will readily lay it down before he has finished it; no one will lay it down without acknowledging the rare gifts of the writer." — *The Times.*

"Is a literary masterpiece, as readable as a novel, remarkable for its compression without dryness, and its brilliancy without any rhetorical effort or display. What American could, with so broad a grasp and so perfect a style, have rehearsed our political history from Columbus to Grant in 300 duodecimo pages of open type, or would have manifested greater candor in his judgment of men and events in a period of four centuries? It is enough to say that no one before Mr. Smith has attempted the feat, and that he has the field to himself." — *The Nation.*

"It is a marvel of condensation and lucidity. In no other book is the same field covered so succinctly and so well. Of the five chapters, the first deals with the Colonial epoch, the second with the Revolutionary period, the third and fourth review the history of the Federal Government to the outbreak of the Civil War, and the fifth depicts the era of rupture and reconstruction. We have marked certain passages for extract, but the truth is that almost every page is enriched with striking comments that cause the reader to carefully reconsider, if not to change, his views of historical persons and events." — *New York Sun.*

"To say that nothing comparable with this most instructive and enchanting volume has hitherto come from Professor Smith's pen, would perhaps be only anticipating the judgment of its readers." — *Toronto Mail.*

"As a whole, has a comprehensiveness of view and a ready grasp of leading tendencies, that should make it particularly useful to the busy man who desires a rapid survey of American political history. By deliberately neglecting details, Professor Smith has been able to fasten the attention upon salient points, and to concentrate interest around the career of the great leaders in our political development." — *Boston Beacon.*

"No pen has ever been more eloquent than his in setting forth the merits of Washington, and Hamilton, and Webster, and Lincoln, and others of America's great citizens. The chapters on 'Democracy and Slavery' and 'Rupture and Reconstruction' deserve thoughtful perusal by every American, North and South." — *Public Opinion.*

MACMILLAN & CO.,

66 FIFTH AVENUE, NEW YORK.

THE AMERICAN COMMONWEALTH.

By the Right Hon. JAMES BRYCE, D.C.L.,

Author of "The Holy Roman Empire"; M.P. for Aberdeen.

In Two Volumes, Large 12mo.   Third Edition, Revised Throughout.

Vol. I. $1.75. *Now Ready.*   Vol. II. *In the Press.*

"Written with full knowledge by a distinguished Englishman to dispel vulgar prejudices and to help kindred people to understand each other better, Professor Bryce's work is in a sense an embassy of peace, a message of good-will from one nation to another."—*The Times,* London.

"This work will be invaluable . . . to the American citizen who wishes something more than a superficial knowledge of the political system under which he lives and of the differences between it and those of other countries. . . . The fact is that no writer has ever attempted to present so comprehensive an account of our political system, founded upon such length of observation, enriched with so great a mass of detail, and so thoroughly practical in its character. . . . We have here a storehouse of political information regarding America such as no other writer, American or other, has ever provided in one work. . . . It will remain a standard even for the American reader."—*New York Tribune.*

"The book should be known by every American who wishes to understand his own country. . . . It is by far the most able, sincere, candid, and impartial study of the condition of the United States that has ever appeared since De Tocqueville's memorable work."—*Boston Beacon.*

"This general outline of Mr. Bryce's most important book is given in the hope that it may help create the conviction that no earnest and intelligent American can afford to remain ignorant of it. His education will be incomplete, as a preparation for his duties as a citizen, if he does not take advantage of the helps to a sound judgment and a noble purpose which are here given."—*N.Y. Evening Post.*

WORKS BY THE SAME AUTHOR.

THE HOLY ROMAN EMPIRE.   Eighth Edition, revised and enlarged. Crown 8vo. $1.00. Library Edition. 8vo. $3.50.

The *Saturday Review* says: "It exactly supplies a want. . . . We know of no writer who has so thoroughly grasped the real nature of the mediæval empire, and its relations alike to earlier and later times."

TRANSCAUCASIA AND ARARAT.   Being Notes of a Vacation Tour in the Autumn of 1876. With Map and View of Mount Ararat. Third Edition. Crown 8vo. $2.50.

The *Times* says: "He has produced a very interesting volume, full of information. . . . In Professor Bryce's bold ascent of Ararat alone, when Kurds and Cossacks alike deserted him, we have a feat of mountain climbing which in itself proves him to be no unworthy member of the Alpine Club. This alone would render the book well worth reading, quite apart from the store of information contained in it."

SOCIAL INSTITUTIONS OF THE UNITED STATES. Reprinted from "The American Commonwealth." 12mo. Cloth. $1.00.

MACMILLAN & CO.,

66 FIFTH AVENUE, NEW YORK.